The Golden Millstones

The Golden Millstones

Napoleon's brothers and sisters

R. F. DELDERFIELD

HARPER & ROW, PUBLISHERS

NEW YORK

CONTENTS

ILLUSTRATIONS

These illustrations appear following page 54

*General Leclerc, Pauline's first husband. A contemporary print.
Bibliothèque Nationale* (Photo: *Giraudon*)

*Jérôme, the youngest of the family, as King of Westphalia, by
Bosio. Private Collection* (Photo: *Bulloz*)

Jérôme in later life. A contemporary print (Photo: *Radio Times
Hulton Picture Library*)

'*The Game of Four Corners or the Five Brothers.' A contemporary
print. Bibliothèque Nationale* (Photo: *Jean-Pierre Vieil*)

PREFACE

THERE WERE SEVEN of them, not counting the man who towered above them from the time he was a boy of sixteen until the day he died. Every derogatory adjective in the Thesaurus has been used to describe them by men and women who walked and talked with them and by historians who have studied their careers. They have been described as failures, degenerates, mountebanks, thieves, rogues and traitors; the policies they pursued as kings and queens have been called futile, dishonest and bankrupt. The four brothers have come down to us as clowns whose loyalty was always in the market and whose ingratitude towards the man who gave them power and position made nonsense of the theory that blood is thicker than water. The three sisters have been called strumpets whose sexual appetites were matched by their lust for money. Almost all the epithets levelled at them are justified or partially so, yet the characters of the four brothers and three sisters of Napoleon Buonaparte continue to intrigue. They were seven millstones hanging from the neck of the most astounding man in modern history but they were, or seem to be, golden millstones and their glow still reaches us across the years. The first of them was born nearly two hundred years ago and the last of them died well over a century ago but somehow they are more alive than some of the sober, useful, distinguished men and women whom we watched on television last week.

BOOK ONE

The Starvelings

CHAPTER ONE

'All this discourages Ambition . . .'

Napoleon, writing to Lucien
from Paris, 1792

ON JUNE 13TH, in the year of 1793, a family of fugitives with no
other possessions than the soiled clothes on their backs stepped
ashore at the French port of Toulon and qualified for the modest
subsistence grant then being paid to Corsicans who had fought
the islanders on behalf of Republican France.

It is hard to say whose plight was the more desperate, the family
that had taken the losing side or the Republicans to whom they
looked for food and shelter. Local representatives of the Convention did their best to assist the mother and children who had
lost the little they owned in an attempt to keep Corsica French but
how could officials be blamed for overlooking such a trivial matter
at such a time? The Republic's frontiers were ringed with the
armies of kings and implacable noblemen who had fled France.
Famine and ruined credit added to the internal pressures. Con-
servative departments in the West and South were either in open
revolt or on the point of ranging themselves against the Republic.
Victories like that at Valmy, eight months before, had staved off
collapse but counter-revolutionaries in the port to which the Corsicans had sailed were now planning to join the sister city of Marseilles and side with the English fleet against the dreamers and
despots in Paris. The future of the young Republic was desperately uncertain and that of Madame Letizia Buonaparte and her
family almost hopeless. Behind them was a homeland to which
they could never return and such property as they had possessed
there was in the hands of enraged Paolists. Of the family of five

3

sons and three daughters, the eldest twenty-five, the youngest not yet nine, only one was earning and all he could contribute was part of a lieutenant-gunner's pay amounting to £55 a year. The eldest and the third son, Joseph and Lucien, had no professions; Louis, the fourth boy, was only fifteen, Jérôme, the youngest, was nine. The girls, Elisa sixteen, Pauline fourteen and Caroline eleven, were dowerless and in rags. Yet Madame Buonaparte, hardened by adversity and by her own unassailable courage and dignity, did not despair. After a brief grumble at the condition of her daughters' bedraggled clothes she joined her second son, Napoleon, in a search for temporary refuge – a cottage, an empty house, anywhere that would give the family a breathing space and the chance to await better times.

Within a day or so she found her base, first in Toulon, then on the fourth floor of a ruined aristocrat's house in Rue Faubourg de Rome, Marseilles. Here, for the next six months, she gathered her family around her, superintending wardrobe repairs and telling the younger children to be quiet whilst fifteen-year-old Louis read aloud from the newspaper. Officials of the Convention paid out the miserable allowance. Joseph and Lucien ranged about looking for work. Napoleon, already acknowledged titular head of the family, took up his appointment of officer in command of the artillery with the ex-painter Carteaux's rabble, in Avignon. Better times were coming but the refugees in Marseilles would have been dumbfounded if they had been given a peep into the future, for no fairy-tale characters enjoyed a reversal of circumstances as spectacular as that awaiting this particular family. In less than a decade the youngest of them was to spend 10,000 francs on a travelling-case containing, among other things, a razor for which he had no immediate use.

Writing to his brother Lucien almost exactly one year before the clan's arrival in France Napoleon, for some time the prop of the family and inclined to relish his authority, criticised the men at the head of affairs in Paris as 'a poor lot' and went on to comment on the general worthlessness of people as a whole and the thanklessness of trying to improve their lot. 'Every individual is out for his own interests and will forward them, if he can, by insult and outrage . . . all this discourages ambition,' he complained.

It was a strange comment from a man who never, until the final moment of his life, renounced ambition or abandoned the ties of a family who already regarded him as a substitute for their dead father. For the whole of his life Napoleon Buonaparte was acutely conscious of family responsibilities and never, for one instant, did he attempt to shift these responsibilities on to other shoulders, or allow brothers or sisters to stand on their own feet. He expended an enormous amount of nervous energy in shaping their personalities and guiding their careers and took appalling risks in efforts to guard them against the consequences of their individual and collective follies. In the end it was they, more than any failure or misjudgment on his part, that ruined him, but Corsican family loyalty proved more enduring than rancour and on his Atlantic rock, with his life in ruins, he thought of them without bitterness. There are aspects of the character of Napoleon Buonaparte that are indefensible, but his lifelong concern for the members of his family is not one of them. He deserved better of them and if he had washed his hands of them all in early life he might have received better.

Carlo Buonaparte, father of the thirteen sons and daughters of Letizia Ramolino Buonaparte, died of cancer in the house of an old friend at Montpellier in the winter of 1785. He left a widow and eight children, five having died in infancy. The family had some claim to Tuscan nobility and in their native Corsica, where possession of a few acres and a small country estate counted for something in a community of peasants and fishermen, Carlo made the most of his ancestry. He was an unremarkable man in every way save one. Few have ever shown more zeal in soliciting patronage.

Carlo had the temperament that often accompanies affability and striking good looks. He was a Mediterranean Micawber and had he not possessed the good luck or good fortune to marry a very remarkable girl when she was fifteen it is doubtful if the world would have ever become familiar with the name 'Buona-parte'. Full of the best intentions, and genuinely liked wherever he went, Carlo never justified the promise of his early manhood and when one searches among his stream of petitions and claims upon authorities one cannot help feeling that here was a man whose essential laziness was the root cause of his failure as a man and a father.

Carlo was educated as a lawyer and used a professional approach in persuading friends, relations and public bodies to accept the responsibilities of educating his numerous family. The early years of the Buonaparte family are studded with appeals and applications of this sort and in the main they were successful, for all five brothers received patronage of one sort or another from govern-mental, military or ecclesiastical departments in France, Italy or Corsica. Carlo died, however, before he had an opportunity to consolidate such gains as he had made in the fields of State-aided education and preferment. From the moment of his death it was Napoleon, then aged sixteen, who shared with his mother the burden of providing for a family who considered themselves privi-leged but were never more than an inch above the borderline of penury.

The story really begins with the death of Carlo during one of his grant-seeking journeys across France and Napoleon, in an ad-mirable letter to his mother, wrote from Paris where he was in Military School: ' . . . comfort yourself . . . the situation re-quires it. We shall be doubly grateful and attentive to you and feel happy if we can recompense you a little for the incalculable loss of your beloved husband.'

This was far more than a formal recognition of the deep affection that existed between the shiftless Carlo and the stern, self-dis-ciplined Corsican woman who had attended her husband through-out the guerrilla war that followed the islanders' revolt against France in the second year of their marriage. Two children died in infancy during this struggle and the third, Joseph, was only a year or so old when the revolt ended. A few weeks after capitulation Napoleon was born, on August 16th, 1769.

Carlo was no martyr. He soon came to terms with the occupying power and in the comparatively tranquil period that followed the revolt Letizia produced a string of children, all of whom were baptised under local names which they discarded before they became the most famous family in Europe. After Napoleon (baptised Nabulione) came a child who died at the age of five, then Lucien, then Maria Anna (later known as Elisa), then Louis, then Pauline, then Maria-Nunciata (known later as Caroline) and finally Jérôme the youngest, who was born two years before his father's death. At the time of Jérôme's birth the prolific Letizia was thirty-five; she lived another fifty-two years, surviving all but five of the thirteen children born of the union.

A large number of people who had long, personal contacts with this astonishing family have been so bemused by the genius of one of them that they have been tempted to dismiss Napoleon's four brothers and three sisters as nonentities. This is very far from being the truth. Of the eight survivors only the eldest, Joseph, deserves such dismissal and even he was by no means the dull, clumsy fellow of Napoleonic legend. Of the rest, each possessed considerable individuality and an exceptionally strong character, whilst all three sisters and one brother, Lucien, possessed above average gifts. Collectively they tend to mask one another's abilities; considered individually they show a very high degree of originality.

If Carlo Buonaparte failed to provide money to support his ever-increasing family by his own personal endeavours he must be judged successful as an importunist. Before he died, in 1785, four of his children were already farmed out and three were being educated either free or under conditions that made modest demands on his purse.

Napoleon had been at the military school of Brienne since he was nine and Joseph, a year older, was training as a priest at Autun. Both were free pupils, Carlo having got them entered in these establishments by pulling every string within reach, notably that attached to the French Intendant of Corsica. The eldest daughter, Elisa, was also receiving a state education at St Cyr outside Paris, where she was to be fed, taught and clothed from the age of seven to twenty and was scheduled, on leaving, to receive a dowry of

7

3,000 francs, a trousseau and 150 francs for travel expenses to her home. Having thus disposed of three of his children Carlo began to solicit on behalf of eleven-year-old Lucien who was brought over to take Napoleon's place as a free pupil at Brienne and study for a military career. Here, however, something went wrong. Perhaps a sour official drew attention to the fact that the Buonaparte family was becoming something of a liability to the State. His suit failed and Carlo was told that Lucien's education would cost him 600 francs a year. This was a serious setback, but Carlo took it philosophically, just as he accepted his eldest son's sudden decision to turn his back on the Church and join Napoleon and Lucien in preparing for a military career. With the object of seeing what could be done about this switch Carlo undertook his final journey to France and here, taken ill at the house of Corsican friends, the Permons, he died. Napoleon at once assumed authority. Within days of Carlo's death the family had an opportunity of learning that the sixteen-year-old gunner cadet was unlikely to show Carlo's forbearance with people who had difficulty in making decisions. His first action as arbiter of the family fortunes was to decree that Joseph abandon both clerical and military studies and enrol himself as a law student in Italy; Napoleon had already assessed his elder brother's capabilities. Nine months before Carlo's death he had written bluntly to his uncle on the subject of brother Joseph. In the course of this letter he remarked: ' . . . he has not the courage to face the perils of an action . . . his health is feeble . . . and he knows nothing of mathematics!' Twenty years later, when Joseph was vacillating in Spain, Napoleon may have recalled this judgment. If he did he would have been well advised to act upon it.

Although Carlo Buonaparte had never been much good as a breadwinner the family felt his death keenly. Their immediate prospects were bleak. The family property in Corsica, consisting of a few acres of mulberry trees which Carlo had hoped to sell to the Government when they matured, was not much of an asset, particularly after the authorities refused to honour their promise. Elisa, the eldest girl, was well provided for at St Cyr and Joseph could expect further help from an ecclesiastical relative but Lucien still had to be supported, little Louis was awaiting a scholarship, Jérôme was an infant and the two younger girls had no prospects of a *dot* when they reached marriageable age. In the meantime Lucien, always the most unpredictable of the family, began to show an independent spirit and announced that he was abandoning his military studies to enter a seminary and study as a priest. If this proved impossible, he told them, he would pursue a literary career. The vagueness of his plans must have enraged his hard-pressed brother.

In February 1787, Napoleon got leave and went home to use his authority in the task of reorganising the family. He applied for and was granted a lengthy extension of leave on grounds of health and he did not return to his regiment, then stationed at Auxonne, until October. He must have had a very easy-going Colonel, for in the four years between February 1787 and February 1791, he obtained three leaves and three long extensions of leave, being absent from his regiment for a total of nineteen months. On New Year's Day 1788, the widow Buonaparte was alone with her four youngest children, Louis, Pauline, Caroline and Jérôme, whose ages ranged between ten and four. Although living in very modest circumstances she kept two servants but there is no doubt that she feared for the future and that she confided in Napoleon, who solved the immediate problem of ten-year-old Louis by taking him back to his regimental barracks, undertaking to feed, clothe and educate the boy.

The two brothers lived together in Spartan style, and after three months of this life Napoleon wrote to Joseph in terms of great affection for the boy abandoned in such cheerless surroundings with no one to look after him but his austere brother. Young Louis, however, made the best of things and employed the Buonaparte charm that each of the boys and their sister Pauline could switch on when necessary. 'All the women in the place are in love with him,' wrote Napoleon, 'and he is working hard at French, mathematics and geography. It is not difficult to see that he will turn out the best of us four. He is a delightful pupil and has the application and judgment of a man of forty.' In this letter we get a picture of Louis that is very different from the sour, misanthropic king who fled from his taskmaster eighteen years later. We hear of little Louis 'apeing the French' and 'making small-talk with the seriousness of an adult' but behind this is another picture that illustrates Napoleon's strong sense of family: he accepted these responsibilities with a purpose that was utterly lacking in their father.

In the meantime events were taking place that were to convulse not only the Corsican family, now scattered, with each of them making unspectacular attempts to equip themselves for the future, but France and all of Europe. In July 1789, the Paris mob stormed the Bastille and in the uneasy period that followed, three-quarters of Napoleon's aristocratic fellow-students at the Paris military academy left the country. For a time it looked as though Louis XVI would continue to reign as a constitutional monarch, but within three years the republican elements in French politics had gained the upper hand. Within a year of Napoleon's return to Auxonne another mob had stormed the Tuileries and France began to slide into anarchy.

One of the most serious results of this latest act of mob violence was the closing down of the *demoiselle* school at St Cyr. 'The Jacobins are lunatics,' raved Napoleon, writing to Joseph in June 1792, and goes on to describe in vivid terms what he had witnessed two days previously in the Tuileries gardens. In August all prospects of Elisa's serene future vanished overnight. The eldest girl was packed off home, bewailing the loss of the promised dowry and almost certainly without the promised 150 francs travelling allowance.

During his frequent visits to Corsica, Napoleon had become deeply involved in a revolutionary movement that aimed at regaining Corsican independence. No one has ever succeeded in unravelling the numerous shifts and evasions of Napoleon and his brothers during the period after the return of the Corsican patriot Paoli and the final defeat by the insurgents of French interests in the island. For a time, it is certain, they dreamed of seconding Paoli and freeing their homeland of the foreigner but as the revolution in France developed they had second thoughts and after two unsuccessful attempts on the part of Napoleon to capture the citadel at Ajaccio there was no alternative to flight. Joseph, still unqualified as a lawyer, had returned from Pisa and the wayward Lucien, still dithering between a military, priestly, literary and political career, had reappeared in Corsica to try his hand at state-craft. When the crisis came Lucien was the first to leave and after hiding out on their little estate for a day or so Napoleon and Joseph followed him, on June 13th, 1793. They took with them their Uncle Fesch, Letizia's half-brother, and all but the two youngest children, Caroline, then eleven, and Jérôme, aged nine, who were left in the care of kinsmen and brought over to the mainland after a brief interval. Within a month the fugitives were temporarily housed in Marseilles. About six months were to elapse before the unexpected success of a gunner's plan to take the neigh-bouring city of Toulon set each of them on the road to the throne-rooms of Europe.

This book is not an attempt to trace the military and political history of Napoleon; its object is much simpler, to follow the careers of the seven millstones Napoleon chose to hang around his neck during the twenty-one years separating the siege of Toulon from the final disaster at Waterloo. Insofar as Napoleon was never absent from the calculations of his brothers and sisters, and that he in his turn tried over and over again to use them as instruments of his policy, he will always dominate the background but this is not Napoleon's story but an attempt to tell seven almost parallel stories over a period of sixty-odd years. Napoleon, the arbiter of their fortunes, was the first of the brothers to die and his brothers and sisters only appear as actors on the world stage so long as he is there. Distance meant nothing to Napoleon. Not for nothing did he earn the soubriquet of 'Longboots' in the camps of Europe and he was no more inclined to let a thousand leagues curtail his guardianship of the family than he was to abandon his marshals in Spain to their own selfish devices. Wherever the members of his family were and whatever they were doing, he kept in close touch with them, missing very little of their secret intentions, their follies and their extravagances. Those among them whom he set up as kings never attained, or even expected to attain, the measure of independence taken for granted by most people on their twenty-first birthday. He loved them all but he never trusted them. He was always pathetically hopeful that one or more of them would mend their ways and when they disappointed him he stormed at them like an enraged parent. To his mother, Letizia, he was always respectful but even she could do little or nothing to soften his attitude towards them when, in his opinion, they had failed in their duty or tarnished the family name. At times he could be merciless in the exercise of this usurped authority but always, on reflection, he returned to them, showing far more gentleness than he received from any one of them. Throughout his entire life after the age of sixteen he identified himself with each of these four brothers and three sisters and when they failed he felt that he himself had failed, when they made fools of themselves in public then it was Napoleon at whom Europe laughed and jeered and this identification with his family caused him some of the most wretched moments in his life. It has been said that without his family Napoleon would have succeeded in retaining his vast Empire and establishing a hereditary line of kings. Perhaps this is true but as a theory it is worthless, for his family pride was such that it is impossible to imagine him turning his back on the least worthy of them at any time in his career. These four men and three women were not simply his brothers and sisters, because in all important respects he was head of the family and his position was nearer that of a father.

Every son and daughter of Carlo and Letizia Buonaparte inherited their parents' good looks. Each, in their youth, had the finely-moulded features and magnificent eyes of their mother, combined with the regularity of Carlo's handsome appearance. Two of the girls, Pauline and Caroline, were strikingly beautiful women and although the face of the younger girl was often clouded by bad temper her sister Pauline was regarded by many competent judges as the most beautiful woman of her time. All of them, Louis excepted, possessed robust health and strong constitutions and in their early 'twenties Joseph, Lucien and Jérôme were exceptionally

handsome men. Later on Joseph put on too much weight but he
never quite lost that air of distinction that clung to each of them
until they reached middle age. Elisa, the oldest of the girls, had
excellent features but her severe cast of features made her less
attractive than her sisters. On the other hand she was more
intelligent than either and had, in addition, a greater share of her
mother's dignity. Temperamentally Lucien was always the odd
man out among the brothers, but physically this distinction
goes to Louis. In early life they all looked very much alike,
but a close study of the large gallery of portraits available pro-
vides a number of clues to the dominant characteristics of each
brother and sister, characteristics which grew more distinct as time
went on. In all his portraits Joseph shows uncertainty, as though
he were forever awaiting somebody else's lead, whilst Lucien's
frustrated ego is clearly visible in his handsome features, and a
wilful temperament is revealed in the half-arrogant, half-obstinate
glance the painter has caught in the eyes. Louis' congenital pessimism and distrust of life is there and so is Jérôme's impudence and
sensuality. Elisa has the face of a woman without much capacity
for affection and the face of Caroline, the youngest girl, is that of a
spoiled child. It is in the features of Pauline, however, that a number of Buonaparte characteristics are revealed, for as an acknowledged beauty she was painted many times and her face has none
of that simpering quality so often seen in the portraits of many
professional beauties. Pauline's face reveals a great deal of personality and a range of expression usually absent in the Buonaparte
portrait gallery. Sometimes her expression is that of a teasing,
capricious woman and sometimes the warm heart which distinguished her from her brothers or sisters is revealed in the soft
lines of her mouth, but every portrait painter for whom she sat and
Canova, who modelled her in marble, has captured her strongest
characteristic, a half-amused sensuality that bewitched almost
every man she met.

All these are characteristics which could be recognised by someone knowing nothing of the personal histories of these seven
Corsicans, but they are vouched for in the millions of words
written about the family during the nineteenth century, when

memoir-writing was a very popular pastime among the French upper classes. Joseph never made a major decision that was not prompted by his terrible brother and Lucien was in a state of rebellion against Napoleon until the two brothers were parted by exile. Louis, who had shared the cheerless barrack lodging with Napoleon in the days when they both subsisted on a few francs a day, was never able to return the affection Napoleon had formed for him during those lean days and although, in some ways, he was as resentful of imperial authority as was his brother Lucien, he lacked the courage which made the family rebel push defiance to its limits. Elisa revealed very few human weaknesses, pursuing a policy of self-aggrandisement with singlemindedness but less ostentation than her sister Caroline or her youngest brother Jérôme. Caroline is the only member of the family whose greed and ambition was strong enough to make her a traitor. Jérôme, the baby of the family, probably committed more acts of folly and indiscretion than any of them but they were never calculated acts of rebellion such as Lucien's, or shameless deceits such as Caroline's. Jérôme never matured, not even when he was old, gross and sole inheritor of the Napoleonic mantle. At sixty he was still dedicated to the pursuit of women and diversions more suitable to a boy in his early 'twenties. Notwithstanding this there remained deep in Jérôme qualities of loyalty and courage that surprised his contemporaries and have the power to surprise us now.

One thing, perhaps only one, did the Buonapartes (Napoleon excepted) possess in common and this was a love of fine clothes and the outward trappings of power. In some cases, Joseph's for instance, this extended to the ownership of rich country estates and fine furniture but in Pauline and Jérôme particularly, and to some degree in all of them, there was a compulsion to load themselves with gorgeous clothes and expensive jewellery in which they could show off. Napoleon's taste in clothes was simple to the point of austerity but to his brothers and his sisters fine clothes were essential. Nothing so slyly illustrates the Spartan simplicity of their youth under the pennywise eye of their frugal mother.

CHAPTER TWO

'I watch life almost indifferently . . .'

Napoleon writing to Joseph
from Paris

THERE ARE MOMENTS in the history of Western civilisation when
it is possible to say 'It was here and in this way that it began; it
was at this precise time and place that circumstances combined to
divert the stream of history into a specified course and to generate
a movement, a nation or an age'. Moments like the one when
Luther hammered his thesis to the church door in Nuremburg, or
Lincoln was elected President on a minority vote – events that
touched off the Reformation and the American Civil War. The
hour of the Buonaparte family, crowded together on the fourth
floor of an exile's home in Marseilles, arrived in December 1793,
when the British fleet abandoned Toulon to the besieging republicans and some of the credit for the unexpected victory passed
to an obscure Corsican gunner whose plan, and his audacity in
carrying it out, had led to the fall of the base.

The importance of this relatively insignificant event to the exiled
family can hardly be exaggerated. Six months had passed since
they arrived in France as fugitives and the period had been a lean
one, far leaner than any of them except Letizia had ever been
called upon to endure. The chaotic state of the Republic was reflected in their prospects. Of the entire family Napoleon alone was
capable of supporting himself without recourse to charity. Here,
in this close-knit family group, was a half-trained lawyer, a young
man who had already tried a military and then a priestly training
and given both up in favour of politics, a half-educated boy of
fifteen, two 'teenage girls of sixteen and thirteen and two hungry

children of eleven and nine. How they lived during this final period of poverty is a mystery. The refugee allowances paid out by the Government were insufficient to buy more than one meal a day and presumably part of this dole must have been spent on rent and replacing the threadbare clothes in which they had fled Corsica. It is known that Joseph and Lucien went out daily in search of work, but whether they found anything more lucrative than an odd job is doubtful. Elisa, who had spent several years at St Cyr and also possessed a keen intelligence, was untrained to do the kind of job a sixteen-year-old girl might find in a Mediterranean seaport and such education as Louis had received from his brother had been sketchy and intermittent. The three younger children, Pauline, Caroline and Jérôme, were liabilities to the communal purse. It is probable that, during the Midi campaign that ended with the triumph at Toulon Napoleon, always conscious of his family responsibilities, sent what little he could afford, but it could not have been much and the family lived from hand to mouth, the girls repairing their clothes, helping Letizia about the house and cooking such food as was available in a city where many people were starving.

Lyons, the second city of France, had revolted against the central government and was under siege, a prelude to the revolting atrocities that attended its capture. In July Napoleon reported to Carteaux's army in Avignon and was attached to the artillery arm. When Marseilles itself revolted and the Marseillais marched to relieve Lyons, he saw his first sizeable action and the Federalists were thrown back and dispersed, Marseilles falling to the republican troops almost at once. In the meantime, however, the Toulon rebels, a mixture of royalists and constitutionalists who were appalled by the butchery taking place in Paris, came to terms with Admiral Hood's fleet and surrendered the town to the British, who at once fortified the heights east and west of the town. General Carteaux, whose qualifications for the command of an army rested on his reputation as a painter of historical scenes, moved on the port in September and here Napoleon had a stroke of luck. In the first day's fighting the artillery commander was wounded and Napoleon took his place. The hill forts were stormed in December and Napoleon was wounded in the thigh by a British bayonet, but the port was recaptured and Admiral Hood sailed away. In his despatch to the convention Carteaux's successor gave Napoleon full credit for his share in the victory and promotion followed. Within two months Napoleon was chief of brigade.

In Paris outrage succeeded outrage. Danton fell and the dictatorship of Robespierre was maintained by terror. Every day tumbrils rattled along the Rue St Honoré to the guillotine but news from Paris was slow to reach the south and when a gang of ruffians, fearing for their own heads, overthrew the dictator, the men of the Army of Italy in Nice, where Napoleon had gone to consolidate his reputation, were bewildered. As the friend and protégé of Robespierre's brother Augustin, Napoleon's own position was dangerous, for the younger Robespierre had written from Nice praising the enterprise and patriotism of the Corsican officer 'Buona Parte, whose property in Corsica had been ravaged by the tyrant Paoli'. After the Thermidor revolt reaction spread outwards from Paris and for a brief period Napoleon was under arrest, but his luck held and a Corsican brother officer intervened. He was released after a fortnight, restored to the active list and ordered to take up a command in the West where provinces were still resisting the revolution.

What had happened meanwhile in the crowded top floor of the house in the Rue Faubourg de Rome, Marseilles? After Napoleon's success at Toulon and his promotion to chief of brigade family fortunes took a sharp, upward turn. Joseph, Lucien and even young Louis were not slow to take advantage of their brother's rising star. Joseph obtained a commissary post with the Army of Italy and Lucien got himself a post as military storekeeper in the village of St Maximin in the Midi, but it was fifteen-year-old Louis who made the most spectacular use of the opportunity by getting himself appointed to the rank of adjutant-major of artillery in the National Guard! Had any of their subsequent biographers been on hand to note the speed with which the three brothers exploited their lucky break, Europe might have been less surprised by Buonaparte opportunism in the years ahead.

There is no evidence that Napoleon actually secured these appointments but no doubt at all that they stemmed directly from his influence or that of Salicetti, a fellow Corsican who had befriended Napoleon at Toulon and secured for him command of the artillery. Promotion to chief of brigade had brought Napoleon a substantial rise in pay and his first thought was for the impoverished family in Marseilles, but important as his advance proved to the family at this time it was not the only factor in their improved circumstances. Within a few months of Toulon the Buonapartes had access to the equivalent of £6,000 sterling; on August 1st, 1794, Joseph, the dull dog of the family, captured an heiress!

It would be interesting to know more of the courtship between the plodding Joseph and the plainer of the two Clary girls, who brought such a magnificent dowry to a man only recently in receipt of government relief. M. Clary, father of Julie and the prettier Désirée (who later came so near to marrying her famous brother-in-law) is variously described as a soap-boiler and a silk-merchant. Perhaps he was both. Details regarding the Clary background are hard to trace for in later years, when both daughters occupied thrones, the Clarys were understandably reticent about their associations with soap and silk. Julie was no beauty and unkind remarks about her imperfect complexion have come down to us, but all contemporaries agree that she was a kind, generous person who would go out of her way to help any one in need. Perhaps Joseph's complacency and pliability appealed to her, or perhaps his good looks triumphed over the suits of more successful men. Perhaps her father was discerning enough to see prospects of an all-round improvement in the Buonaparte fortunes after the groom's brother had made a reputation for himself in the South. In any case the match received papa's approval and the dowry was paid. For the time being at least Letizia and the four youngest children could be sure of a meal.

Napoleon was understandably delighted. For years he had been contributing the greater part of his meagre earnings to the bed and board of mother, brothers and sisters, and although he had never complained, news of the substantial Clary dowry must have come as an immense relief to him.

Louis' appointment as adjutant-major in the National Guard did not last very long. Somebody, possibly Napoleon himself, realised that promotion at this speed should not be encouraged in a fifteen-year-old boy and he was hauled out of the National Guard and packed off to Chalons to serve as a cadet and complete his interrupted education. In late summer, 1794, it must have seemed to all of them that luck had turned and that they could look ahead with a certain amount of optimism. They were wrong. The summer of 1794 was a false dawn. In less than a year their prospects were as bleak as ever.

The wave of reaction sweeping down from Paris after the overthrow of Robespierre very nearly engulfed the Buonaparte family. Suddenly and inexplicably terror was unfashionable and those who had subscribed to it found themselves the hunted instead of the hunters. Napoleon had never been a terrorist but he had been a close friend of Robespierre's brother and Lucien, who rarely did anything halfheartedly, drew attention to himself by adopting the extreme republicanism popular during the period preceding the tyrant's death.

Napoleon had managed to escape the fate of a number of Robespierre's executives in the provinces. The bloody Carrier, butcher of Nantes and inventor of republican 'marriages' (in which victims were tied two by two and drowned in the Loire), had been brought to justice; so had Fouquier Tinville, the impassive monster whose nod as Public Prosecutor had sent hundreds to the guillotine. Reaction against senseless butchery, however, was not the only factor that checked the family's advance that summer, for with it came a slackening of the national will to crush the coalition threatening the Republic. A mood of frivolity succeeded one of strident patriotism and the impetus of revolution lost. Down in the south, where Napoleon had gone as inspector of coastal defences, the armies were shoeless, ill-equipped and wildly undisciplined. An expedition to recapture Corsica was launched and Napoleon played a part in it, but it ended in failure and part of the ignomity adhered to the victor of Toulon.

Madame Buonaparte, with her three pretty daughters and her youngest boy, had moved to Nice in order to be close to the man they regarded as head of the family. Elisa and Pauline, now respectively eighteen and fifteen, were already attracting a swarm of suitors and their association with so many young army officers was giving Letizia a certain amount of anxiety. Elisa particularly had won the reputation of a flirt whilst Pauline's beauty aroused lively interest among her brother's associates. It was Lucien, however, who caused Madame more serious concern, for word reached her that, notwithstanding the fate of the extremists in Paris, he was earning a reputation as a local firebrand.

A study of Lucien's behaviour during this period of his life, when he was no more than a humble military storekeeper, goes some way towards establishing later claims that he was bitterly jealous of Napoleon and was determined, somehow or other, to build himself a reputation equal to that of his brother. He styled himself 'Lucius Brutus' and his cronies, dazzled by his clownish behaviour and bombast, called him 'Little Robespierre'. What might have happened to him when his reputation spread beyond the confines of the district can be conjectured without difficulty, but fortunately for himself he now succumbed to a new and less dangerous enthusiasm. He fell madly in love with the pretty daughter of the local innkeeper and before either of his elder brothers or his mother could advise him he married her. At the same time he did not altogether abandon politics, for we hear of his strenuous efforts to rename St Maximin 'Marathon'.

His bride, Christine Boyer, was illiterate but her contemporaries unite in paying tribute to her prettiness and sweetness of nature. Madame Junot, who came to know her well in the following years, describes her as 'an angel of light' and there is no doubt that Lucien not only courted her with the enthusiasm he brought to everything but developed for her, during the few years she survived their marriage, a deep and genuine affection. Within a year of the marriage Christine had presented her husband with a girl named Charlotte. She was the first of the Buonaparte grandchildren.

In the meantime Louis, now sixteen had been appointed his

brother's aide-de-camp in Nice. Had the abortive Corsican expedition been successful he would have shared Napoleon's delight in punishing the men who had driven the family from their home. Napoleon had already begun to assemble round him a little knot of soldiers who saw him as someone possessing above-average talent and the bond forged between the two brothers during their lean days together in Auxonne encouraged Napoleon to keep his younger brother near him and supervise his training in the field. By spring 1795, however, all hopes of a triumphant return to the homeland had faded and Napoleon, disgusted with the Government's neglect of the forces in the south, decided to try his luck in Paris.

He left the south in May, taking Louis with him, and before long the sixteen-year-old lieutenant of artillery was back at school in Chalons. Napoleon had made up his mind that only by remaining in the capital, where he was in close touch with events and politicians, could he hope to exploit any further opportunities that might arise, and having made this decision he stuck to it, regardless of risks. Orders came for him to take up a command in the West where civil war was still raging and the central government had failed to crush the counter-revolution of a few thousand peasants. The war in the west was the graveyard of military reputations. Whole divisions disappeared into the forests of La Vendée and most of them, harried by expert partisans like Charette, were cut to pieces without having achieved anything. Napoleon weighed his prospects carefully and then pleaded illness. He knew that in times like these his luck could change if he managed to remain in Paris, and when renewed orders came for him to take up his post he fell back on further evasions and continued to watch events in the capital. He was risking a court martial, but to a man who had once overstayed leave by nine months, a delay in taking up an unwanted appointment presented few difficulties. He had influence of a sort among the shoddy politicians who had succeeded Robespierre and, as he wrote to Joseph, 'Plenty of soldiers will make better brigadiers than myself but few can command artillery so well.' He wrote a great deal to his brother Joseph this summer, describing the moods of Paris, discussing a possible match between himself and his sister-in-law Désirée, and interesting himself in Joseph's half-formed decision to obtain a Government post in Genoa. As always he was confident of his ability to pull the necessary strings and Joseph, who had lost his commissary position and now had a wife to support, waited hopefully, happy to let his dynamic brother chart his destiny.

In the meantime, as everyone had prophesied, Lucien got into serious trouble. He was arrested and thrown into prison at Aix. In the same town was Uncle Fesch, Letizia's half-brother, who had fled with the family from Corsica but he does not seem to have made much effort to get Lucien out of gaol. Fesch was miserably homesick for Corsica and Napoleon wrote contemptuously from Paris: ' . . . he is just what he always was, building castles in the air and writing me six-page letters on some meticulous point of speculation. The present means no more to him than the past, the future is all in all.'

By August, in the steamy heat of the capital, Napoleon was growing desperate and his letters show more despondency than those written during the days preceding Toulon. The family was scattered and he could draw no comfort from that sense of kinship with mother, brothers and sisters that had sustained him when they were all in the south. With Joseph out of work, Lucien in gaol, Louis in Chalons and his sisters lacking dowries his splendid visions began to fade, but he hung on with quiet desperation, parrying the demands of exasperated superiors who would have packed him off to the reeking villages of La Vendée. In an almost suicidal mood he wrote again to Joseph: ' . . . I watch life indifferently . . . at this rate, my friend, I shall end by not stepping out of the way of a passing carriage.'

Then, quite suddenly, everything changed again. In place of Carnot, the Republic's organiser of victory, Napoleon was appointed to the topographical bureau of the Committee of Public Safety, a body responsible for planning the strategy of the distant armies. He was excited and flattered, for here was proof at last that authority was beginning to recognise his administrative talents. Joyfully he wrote to Joseph, advising him that it might be a good idea to apply for the Turkish Consulate, and a week or so later the

threat of a posting to the West was finally removed and his appointment to the topographical bureau confirmed. One month was to
pass before an event took place in Paris that set the entire family on
the second rung of the ladder to affluence and splendour.

The opportunity for which Napoleon had been waiting, and for
which he had twice risked dismissal from the army, arrived on
the evening of October 5th when – for the last time in almost a
generation – the mob was out on the streets of Paris and Robespierre's successors were obliged to defend themselves against men
and women who did not care who was in power so long as they
brought bread, solvency and some kind of order into civil affairs.
Among the enemies of the Convention were royalists who wanted
the return of the Bourbons, constitutionalists who wanted a Parlia-
mentary régime on the English pattern, Jacobins who distrusted
the mediocrities who had replaced Robespierre and (by far the
majority), men like Napoleon himself who realised that if the
gains of the revolution were to be consolidated the country must
have a governing body alive to its responsibilities.

The story of Buonaparte's share in the comparatively mild riot
known as 'The Whiff of Grapeshot' is well known. It was all over
in a matter of hours and the Convention, headed by the cynical
Barras, gained a four-year respite. When the Directory that succeeded it disappeared, the name of 'Buonaparte' was a household
word in Europe, but in the interval Napoleon was the most popular
soldier in Paris. Once again his family had been plucked from
poverty and obscurity.

For each of them the situation improved overnight. There was
no more talk of Joseph drifting off to Genoa or Constantinople as
a diplomat. Lucien talked himself out of gaol in Aix. Madame,
her two flirtatious daughters, and the two youngest children,
Caroline and Jérôme, were summoned to Paris. Joseph and his
wife also arrived and settled themselves in a pleasant house in the
Rue de Rocher, where young Louis was sent with his brother and
sister-in-law. If one studies the immediate demands made by
Napoleon within hours of saving the Government the true value
of his service on October 5th can be estimated. The last of the

rioters had dispersed by dawn on the 6th. The same day Napoleon was made General of Division. By October 26th he was General of the Army of the Interior, demanding and getting 60,000 francs for his mother and sisters, a consulate appointment for Joseph, a substantive lieutenancy for Louis as aide-de-camp and the Commissary of War for Lucien, just out of gaol! No one could accuse him of failing to take family responsibilities seriously, even if he had nothing but contempt for the men he had saved from lynching.

Having disposed of his family problems for the time being he began to take stock of his own future. In the weeks immediately succeeding Vendémiaire he met and fell in love with a thirty-two-year-old widow, Josephine Beauharnais, lately the mistress of the politician Barras. After spending one night in her arms he wrote, 'I awake all filled with you. Your image, and the intoxicating pleasures of last night, allow my senses no rest. Sweet and matchless Josephine how strangely you work upon my heart!' That was in December. By March 5th the following year, they were man and wife, Napoleon having gallantly advanced his age to help close the six-year gap between them. On his marriage certificate he gave his place of birth as Paris and in a carriage that had once been owned by the dead King Louis the couple drove off to spend a three-day honeymoon at Josephine's house in the Rue Chantereine.

By this time the family had gathered in Paris to await further advantages from their blood relationship with the man of the hour and such advantages were soon apparent. Early in the new year Napoleon was appointed to command the Army of Italy and was regarded by all (except his bride) as the coming man in military circles. The Buonapartes accepted his patronage coolly, for his whirlwind courtship had frightened them. They did not know much about this Beauharnais woman. They heard that she was a free-spending harlot who was sparing with her smiles in the hope of concealing her bad teeth, and for the time being they reserved judgment. Within a few days of the civil wedding, which none of them attended, he had gone to Italy to astonish the world in a forty-three day campaign that was to write his name in history. Mother, brothers and sisters settled down to await news of triumphs, Letizia and her two elder daughters at a house in the Rue Verte,

Joseph and his wife at their house in the Rue de Rocher, Lucien to make as many bombastic speeches as he liked in the House of Representatives and the two youngest, Caroline and Jérôme, at their new schools.

Caroline, already a beauty, was enrolled at the general establishment of Madame Campan where Josephine's daughter Hortense was a pupil. Jérôme went to the Collège Irlandais in St Germain-en-Laye, where he had as a model scholar Josephine's son Eugène. These two step-children of Napoleon were to play important parts in the Buonaparte story. Hortense was to become the disillusioned bride of Louis, Eugène was to remain all his life the *bête noire* of the pleasure-loving and improvident Jérôme.

CHAPTER THREE

'Like a torrent you have rushed down from the Appennines!'

Proclamation of Napoleon to
the Army of Italy, 1796

'SOLDIERS, like a torrent you have rushed down from the Apen-
nines; Milan is yours' ran the proclamation of the conqueror to
his loot-hungry battalions at the close of the first stage of his Italian
triumphs. It had all happened with a speed that stupefied the slow-
moving, slow-thinking professional soldiers schooled in the gavotte
of eighteenth-century warfare. In March, Napoleon was at Nice.
In May he was at Milan, with the whole of Northern Italy at his
feet. Before the end of the year members of the Buonaparte family
were enjoying oriental luxuries at the Commander-in-Chief's
headquarters in the castle of Montebello, near the northern capital.
Milan was theirs as well.

Nothing like this had ever happened before, not to them, not
to France, not to any European state engaged in a war of conquest.
To politicians like Barras, to Josephine flirting in Paris, to the reassembled Buonapartes uncertain that the whiff of grapeshot was
not another false dawn, it seemed hardly more than days between
the departure of the newly married general for the south and the
arrival in Paris of couriers with news of astounding victories, each
more sensational than the frontier victories of the Republic in '93.
Only Louis, the protégé of the famous man, could claim a personal
share in his brother's triumphs, for Louis had gone down into
Italy to serve on the Commander's staff and at Arcola, a narrow
victory, Napoleon had a chance to evaluate the young subaltern's
qualities as a soldier. It was Louis, helped by Napoleon's academy
comrade Marmont, who plunged into the slime beside the

embankment when the bridge over the river had been swept by Austrian crossfire and the General, running forward to rally his grenadiers, had been half drowned in the mud of the dykes. The comradeship of these two brothers, so utterly unlike in temperament, had now been tested in the field.

The rest of the family played no active part in the campaigns. Joseph and his wife stayed at their comfortable house in the Rue de Rocher and Madame Buonaparte spent her time getting rid of undesirable suitors at the Rue Verte. Lucien, still an army commissary and smarting under his brother's displeasure for marrying the daughter of his landlord, was home again from Germany, trailing his pretty wife and one of her cousins who had attached himself to the pair. Caroline was studying geography, drawing and deportment at Madame Campan's establishment in St Germain-in-Laye and close by, at the Collège Irlandais, Jérôme was being urged by everyone except Josephine to model himself on his blameless schoolfellow Eugène Beauharnais and win prizes offered by Patrick MacDermott for good behaviour and scholastic achievements.

The year 1796, a time of triumph, was a bad year for domestic relationships within the Buonaparte-Beauharnais circle. In that year Caroline and Hortense conceived an active dislike for one another at Madame Campan's and Jérôme, who had already made up his mind that life was an oyster, regarded Eugène with the contempt backward students reserve for the ones who win prizes. Little Hortense, a timid girl, tried hard to win Caroline's friendship. The terrible ordeal through which she had passed during the Terror had left her a nervous, highly-strung child and she saw Caroline as a means of ingratiating herself with her formidable stepfather, but her approaches came to nothing. She touched up Caroline's drawings in the hope that they would win awards; she explained to giggling little girls that Caroline was not really so backward as she appeared, but had lost educational headway during her constant moves up and down the country, but instead of being grateful for this chaperonage Caroline told stories of her little relative's haughtiness and when challenged by Hortense excused herself by declaring that she was madly in love with a member of her brother's staff and wanted to leave school and share the gay life her brothers and sisters were enjoying in Paris. She also drew attention to the pace set by Hortense's mother who, at that time, was making the most of her unique role as Our Lady of Victories. All Paris was aware that the astonishing little General was hopelessly in love with his elegant wife and wrote to her every day in terms of the most extravagant affection. Those who knew Josephine were also aware that most of his letters went unanswered and that Josephine's day was far too full of fêtes, parties, carriage drives, presentations and flirtations to waste time penning more than a few casual lines to her lovesick husband. Her indifference to him and, what was more to the point, her wild extravagance, did not go unnoticed by the Buonaparte clan. Joseph complained about her daily visits to the dressmaker and the more expensive Paris jewellers and Madame Letizia, who could look back on a blameless life as wife and mother, frowned whenever the name of Napoleon's aristocratic wife was mentioned. She had heard that there had been a public scandal in the Beauharnais family years before the guillotine had made Josephine a widow and that Hortense was the result of a brief reconciliation between man and wife. This was bad enough but worse had followed, for it was also rumoured that whilst awaiting the guillotine in the Carmelite prison Josephine had been the mistress of General Hoche. After that there had been the association with the voluptuary Barras, who had tired of her and passed her on to Napoleon. It was not an encouraging recommendation to a mother who had borne thirteen children in twenty years of married life and had never, either before or since her husband's death, so much as smiled at another man. Discussing 'the Creole' as they called her, the Buonapartes forgot their private jealousies and decided that something would have to be done about this ridiculous marriage, but they were aware that very little could be done at the moment, for Napoleon's infatuation was the joke of Paris. Sooner or later, however, a fever of this intensity must cool and then, perhaps, some of the money that Josephine was pouring away on clothes, jewels, furniture and loans to her friends could be rediverted into family channels.

*

It might have been the need to close family ranks that disposed Madame, the kindly Joseph and even the two elder girls to behave charitably towards Lucien's wife. When Napoleon first heard of Lucien's marriage he flew into a rage and declared that he would never receive Christine and would not speak to Lucien again until he had put her aside. In Napoleon's absence, however, Lucien managed to persuade the rest of the family to accept Christine as a bona fide daughter and sister-in-law and it is probable that Christine's personal charm did more to achieve this than Lucien's open defiance of his brother's decree. For a time the couple lived in Paris, partly with Joseph and partly with Madame and the girls, and the family's main worries at this period were young Jérôme's precocity and the difficult business of selecting two likely suitors from the men swarming about Elisa and Pauline. Pauline, particularly, was proving very troublesome, for sometimes it seemed to the stern Letizia that the girl had no moral sense at all and it was clear to her that she must get her married. This was a problem that could be solved as soon as Napoleon sent for them to share his triumphs but for Jérôme, still slacking at school, there was no easy solution, for the boy had such charm that everyone spoiled him, including Josephine.

Jérôme spent his school holidays in Paris, flitting between the homes of his mother, his eldest brother and his sister-in-law's house in the Rue Chantereine, and it was at the latter establishment that he was given the maximum freedom, for Josephine was looking for a flaw in family unity and the possibility of a match between Jérôme and her daughter Hortense had already occurred to her. Jérôme's precocity was such that he is said to have formed a romantic attachment some time before he left the Collège de Juilly at the age of fourteen. Whether this is true or not, it is at least certain that he pledged his brother's credit and incurred debts that were paid by Josephine.

In the meantime success followed success in Italy, and the arrival of captured battle flags became a daily occurrence. Towards the end of the year the summons for which they had all been waiting arrived and the older Buonapartes set out for Milan. Josephine had already gone there in response to repeated demands from her frantic husband.

Down here, in the atmosphere of a court, an era of splendour dawned for every member of the little group that, three years before, had disembarked without luggage at Toulon. Joseph, now a seasoned administrator of twenty-eight and a man of some real ability as a diplomat, was given a chance to see what he could achieve in Parma and Rome. Lucien was earmarked as a politician and went to the Council of Five Hundred where, in a matter of four years, he made his mark and was president at a time when his brother was desperately in need of a powerful political ally. Louis remained in the army with rapid promotion assured, not only because at that time he was the Commander-in-Chief's favourite brother but also because he had proved himself as a soldier. Then, with a certain gusto, Napoleon addressed himself to the problem of finding suitable husbands for the two eldest girls.

The Napoleon who presided over family councils at Montebello was a very different person from the shabby brigadier who had done what he could for his family after Toulon; he was changed too from the man of the hour who, a few months before, had set out for Italy with his way still to make in the world. Almost every observer close to him in the spring and summer of 1796 comments on the great change that came over him after the victory at Arcola where he came so near to losing his life. The change showed itself in a number of ways, in his manner of addressing subordinates, in an increased grasp of fundamentals on the field and in the conference chamber, by a thoughtfulness that sometimes softened his expression to such a degree that strangers could mistake it for affability. After Arcola he spoke quite openly of his 'star', of the certainty with which he would shape coming events, and those near him, men like Joseph and dashing blades like Junot and Murat, began to moderate their approach to him, their admiration already tinged with awe. This was not only the result of triumphs in the field, for some had been close enough to see that several victories had come very near to disaster. It was due to something in the man himself, an air of tremendous confidence that he wore with modesty, as though his achievements so far would soon be eclipsed by far more spectacular events. Nowhere is this dignity and authority more apparent than in his dealings with his family. Deeply

immersed as he was in consolidating victories, re-shaping Northern
Italy, granting interviews, looking after the men who had won
those victories, and dealing with a mass of correspondence, he
still had time for the family, giving careful consideration to Joseph's
appointments as a diplomat, to Lucien's future as a politician and
even to Jérôme's education. Above all he was concerned with the
future of the girls – what kind of men they should marry and in
what spheres they would best acquit themselves as wives. As a
man deeply in love with his wife he was inclined to favour love-
matches, although only his mother had succeeded in moderating
his anger at Lucien's entanglement. Here at Montebello he was
immersed in statecraft and hardly a detail escaped him, but now,
as later, his deepest thoughts were reserved for his family. His
mother, brothers and sisters, aware of this for years, were content
to await his decisions and accept his judgments.

Among the suitors for Elisa was Admiral Truguet, a fine seaman
and an excellent match, but Madame Buonaparte had a prejudice
against the sea, evident later in her opposition to Jérôme becoming
a sailor and which had, in fact, revealed itself years ago when there
was talk of entering Napoleon at a naval academy. For this reason
if for no other she was against Truguet and favoured the suite of a
fellow Corsican, a young man called Felice Pasquale Bacchiochi,
whom Elisa herself preferred. Looking into the future, and contemplating some of the splendid matches arranged by Napoleon
for the younger children and for comparatively distant relatives,
it seems odd that Napoleon should have approved of this marriage.
Most of his staff officers would have been glad to enter the family
circle and Bacchiochi, a mere major of infantry, was slipshod, dull
and talentless, his heavy features the outward signs of a ponderous
mind. There is one other reason why he should have been sum-
marily rejected in favour of a more promising husband. He was
closely related to the Borgo family, also of Corsica, and the Borgos
had at one time feuded with the Buonapartes. It is possible that
the marriage ended the feud but if it did traces of it lingered over
the next twenty years, for one of Bacchiochi's relations distinguished himself in the service of several European governments
by his hatred of the Buonaparte clan.

In spite of this, and believing no doubt that the forceful Elisa might make something of the groom, Napoleon approved the match, which took place at Montebello on May 1st, 1797. Elisa brought her husband a dowry of 30,000 francs. This was not, as has been suggested, part of the loot of Lombardy but her share of the Buonaparte property in Corsica, recently recovered from the Paolists. Within six weeks Pauline was also married. There had been five Buonaparte weddings in less than three years.

The choice of Pauline's husband presented difficulties. Recently she had been having an affair with a prominent politician called Fréron and it was rumoured in Paris that she already had as many as half-a-dozen lovers, including her brother Napoleon. This rumour started with lighthearted remarks made by Pauline herself, who is said to have declared, 'I am on excellent terms with my brother, I have slept with him twice.' Since Pauline often made scandalous remarks of this kind and went through life shocking friends and relatives by comments that embarrassed everyone within earshot, very little reliance can be placed on the statement, particularly as Napoleon was also accused of incestuous conduct with his youngest sister, Caroline. There can be no doubt, however, that Pauline lost her virginity at an early age. Mounier, a secretary of Napoleon, declares that he was one of five lovers whom Pauline entertained under one roof at one time and either then or later she certainly obliged the Marshal Macdonald and General Montholon, who accompanied Napoleon to St Helena. Her subsequent liaison with Macdonald became an imperial scandal. The pair are said to have locked themselves in an apartment for three days and had food and drink sent in at intervals but at the time of her marriage she was deeply in love with Fréron, the well-known Jacobin, but it was his reputation as a terrorist that turned Napoleon against the match and led him to substitute General Leclerc. Madame Mère, who was aware of her daughter's fall from virtue, was extremely anxious that Pauline should be married as soon as possible and certainly communicated her wishes to Napoleon. Anxious to use his sister to further his political interests, Napoleon promptly offered her to his oldest friend, Marmont, who politely declined the honour. A closer look at the character of this man leads one to

understand why he rejected this chance to marry into the Buonaparte family. Auguste Fréderic Marmont was an extremely shrewd,
calculating officer who had estimated Napoleon's talents when
they were both cadets and had extended hospitality to him in the
days when he was in need of a free lodging and a square meal.
Since then they had been inseparable and were to remain so until
Marmont played Judas and earned the contempt of every Buonapartist in France. He was the last marshal to survive and this alone
singles him out as a remarkable judge of events and character. He
had little difficulty in estimating what kind of wife Pauline was
likely to prove and cheerfully sacrificed her to another distinguished
officer, Adjutant-General Victor-Emmanuel Leclerc, whose reputation stood high among the veterans of the army of Italy.

They were married in Milan on June 14th, and the wedding was
celebrated with a pomp entirely lacking at the shabby little ceremony that marked Napoleon's marriage to Josephine fifteen
months before. Pauline at this time was attracted to her husband
but it was not long before Leclerc found himself obliged to choose
between a scandal that would injure his career, or the prospect of
sharing Pauline with others. Already, at the age of seventeen, the
beautiful Corsican girl had a reputation for sensuality. Within two
years of her marriage she was regarded by many as a nympho-
maniac.

In the meantime Napoleon's own marriage was floundering.
Josephine, who made no secret of the boredom Napoleon's passion
produced in her, began flirting with a gay young man called Hippolyte Charles. Hippolyte was everything Napoleon was not,
handsome, athletic and with a reputation for wit and high spirits.
The family saw in this indiscretion an opportunity that might be
turned to account and lost no time in acquainting the harassed
Commander-in-Chief with the details. Napoleon, however, was
still too much in love with his wife to be influenced by gossip and
dealt with the situation promptly by sending his rival back to
Paris. The Buonapartes were bitterly disappointed at the failure of
their first attempt to destroy the Creole but they did not despair.
Hippolyte Charles was a card to be kept up the family sleeve and
we shall hear more of him in the near future.

With two of the girls married, Joseph launched upon a promising career, Louis making progress in the army, Lucien more or less forgiven and the two youngest children at good schools, Napoleon now turned to the business of making peace with Austria and consolidating his position as the first soldier-negotiator of the Republic. Montebello was the third milestone in the march of the Buonaparte family towards the thrones of Europe. There had been Toulon, then Vendémaire and finally Italy. From now on there were no more false dawns and no more waiting in scattered little groups for something to turn up. They had arrived and there was not one of them save Letizia who did not regard the future as assured. From Joseph in Parma to Jérôme at the school in Juilly, they looked ahead with confidence. They had a champion and a provider far superior to the man who had importuned on their behalf as children, for whilst the journeys of Carlo Buonaparte had sometimes borne fruit, those of his second son led not to sinecures but to Aladdin's cave. The man upon whom the paternal mantle had fallen thrived on responsibility. In this respect, as in others, he was unique amongst the family.

BOOK TWO

The Arrivals

CHAPTER FOUR

'I am tired of Glory at twenty-nine . . .'

Napoleon to Joseph in
Egypt, in 1799

THE TIDE WAS FLOWING strongly now, but it was still no onrush
that swept everything before. Here and there were islands of resistance, scattered and not readily recognised by a family enjoying
the services of such a pilot, yet each obstruction capable of wrecking
the ship if approached without patience.

France was now controlled by a group of five Directors, consisting of one opportunist, one theorist and three honest nonentities.
None would willingly yield power to a young man of twenty-
seven. There were still the old republicans, men like Augereau
and Jourdan, who would resist any attempt at dictatorship, and
there was Moreau, whose reputation as a General most nearly
approached that of Napoleon. There were also the fence-squatters
centred round Bernadotte, who had married Napoleon's old sweet-
heart Désirée Clary and was encouraged by her to oppose the
ambition of the Buonapartes. None of these opposition parties
had joined forces but if they did anything might happen and the
Buonapartes might be thrust aside.

Napoleon came home from Italy on December 5th, 1797 and
the modesty of his behaviour during his appearances in the streets
of the capital disconcerted his enemies and dismayed the more impetuous of his supporters. Some thought he should seize control
at once, capitalising on his triumphs and sweeping to power on a
popular vote, but his sure political instinct made him hold back,
knowing that the time was not ripe and that the success of such a
coup could not be guaranteed. He had a profound distrust of mobs

and wanted to come to power by constitutional means. He was ingratiating with everyone, and when the Directory suggested that he should take command of the army in the North and prepare for the invasion of England he travelled to the Pas de Calais and inspected harbours and ships, weighing the chances carefully and deciding that the scheme was impracticable so long as Britain commanded the seas. Instead he turned his thoughts to Egypt and the Directors, eager to get rid of such a dangerous man, encouraged him in the enterprise. By spring 1798, plans for an Eastern campaign were well advanced and forty thousand men gathered at Toulon and nearby ports with the object of outwitting Nelson, who patrolled the Mediterranean, and landing in Egypt in order to disrupt British trade in the East. It was a harebrained scheme but it caught and held his imagination. The youthful dream of becoming a second Alexander had never quite faded.

Before he rode south again there was a picnic in the woods outside Paris. Napoleon and his wife called at Madame Campan's Academy and collected Caroline, Hortense and a pretty relative of Josephine's, Emilie de Beauharnais, who was also a pupil at the establishment. Accompanying the General that day was Lavalette, one of the eager young men with whom he had begun to surround himself and the soldier paid court to Emilie, whose response was apathetic. This particular picnic had been arranged for the purpose of bringing these two young people together and the fact that it achieved its object had powerful repercussions in the future, for soon after his return from Italy, Louis Buonaparte had called at Madame Campan's on a visit to Caroline and here he had fallen in love with the dark, slender Emilie de Beauharnais whose aristocratic parents were not only prescribed but divorced and whose mother had remarried, choosing a coloured man. Hearing of Louis' infatuation, and determined to prevent Louis from imitating the reckless conduct of Lucien, Napoleon took matters in hand and brusquely informed his aide-de-camp Lavalette that he must marry at once and that his Commander-in-Chief would provide the bride. Lavalette protested that he had no money and that he was due to embark for Egypt in a fortnight and might well be killed in action. Napoleon agreed that this was more than a possibility but that he himself would provide money and that the State paid pensions to the widows of soldiers killed in action. He added that Lavalette could easily be married in a week and that it was his duty to father children 'for without them there is no meaning to life'. Fortunately for Lavalette the handpicked bride was an attractive girl and the wedding did in fact take place within seven days. Years later the devotion of this couple became a legend in Europe after Emilie had stagemanaged a spectacular escape from prison on behalf of her husband the night before he was due to be shot for his part in the Hundred Days.

Louis was furious at seeing the girl of his choice whisked out of his reach and it is doubtful whether he ever forgave his brother for this particular piece of matchmaking. Hortense Beauharnais, who had the misfortune to marry this sullen, brooding Buonaparte, declared that Emilie returned Louis' love and if this is true the incident goes some way to explain the miserable failure of her own marriage and also the future relationship of the brothers.

Josephine accompanied her husband down to Toulon to see him set sail and then, with relief, she returned to her beloved Paris and bought a pretty estate at Malmaison. Here she settled down to enjoy her hobby of gardening and her infatuation with the irresistible Hippolyte Charles. Within weeks all Paris was convinced that he was her lover.

Joseph, back from Rome, was consolidating his position in political circles. He and his plain, pleasant wife Julie bought a magnificent estate at Mortfontaine and used the house as a rallying centre for the Buonapartists. Sometimes Jérôme went to receive a mild lecture on his extravagance and what his despairing tutors described as 'giddiness and an inordinate love of display'. Jérôme was always willing to sit through a lecture if, at the end of it, he could borrow a few thousand francs from his mentor and settle the more pressing of his debts. He was very happily placed for this kind of manoeuvre. If Joseph and Julie failed him he fell back on his mother and if Letizia was not in a generous mood he could always call upon Lucien or upon one or other of his married sisters. In the last resort he could touch Josephine for a loan. As regards friends in need Jérôme had no special favourites.

In his mind at least there was every excuse for his extravagant way of living. The boy was nursing a bitter, personal disappointment, for he had hoped that his brother would have enrolled him in the Army of Egypt and given him an opportunity to share in the glory of conquest. He was still only fourteen, but many boys of his age were enrolled as powder-monkeys on the men-of-war accompanying the expedition, and Eugène Beauharnais, the model schoolboy, had left school to serve on headquarters staff. Napoleon, however, would not hear of such a project. Jérôme was told to forget it and apply himself to his studies. He had won a prize for geography but it was not much to show for two years of study at the best college in the land.

Lucien was now making spectacular headway as a legislator. The only member of the family capable of making a lucid and persuasive speech, he was the right man to recruit support among professional politicians. In the Council of Five Hundred his reputation increased daily and when, eighteen months later, his brother unexpectedly returned from Egypt, he was Minister for Home Affairs. Soon the family was to owe him almost as much as they owed his elder brother.

Louis had accompanied Napoleon on the expedition, but within six months he was invalided home. It was said at the time that he had contracted syphilis and he was not present with the other Italian veterans when the French Army trailed across the desert, were halted under the walls of Acre and trudged back again to throw the Turks into the sea at Aboukir. Louis' pessimism was already apparent. He had never been as strong and resilient as the other Buonapartes and whether or not he suffered from venereal disease the rigours of the Italian campaign had left their mark on him.

Elisa was finding her husband Felice unutterably dull and her frustration showed in a propensity to gossip, sometimes about the amours of her sister Pauline but more often about the scandalous behaviour of Josephine at Malmaison. Recognised as an intelligent woman, with excellent literary and artistic tastes, she did not possess the temperament to enjoy the Buonaparte good fortune. When she was not intriguing against her detested sister-in-law she was presiding over a salon of writers and painters. She kept Joseph, as temporary head of the family, well informed on everything that was taking place at Malmaison, but although the animosity between the Buonapartes and Josephine was discussed in every drawing-room in Paris there was no open breach as yet but only a war of innuendo. For instance Elisa commented on Josephine's failure to produce an heir. 'It may be Napoleon's fault,' complained Josephine, to which Elisa replied: 'Ah sister, I know you have had two children but after all, you were young then!'

The scandal at Malmaison soon grew to such proportions that Joseph was persuaded to report the facts to Napoleon. His letter got through the tight British blockade and General Junot broke the news to his Chief. Bourienne, Napoleon's chief secretary, has left a moving picture of how the Commander-in-Chief took the blow. He saw Napoleon walking agitatedly up and down with his friend Junot and says, 'There was something convulsive in his features and wild in his looks; several times he struck himself on the head. Later he said to me – "If you were attached to me you would have told me all I have just heard from Junot! There's a true friend. Josephine . . .! and I am six hundred leagues away . . . to deceive me like that! Woe betide them! I'll exterminate that race of whipper-snappers and fops! As for her, divorce, yes, a resounding public divorce!"' It looked very much as if Joseph's letter would have the desired effect.

But it was not infidelity alone that worried the Buonapartes, for only the stern Letizia regarded the marriage tie as binding. What concerned them far more was Josephine's terrible extravagance, and every day Elisa came bustling up with stories of the Creole's gigantic shopping sprees. They decided that a divorce must follow Napoleon's return.

So they watched and worked and waited against the reappearance of the hero in Paris. Unlike the Directors and Josephine they were confident that he must return, since he had so many responsibilities. In her heart Josephine held the opposite view. She respected her husband but had very little genuine affection for him and she had seen too many die during the Terror to share Letizia's anxiety for the dangers Napoleon was facing. On an evening in early autumn 1799, when Josephine was dining alone with Gohier, one of the Directors, a courtier arrived with the news of his landing at Fréjus after running the gauntlet of the British cruisers all the way from Alexandria. She was shocked and dismayed but she knew at once what to do. Summoning her coach and outriders she rushed south, determined to get to him before his mind was poisoned by the malice of his family.

It was a judicious decision but she was unlucky, choosing the more easterly route and missing his progress north. Furiously she turned back but she was too late. When she arrived it was to find her trunks packed and roped in the hall of the house in the Rue Chantereine. The family had had their say and he was determined to divorce her.

She had survived a worse crisis in the Carmelite prison before Thermidor had reprieved those awaiting the guillotine. For hours she stood outside his locked door, banging and pleading and at length asked Hortense and Eugène to plead on her behalf. At last the door opened and he embraced her, the tears running down his face. The family had lost a major battle but the war was to last another ten years.

In the meantime a truce was imperative. Every member of the Buonaparte-Beauharnais clan, together with every friend and dependent they could muster, was needed for a more immediate task, to make Napoleon the master of France, replacing Jacobinism, neo-Royalism, Égalitairism, Constitutionalism and every other party that had bedevilled France during the last decade. Such an attempt might have succeeded before he left for Egypt but now, with his Italian policy in ruins and the country crying out for strong government, a decisive move to put himself at the head of affairs was almost certain to succeed – providing it was carefully stage-managed. Within hours of his return he sounded the Directors, and when he found them all unresponsive to his suggestion that they should retire he decided upon a *coup*.

In a world of shifting loyalties, where political clap-trap replaced the swift decisions of the field Napoleon was unsure of himself and badly in need of experienced politicians to advise and guide him. Fortunately they were at hand and the house in the Rue Chantereine became the rendezvous of half the political opportunists in Paris. Good timing and at least a semblance of legality were essentials and the Buonapartes, helped by Josephine, went to work on everyone thought to be politically useful.

Pre-eminent among the conspirators were Joseph, now experienced in these matters and regarded by men of all parties as a steady, reliable man of affairs, and Lucien, whose talents in this field were unquestioned but whose reputation was anything but steady and reliable. In the weeks between his return to Paris and the *coup d'état* known as 'Brumaire' because of its place in the republican calendar, Napoleon relied more on these two than at any time in his life. Joseph and his wife Julie were particularly useful in the early stages, for they stood well with uncommitted politicians and soldiers, whilst Julie's sister, Désirée, had just married the enigmatic Bernadotte, a possible rival to Napoleon. Lucien went to work on the Council of Five Hundred and succeeded in recruiting about fifty deputies who could be relied upon to support the plot. Josephine used her blandishments to good effect on three of the five Directors and on the Machiavellian Talleyrand. The Abbé Siéyès, theorist of the Directory, already favoured Buonaparte's seizure of power and another Director, Roger Ducos, was soon won over. Barras, then the most powerful man in France, was ready to retire to his country estate and enjoy the fortune he had amassed, so that this left only two, Gohier and Moulins, both exceptionally honest men who could not be bribed and would have nothing whatever to do with a palace revolution. Napoleon felt he could be sure of most of the soldiers, although three of the old republicans, Augereau, Jourdan and Lefèbvre, caused him some anxiety at the last moment. Pauline's husband, Leclerc, was already his man and nobody seems to have told Elisa's husband Bacchiochi that anything unusual was going on. Bernadotte remained unpredictable, in spite of strong pressure from Josephine and his brother-in-law Joseph. Louis, as a professional soldier, could also be relied upon and the two younger children, Caroline and Jérôme, were still at school and safely out of the way.

On November 18th, thirty-four days after his reappearance in

Paris, the conspirators went into action, the two Chambers, the Council of Ancients and the Council of Five Hundred adjourning their sittings and moving out to the Palace of St Cloud on the pretext of a Jacobin plot to seize power. Buonaparte's officers took up their positions at strategic points of the city and at first it looked as if the *coup* would be almost effortless. Then the trouble began, and the badly botched stages of the conspiracy can only be blamed on the central figure, who was completely out of his element in this type of situation. When he addressed the Council of Ancients, warning the Councillors of the non-existent plot, his speech was so banal that his friends drew him out of the hall. Worried and uncertain, the legislators argued, dithered and delayed. The resignations of some of the Directors did nothing to enlighten them as to what was going on and in the Orangerie below, where Lucien was buying time by haranguing his colleagues in his best republican style, it began to look as though the carefully-mounted conspiracy would fade out in gusts of derisive laughter.

In the Council of Ancients this had already come close to happening. Napoleon ranted about the God of Battles and the Goddess of Fortune until Bourienne, his secretary, whispered, 'Do stop, General, you don't know what you are saying!' But there was no laughter in the Orangerie where Lucien was fighting the battle of his life. Instead came isolated shouts of 'Outside the Law!' from indignant deputies, and protests multiplied when Napoleon appeared, so that soon neither he nor Lucien were able to make themselves heard. Deputies scrambled up and surged round the stammering victor of Italy, shouting for his expulsion and jostling him, and at last Napoleon stumbled out, shouting that they had tried to assassinate him. Lucien mounted the rostrum and in his capacity as President (he had been elevated to the chair in honour of his brother's return only a month before) jangled his bell and begged for audience. It was useless. Thoroughly roused, and gaining confidence by their apparent victory, his opponents made speech impossible and Lucien did the only thing left to him, tore off his insignia and hurried out of the Chamber.

Outside in the court it seemed as if all was lost, and it would have been if Lucien's nerve had not been better than his brother's.

Seeing the ranks of the Council Guard drawn up he leaped on to his horse and turned his oratory on the soldiers. His imagination gathered momentum and the stolid Grenadiers began to waver under the torrent of words. 'I tell you that in there a majority is being terrorised by a handful of armed Jacobins!' he shouted. 'These rascals are in English pay! They have dared to outlaw your General . . . they have actually tried to assassinate him! Look at his wounds! Use your bayonets to guard him against their daggers . . . recognise as deputies none but those who come with me into the midst of your ranks!'

Napoleon, still pale and shaking from his ordeal in the Orangerie, listened to his brother's appeal. The 'wounds' to which Lucien referred were a few scratches that some say Napoleon had inflicted on himself in his agitation but now he joined in, beginning 'Follow me . . . I am the God of Battles . . .!' whereupon the breathless Lucien snapped, 'For God's sake hold your tongue!' but when the brothers turned back towards the Chamber the cheering soldiers followed. In five minutes it was over, with deputies leaping out of the windows and escaping into the gathering darkness, and Lucien rushing about trying to stop those he needed to ratify Napoleon's appointment as a Director. He collected about fifty and with this minority the democratic conscience of the nation had to be content. By the following day Siéyès, Ducos and Napoleon were a triumvirate. Within a few weeks both Siéyès and Ducos had disappeared into private life and two new nonentities replaced them, Napoleon assuming the role of First Consul. He had triumphed but the credit, such as it was, belonged to Lucien.

There was excitement in the dormitory at Madame Campan's establishment for young ladies that same night. The quiet evening in the residential district was disturbed by the sound of hooves as four horsemen approached the school and took up guard positions for the night. They had been sent by Murat, one of Napoleon's inner circle who had been prominent in the expulsion of the deputies from the Chamber. 'The General's youngest sister must have special protection,' he declared and Caroline, who had long coveted this handsome Gascon and was determined to marry him and escape the tiresome restrictions of life in a finishing school, was delighted with the compliment. She lost no time in telling her schoolfellows the reason for the special guard and the name of the soldier who had mounted it. In less than a year he was to be her husband, and together they were to begin a long journey into Cloud Cuckoo Land, a journey signposted with folly, arrogance, self-deception, greed and treachery.

CHAPTER FIVE

'Not exactly a court but no longer a camp ...!'

FROM NOVEMBER 1799 until February 1800 Napoleon lived in the Luxembourg Palace where the Directory had sat for so long. In the early spring of the new year he moved to the Tuileries where, as one observer puts it, 'we were not exactly a court but no longer a camp'. On this, his second decisive step towards the assumption of regal power, his attitude towards his family underwent a subtle change. Dropping all pretence at being only a brother anxious to help his family and further their careers, he became the arbiter of their private lives. This period, between Brumaire and his assumption of the imperial title four and a half years later, was known as the Consulate, and it was then that he took upon himself not only the control of France and the cares of State but complete authority over his four brothers and three sisters. From this time on not one of them was allowed to make a major personal decision without his approval.

They reacted to this dictatorship according to their individual temperaments but in the main, though they often resented this interference, they accepted his authority. Only Lucien found the bonds insupportable, but even he submitted for the time being. Their general submission to him can be readily understood for the rewards of obedience were considerable and the price of defiance more than any of them, at that time, were prepared to pay.

The first family event to mark the new period was the marriage of Caroline, now approaching her eighteenth birthday. To her delight she was allowed to leave the hated academy for young ladies and marry Joachim Murat, once a Gascon stable-boy, now a celebrated General and a close personal friend of Napoleon.

Caroline had met the handsome cavalry officer in Rome and the couple had been attracted to one another from the start, but by then Napoleon had already made up his mind that all the unmarried Buonapartes were under an obligation to strengthen his position and when he returned from Egypt, in the autumn of 1799, there was talk of Caroline being offered to General Moreau, victor of Hohenlinden and Napoleon's most dangerous rival in the army. Like Marmont before him Moreau declined, and the decision altered the course of his life, for after being involved in a Royalist conspiracy he was exiled and years later, when serving in the ranks of the enemies of France, he was killed at Dresden. At about this time there was also talk of marrying Josephine's daughter Hortense to General Duroc, another prominent Buonapartist, but Duroc also refused. By a strange coincidence he died in the same campaign, but the ball that killed the amiable Marshal of the Palace was fired from an enemy gun.

So Caroline married the innkeeper's son and told everybody that she was madly in love with her handsome husband. Throughout the period of the Empire, Murat won a brilliant reputation as a Commander of massed squadrons in the field and in this sphere he has never been surpassed; along with this reputation however went another, that of a man with the heart of a lion and the political judgment of a sheep. His wife, clever, pitiless and at all times utterly unscrupulous, was to take full advantage of this contradiction.

Murat owed his present position to no one but himself. Without education or influence of any kind he had been destined for the church but had run away from home as a boy and enlisted in the Revolutionary Army as a hussar. He attracted attention at the very outset of his career by clownish behaviour, flamboyant clothes and extreme personal bravery. He was well-built, a superb horseman, a braggart, a dandefied ass and, off the battlefield, a complete fool, but none of the enemies he made during his career as soldier and king have ever accused him of being reluctant to risk his life at the head of his men in action. Whenever there was a charge to be made Murat led it (exchanging his sabre for a golden wand). He often rode into action bareheaded with his black curls flying

48

in the wind, and his spectacular uniforms and extravagant gestures made him half a legend and half a joke among the veterans of the Grand Army. At the time of their marriage Caroline adored him, but it did not take her long to assess his capabilities. With a certain amount of judicious prodding and as much nagging as he could stand, she decided that their chances of outstripping the rest of the family were good, for Napoleon was known to favour old friends and when he had stood in need of guns on the night preceding the famous 'whiff of grapeshot' it had been Murat who found them. Ever since then he had stood at Napoleon's elbow and no one doubted his ability to handle large masses of cavalry so that when France found herself at war again, and the First Consul crossed the Alps to win a narrow victory at Marengo, his new brother-in-law rode with him and won fresh laurels. Caroline noticed with approval that at the reviews and levées which were just coming back into fashion her husband cut a very striking figure in his gorgeous uniforms, attracting more attention than a modest soldier like Pauline's young husband Leclerc, and far more than Elisa's stupid Bacchiochi. She made up her mind that when fresh rewards were being distributed she would put in a word for Joachim and perhaps, through him, triumph over Pauline, who was regarded as Napoleon's favourite. In less than a year Caroline had gained an initial advantage over them all; she gave birth to the first Buonaparte grandson, Achille Charles Louis Murat. Joseph's wife Julie eventually presented her husband with two daughters, but the first of these was not born until later that same year. Elisa and Pauline had no children at this time (Pauline, despite two marriages, died childless) and Lucien had two daughters but no sons by his first wife, Christine Boyer. With the birth of Achille, and Napoleon still without an heir, it seemed to Caroline that her prospects of taking precedence over sisters and brothers were assured, but her hopes came close to being dashed shortly before the child was born. Riding to the Opera to hear a performance of Haydn's *Creation* on Christmas Eve, Caroline's carriage passed a harmless-looking donkey-cart tethered to some railings. As the consular procession drew level there was a shattering explosion. Bystanders, escorting troopers, glass, stones and beams were hurled across the district, and when the dust settled the area around the Hotel Longueville was a shambles, dead and wounded littering the street. Horse and cart, the hiding place of an infernal machine placed there to destroy the First Consul, had disappeared. 'I believe those rascals are trying to blow me up' was Napoleon's comment when he arrived at the theatre and received the cheers of the audience, but Caroline, in an advanced state of pregnancy, seemed in great danger of losing her child. She was lucky and Achille, a healthy boy, was born while hundreds of arrests were being made all over Paris. The child was a source of tremendous satisfaction to his mother but in the years ahead, when all hope of producing a child had faded in Josephine, he was to prove a source of friction between Caroline and the timid Hortense who had once tried to curry favour by helping her to win prizes at school.

Elisa and Lucien were in trouble again. As in all large families, the Buonapartes had their brother-sister alliances and the malicious Elisa had always sided with the stormy and unpredictable Lucien. During the Consulate period it was these two, as well as Jérôme, who caused Napoleon anxiety by their involvement in family scandals. A scandal inside the family was something he feared more than an alliance of kings, or open opposition to his policy. He could deal with coalitions and political opponents but he was extremely sensitive to criticism of his family and the knowledge that his brothers or sisters were being discussed in public was always sure to infuriate him. Between them Elisa and Lucien set themselves up as leaders of the dramatic, literary and artistic coteries in Paris and for the most part their activities were harmless enough, although they were inclined to encourage their friends to regard the First Consul as a Philistine. Napoleon bore with this for a time but his wrath descended on them when he learned of an amateur theatrical show in which brother and sister appeared on the stage in pink, skin-tight and transparent pantaloons. 'I will not tolerate this disgraceful behaviour!' he thundered. 'While I am wearing myself out trying to make people moral and respectable once more my brother and sister appear before the public almost naked!' His outburst was justified. He was then working fifteen hours a day codifying the law and the knowledge that his detractors were smirking at Elisa's ample behind during an amateur pantomime must have been extremely galling to him. His denunciation, however, was to serve no purpose. They were soon engaged in further antics and it was even said that they played the fool deliberately to spite the man to whom they had been indebted from the day they first arrived in France.

Another and far more serious cause of friction between the brothers came when Napoleon decided to sell to the United States the French territory of Louisiana. Lucien, as Minister for Home Affairs, had been personally engaged in negotiations to exploit this territory and news of its impending sale infuriated him, not from patriotic motives but because he was enriching himself in this sphere by the sale of monopolies. He enlisted his brother Joseph's support, and they hurried to the Tuileries where they challenged the First Consul whilst he was taking a bath.

The scene that followed was farcical. Joseph and Lucien declared that the Chambers would not consent to the sale, whereupon Napoleon announced that he would sell with or without the consent of the Chambers. Joseph, roused from his customary lethargy, shouted that if Napoleon committed such an unconstitutional act he, Joseph, would put himself at the head of the opposition and crush him, in spite, of their relationship. To be threatened by Joseph like this drove Napoleon into a frenzy. Jumping out of his bath he shouted that they were insolent fellows and he would have them arrested. Splashed with bath water the brothers retired, but there was a second scene in the library that same day when Joseph and Lucien renewed their protests and Napoleon, again losing his temper, hurled a valuable snuff-box to the ground and smashed it. It was wasted breath on the part of all three. Louisiana was sold for twelve million dollars and France lost its footing in the new world.

Joseph's temper soon cooled, but Lucien's did not and he continued to oppose his brother's policies. Shortly after the bathroom quarrel we hear of him contributing to the authorship of a pamphlet advocating the reintroduction of an hereditary sovereign under a constitution, on the English pattern. Nobody can be sure if, at this particular time, Napoleon had made up his mind to offer himself as Emperor of the French or would have been content with the role of kingmaker, but whatever his secret plans during the first years of the Consulate he would not tolerate prompting from salon politicians of the kind that surrounded Elisa and Lucien. A renewed outburst of rage ended in Lucien being deprived of his ministerial position and sent as envoy to the court of Madrid.

If Napoleon thought this would be the end of his brother's intrigues he was mistaken. Down in Spain the young man soon made a fortune, so that Napoleon was obliged to find some other way of patching up the rapidly deteriorating relationship. He was encouraged by the death of Lucien's wife Christine, and on learning of this Napoleon at once decided that Lucien must remarry, this time choosing a royal heiress, the widowed queen-mother of Etruria.

Christine Buonaparte, née Boyer, the charming illiterate whom Lucien had wooed during his stay in the Midi as a storekeeper, had paid a high price for her surrender to the young man who had alarmed her village with his fiery speeches during the last days of the revolution. For a long time her famous brother-in-law had refused to see her and only gradually had Letizia and Joseph managed to persuade Napoleon to receive her as a sister-in-law. Since then Christine had been caught up in a rush of events that were beyond her limited comprehension, but she had continued to worship Lucien and had borne him two daughters. Her third pregnancy, terminating at five months, undermined her health and she lost the will to live. Friends who visited her shortly before she died found her lying beside an open window on a narrow camp bed. She said she could not breathe in the great bed provided by her husband and that the rough couch reminded her of her little bedroom in the village of St Maximin. It was her way of telling them that she felt desperately unhappy surrounded by luxury and splendour, and a day or so later she died. Lucien soon consoled himself, taking as mistress another beautiful woman, this time the abandoned wife of a Paris banker, called Jouberthon. Lucien was very fortunate in love. Madame Jouberthon proved another sweet-natured woman and in 1802 he married her at a

ecret civil ceremony. It was not before time. Madame gave birth
o a child the day after the ceremony but somehow Napoleon was
kept in ignorance of the facts and announced that Lucien was to
be appointed ambassador to Etruria, where his marriage to the
queen-mother would be a foregone conclusion. When at last
Lucien was forced to tell his brother the truth the First Consul's
rage was terrible. His first action was to send for the notary who
had presided over the marriage and the official seems to have been
a man of remarkable imperturbability. To Napoleon's accusations
that the marriage was illegal the notary replied that it was perfectly legal since the groom was over twenty-one and was under
no obligation to obtain anybody's permission to wed. Having
said this he took his hat and left, perhaps the only man of his time
whom Napoleon had failed to astonish. The First Consul then
turned to Lucien and taunted him with marrying a widow, but
Lucien flung back at him with characteristic daring, 'So did you
marry a widow, but mine is not old and smelly!' What Napoleon
replied to this insult is not recorded, but it probably helped to
harden his heart against this impossibly arrogant man.

In spite of the pleas of Joseph and his mother, Napoleon stood
by his decision to exile his brother and did so, Lucien retiring at
once to the Papal States. To Napoleon's annoyance Letizia insisted on going with him, preferring to exchange the excitements
of Paris for a country where no one would notice or remark
upon the fact that she had been unable to master the French language.

In the midst of his tussle with Lucien, but before it had reached
its climax, Napoleon had trouble with his favourite, the exquisite
Pauline.

In December 1802, when he had been master of France for just
over two years, Napoleon violated the principles of the revolution
by sending a large army and fleet to the island of San Domingo,
where the black population had recently revolted and were now
proclaiming liberty and equality under the leadership of one of
the most gifted negroes of all time, the statesmanlike Toussaint
L'Ouverture. In command of this expedition was Victor-Emmanuel Leclerc, soldier husband of Pauline, and the General was

instructed to reintroduce slavery on the island on the grounds that negroes were happier when in bondage. Napoleon, who had very strong views about the responsibilities of wives, insisted that Pauline should accompany Leclerc and remain with him during what promised to be an arduous campaign in a very trying climate. Pauline was horrified. Between outbursts of weeping she declared that her complexion would be ruined, that the islands of the Antilles did not cater for women of fashion, and that she was being banished by a cruel brother to live among serpents and savages. Her tears achieved nothing and Napoleon remained adamant. A wife's place, he told her, was beside her husband and even Leclerc's reluctance to be saddled with this extra responsibility did not persuade him to cancel the order.

Laurette Permon (later the celebrated Madame Junot) called upon Pauline during this crisis and tactfully suggested that Pauline's taste for exotic clothes would have free rein in San Domingo, whereupon Pauline at once cheered up and ceased to wail about savages and serpents. The word 'serpent' gave Laurette another persuasive idea and she pointed out that there were no snakes in the West Indies, and that Pauline would be sure to create a sensation in the capital wearing a Creole turban and striped muslin. Seeing that there was no alternative Pauline dried her tears and began to pack. It occupied her for a considerable time. The amount of luggage she sent to Brest caused great embarrassment to the captain of the Commander-in-Chief's flagship. Before Christmas they sailed away and in late January a frightful campaign of bloodshed and horror began that lost Napoleon an excellent chance of weakening the maritime ascendancy of Britain by encouraging revolutions in every slave-populated island of the West Indies.

Toussaint L'Ouverture fought desperately but the most deadly enemy of the Europeans was the climate. Soon yellow fever was at work, filling the hospitals with sick and dying men. Among the victims was Leclerc himself, and Pauline was a widow when the remnants of the French Army surrendered to the British fleet and were ferried home, a short-lived peace having been signed with Napoleon's arch-enemy.

Pauline Leclerc was not a woman to waste her youth mourning

'I do not think any man was ever more unfortunate in his relations than I!'
Napoleon's comment on the above assembly.

LETIZIA, Napoleon's stoic Corsican mother, who regarded the entire Napoleonic adventure as a temporary phase and saved money against the inevitable anti-climax. She outlived most of her children but would never return to France unless the invitation was extended to the whole family.

JOSEPH, NAPOLEON and LOUIS as young men.

LUCIEN, the only member of the family whom Napoleon could never dominate. He lived a country gentleman's life in England for several years but rallied to his brother before Waterloo.

JOSEPH, Napoleon's elder brother, who wanted nothing better than to live quietly on a country estate but whose life as a king was a record of disaster. After Waterloo he lived happily in America.

JULIE CLARY, the soap-boiler's daughter, whose dowry, when she married Joseph, saved the Buonapartes from penury. She was a loyal and faithful wife throughout her husband's misadventures.

ELISA, Napoleon's oldest sister, engaged in her favourite pursuit—patronising artists and men of letters. Napoleon usually had a spy on hand to record spiteful gossip regarding himself.

ELISA as she liked to see herself,
in classical pose.

Louis, as King of Holland, who, as a boy, shared Lieutenant Buonaparte's barracks lodging and grew up a sour intractable man, at odds with everyone.

Hortense (Napoleon's step-daughter) and her two sons. Her marriage to Louis was perhaps the unhappiest of all Buonaparte marriages.

MARSHAL MURAT, probably the most famous cavalry leader of all time, a lion in battle, the tool of his scheming wife in all other spheres. He died facing a firing squad.

CAROLINE, the most treacherous of the clan, seen with her daughter when
Queen of Naples. Her mother never forgave her betrayal of the family interests.

One of the most spectacular events of the Empire in its heyday, the marriage of JÉRÔME to the amiable Catherine of Württemberg, who never ceased to adore him. Napoleon's sisters, seen on the steps of the throne, were at this time plotting Josephine's downfall. Soon after his marriage, Jérôme began his astounding reign in Westphalia.

Canova's famous statue of PAULINE. Asked if she was not 'uncomfortable' posing semi-nude, she is reported to have replied, 'Oh, no! There was a fire in the room!'

PRINCE CAMILLO BORGHESE, Pauline's wealthy second husband. He was the Empire's most celebrated practical joker.

GENERAL LECLERC, Pauline's first husband; he died of fever during the St Domingo campaign.

JÉRÔME, youngest of the family, in the days of his splendid bankruptcy, as King of Westphalia. He was always the best dressed of the Buonapartes, but seldom paid his tailor.

The unreformed rake: JÉRÔME in later life, last survivor of the Buonaparte clan.

A contemporary view of the Buonapartes, as seen by their enemies. This was
entitled 'The Game of Four Corners or the Five Brothers.'

a man carried off by yellow fever. When she reached France her hair had been cut short and she was wearing black, but within days she was looking for another husband. Before the year was out she found one, a far better match than the unfortunate Leclerc inasmuch as he was not only a prince of ancient lineage but very rich as well. Camillo Borghese could indulge her every whim and Madame Junot tells of calling upon Pauline shortly after her return from San Domingo. 'She looked angelic in widow's weeds', says the diary, but in spite of this Pauline was impatient of the temporary retirement that convention had imposed upon her and told Laurette 'If my brother determines to shut me out I shall make an end to my existence.' In passing it is interesting to note the tendency of all the Buonapartes to threaten suicide whenever they were frustrated. Pauline, Lucien and Jérôme were all addicted to threats of this kind and Napoleon himself was not unknown to make use of them. Pauline's retirement, however, was very short-lived and she was soon attempting to outdress the First Consul's wife, at that time the acknowledged leader of Paris fashions. On a visit to Josephine she succeeded spectacularly, appearing at St Cloud in a robe of green velvet upon which, declares Madame Junot, 'were displayed all the diamonds of the house of Borghese!' On that particular occasion Pauline's taste was sacrificed to display. Her head, neck, ears and arms were loaded with diamonds and she was a dazzling mass of jewels. Flushed with triumph she revelled in the impression she made and after she had paraded the room like a model at a fashion show she sat down beside her friend, nodded at the gaping courtiers, and exclaimed: 'Laurette, my little Laurette, only look at them! They are ready to burst with envy but no matter, I am a princess and a real one!'

In the meantime the Buonaparte and Beauharnais families had been linked by another marriage. On January 3rd, 1802, Josephine persuaded her husband to form the alliance that had been in her mind ever since Buonaparte gossip had almost succeeded in wrecking her marriage after Napoleon's sudden return from Egypt. Hortense, the nervous seventeen-year-old daughter of the First Consul's wife and the aristocrat who had perished under the guillotine, was married in the presence of the family to Louis, the brother for whom Napoleon possessed a special affection by reason of their close association in the past. It was a match which both Napoleon and Josephine regarded as a possible solution to their difficulty regarding an heir. They had been married nearly six years and had both come to the conclusion that they were very unlikely to have a child. Josephine was now thirty-eight and when the marriage of Louis and Hortense was mooted Napoleon brought her hopes and fears into the open by saying that he looked upon Louis as a son and was sure that his wife cherished her daughter, 'so that their children shall be ours'. Before Josephine could express her relief he went on, 'We will adopt them and this adoption will console us for not having children of our own. It is necessary, however, that our plan meets with the approval of the young people.'

It did not meet with their approval but this was no reason for its rejection. Louis was no Lucien, and Hortense realised how much this marriage would strengthen her mother's hold on Napoleon. It was for this reason, and this reason alone, that she finally consented to accept Colonel Louis Buonaparte as her husband and it was a decision that she was to regret for the rest of her life. Marriage with Louis was to change Hortense from a healthy girl into a miserable neurotic who made a fetish of personal woes.

Louis, now aged twenty-two, had been living at the Tuileries since Napoleon had moved to the Bourbon palace, but he does not seem to have embarrassed his brother with indiscretions of the kind practised by Elisa, Pauline, Lucien or Jérôme. His silent and suspicious nature prevented him from extracting much satisfaction from the family's improved fortunes. He did not run into debt, took no part in the amateur theatricals, and did not even entertain on the scale of Joseph and his wife Julie. He had very little of Jérôme's taste for personal display and none at all for intrigue like his youngest sister Caroline. He kept very much to himself and took his profession seriously, but not seriously enough to make a reputation in the army or fulfil the promise of his youth on the bridge at Arcola. Syphilis might well have accounted for his gloomy and introspective nature but there seems to be no real proof of this, although it is reasonable to suppose that he suffered from ill-health and early in life had developed a partial paralysis that made him limp and added to his habitual gloom. He raised no objection to the match and Hortense, after a week of deliberation, informed Napoleon's secretary Bourienne that she would consent to the proposal. After this there was a good deal of excited activity, and Napoleon, meeting Hortense a day or so later, remarked: 'Well well! So Louis is courting you, is he? That ought to suit you and your mother,' adding, with jocular hypocrisy, 'There, I give my consent!' a remark that must have astonished the unhappy girl.

Napoleon was a lavish giver of wedding presents and on this occasion sent his step-daughter some valuable diamonds, but she would not wear them for the ceremony, preferring to appear at the civil ceremony in white crepe relieved by pearls and a small bouquet of orange blossom. Reading her own listless account of the occasion one is tempted to think that she would have preferred to wear mourning.

In spite of the relief she felt Josephine wept, but tears came very easily to Josephine. When the civil formalities were over the couple drove to their new home in the Rue de la Victoire, where Cardinal Caprara, who had recently arrived in France to take part in the restitution of the Catholic faith, gave them the blessing of the Church. The same blessing was extended to another young couple – Caroline and her husband Murat, who had been civilly married before the faith had been re-established in France and now came forward to take advantage of this opportunity. Hortense viewed their participation in the ceremony with a certain bitterness. Her former schoolfellow, she noted, was in love with her husband and he with her, but Hortense tried to reassure herself with the knowledge that Louis 'was considered a kind young man who would treat her with gentleness and consideration'. She was soon disillusioned. That same day Louis mumbled that his bride was not showing sufficient interest in the magnificent display of wedding-gifts and later, during the honeymoon at Malmaison, they had their first quarrel. Observing a gawky officer engaged in solving a puzzle the bride and a girl companion got the giggles. Louis, always ready to take offence, assumed that they were laughing at him and said as much. Recriminations followed, Louis looking up from a novel he was writing and growling, 'I warn you, only a woman of light morals dares laugh at her husband and make fun of him! I would rather leave you than allow myself to be humiliated!' whereupon the poor bride burst into tears – and who could blame her? It was a remark that did a little to acquaint Hortense with the kind of man she had married and the prospect of the years ahead terrified her. 'After this,' she declares, 'Louis roused in me only one feeling. It was fear.'

Soon after the wedding Napoleon and Josephine drove south to Lyons where they were received with enthusiasm by a city that, more than any centre in France, had suffered from the cruelties of fanatical republicans. Perhaps the Lyonnais saw in this man a ruler who was soon to stop all pretence of flirting with republicanism and reveal himself as a passionate upholder of order, commerce and a carefully graded society. He had already done much for France and if his enemies abroad gave him a chance he would undoubtedly do more. In two months bonfires were to blaze and fireworks soar in honour of the peace with England – peace after a war lasting more than nine years. Meanwhile it is probable that the man himself hoped for peace within his family circle. At that time Joseph's reputation as a diplomat was growing, Lucien, soon to be banished, was far away in Spain, Louis was safely married and might produce an heir, Elisa, Pauline and Caroline were off his hands. Only one Buonaparte remained unmarried, young Jérôme, now learning his trade as a sailor. As he drove south after Louis' wedding Napoleon thought about finding a suitable wife for Jérôme, someone who would encourage the boy to turn his back on 'giddiness', the word that featured so monotonously in all Jérôme's reports.

At that season, early spring, 1802, Jérôme was within a year or so of marriage. Unfortunately for everyone concerned it was a marriage that did nothing whatever for the dignity of the family name.

*

Napoleon's decision to enrol Jérôme as a midshipman in the French navy was part policy, part prudence. As leading citizen it was necessary that Napoleon should encourage his brothers to show a good example in as many fields as possible, and as there was already one in the legislature, one in the diplomatic corps and one in the army it seemed advisable to send the youngest Buonaparte to sea, particularly as, at that time, France was desperately short of naval officers. Political considerations aside, it was becoming obvious that if Jérôme was allowed to grow up without a taste of discipline he would lose no time in bringing disgrace upon himself and the family. At seventeen he was a spoiled and slightly vicious adolescent whose natural high spirits, plus a close relationship to the most powerful man in France, promised to destroy such gifts as he possessed. His taste for extravagant living and debauchery had been noted by his mother and by Joseph but he was less to blame for this than those who had indulged him during Napoleon's prolonged absences from home. Every member of the family circle had at one time or other lent him money to supplement his liberal allowance and even his mother, stern enough in most respects, spoiled Jérôme the moment Napoleon's back was turned. In one respect his precocity was understandable. He was the only male among the Buonapartes who had been a child when the good things of life became available. Unlike all the others, Caroline included, he could recall very little about the lean days before the capture of Toulon. A studious boy with a natural inclination to win the praise of adults might have benefited from the education offered at the two excellent schools he had attended, but Jérôme was not studious and as long as he got his own way in trivial things he did not care a row of beans what his elders thought about his behaviour or scholastic achievements. He was a gay, enterprising, likeable, lively young scamp, with a sense of humour lacking in all the other Buonapartes except his sister Pauline, but he had plenty of Buonaparte obstinacy and as much courage and ambition as any of them. His one desire at this time was to emulate his famous brother on the battlefield and when his step-brother Eugène and his brother Louis had gone as aides to the General, leaving him behind with his hated school books, he had reacted in a way natural to a boy of his age and temperament, substituting high spirits for the glory he was convinced he would have won if given the opportunity.

In the spring of 1800, a few months after Brumaire, Jérôme suffered the mortification of being left behind a second time when the army marched over the Alps to Marengo. On this occasion he sulked for weeks and would not speak to Napoleon when the First Consul returned to Paris in triumph. Napoleon understood the boy's disappointment and presented him with a sword he had carried at Marengo and the kindly act re-established him in Jérôme's heart, but in the following period, when Napoleon allowed him to leave school and join the Consular Guard stationed at the Tuileries, he was soon in trouble again, first on account of gross, personal extravagance, then as a result of a duel that might have cost him his life.

One of the first things Napoleon did on his return to Paris after a campaign was to study his wife's debts and when these had been sorted out he usually turned to those of his youngest brother. On returning from Marengo he was amazed to find an item among Jérôme's papers claiming 10,000 francs, which had been spent on the purchase of an exquisitely wrought dressing-case. When he sent for Jérôme and demanded an explanation the boy was defiant. 'I'm like that,' he said carelessly, 'I only love beautiful things!' Napoleon examined the case and discovered that it contained two razors. 'How dare you spend this amount before you need to shave?' he roared, but Jérôme would make no promise to mend his ways. The incident passed over, but within weeks he was again before the First Consul, this time to explain a pistol duel with a fellow guardsman called Davout. Jérôme explained that the two had quarrelled and had decided to settle the matter by an affair of honour, facing one another with a pocketful of cartridges and firing pointblank until all the ammunition was expended or one of them was hit. Davout must have proved the better marksman for Jérôme came off with a ball in his breast and it remained there for the rest of his life, to be discovered by a surgeon after his death sixty years later. Napoleon was shocked by this foolhardy incident and decided to send him to sea. He was frank about his reasons. If any member of his family was going to die from gunshot wounds then he, as First Consul, should at least be able to claim that a Buonaparte had laid down his life for France.

Letizia objected. She had always hated the sea and the prospect of her youngest child being exposed to the risks of action and shipwreck alarmed her, but Napoleon paid no attention to her objections and Jérôme was despatched to Brest to serve under Admiral Ganteaume, who was then on the point of leaving for Egypt to revictual the remnants of the army Napoleon had abandoned the previous year. Steps were taken to ensure that Jérôme received no preferential treatment. 'I send you,' wrote Napoleon to Ganteaume, 'Citizen Jérôme Buonaparte to serve his apprenticeship in the Navy. You know that he needs to be treated strictly and to make up for lost time. Insist on his carrying out exactly all the duties of his profession.'

After various delays due to violent storms (all his life Jérôme was to run into storms of one kind or another) the squadron passed Gibraltar and sailed to the eastern Mediterranean, but a landing proved impossible and the army was left to its fate, Ganteaume returning home with his mission unaccomplished. Young Jérôme, uninhibited by his youth and total lack of experience, wrote a letter severely criticising his Admiral for the handling of the expedition, but it would seem that Ganteaume did not take Napoleon's instructions about his brother's treatment very seriously, for when the French had the luck to capture an isolated British warship, the *Swiftsure*, it was seventeen-year-old Midshipman Jérôme Buonaparte who was sent aboard to receive the British officer's sword. Napoleon, hearing this, was delighted. 'Let me be told that you are as active as a cabin boy,' he wrote, 'and don't allow anyone to do your work for you!'

After nine months at sea Jérôme returned to Paris and was received with open arms, but Napoleon was not disposed to waste such a promising apprenticeship and allow the swaggering midshipman to return to a life of dissipation in the city. Within three months he was off again, this time accompanying Leclerc's fatal expedition to San Domingo. He served abroad the flagship *Foudroyant* and left Rochefort in mid-December, 1801.

The naval section of the expedition was under the command of Admiral Vallaret-Joyeuse, who was even more tactful than his predecessor. One of his first acts was to promote Jérôme to the rank of ensign and the young man was not slow to exploit his promotion. Sent ashore with a message for General Leclerc at Cap Haitien, the French Headquarters, Jérôme astonished everyone by appearing in the brilliant uniform of the Berchiny Hussars! Leclerc stared at the young man bleakly and when he had recovered from his surprise pointed out that a hussar uniform was hardly suitable for a very junior naval ensign.

Jérôme's luck held. When the General required an officer to convey despatches to France he naturally selected the First Consul's brother and the hussar-ensign set off for Brest once more, arriving in April and proceeding by coach to Nantes. The manner of his arrival into this city was recalled years afterwards, for a dispute arose with the postilion and when the man refused to continue Jérôme climbed on one of the coach-horses and cantered into the city dressed in knee breeches, silk stockings and flourishing the postilion's whip. With him was Lieutenant Hagan, who had commanded the brig *Epervier* in which they had travelled from San Domingo, and on arrival in Paris Jérôme persuaded his brother to give his friend command of the brig on which they were to return to the West Indies.

Back at Nantes the two young seamen discovered that their vessel was not yet ready for sea, so thay spent a very agreeable period of waiting, frequent demands for more money being despatched to Paris. In one of his brusque replies to these appeals Napoleon wrote: 'Die young and I shall be consoled for it; but not if you live sixty years without glory, without use to your country, without leaving a trace of your existence. It would be better not to have existed at all.' Jérôme survived this advice by just short of sixty years. During that period he was of little use to his country but he did leave behind a single day's glory. It was acquired at Waterloo.

There is little profit in following Jérôme's jaunts during the next ten months. With his friend Hagan, and several other gay young men who had attached themselves to him, he drifted about the islands of the Caribbean, sometimes conforming to the orders of the patient Villaret-Joyeuse but disobeying them or adapting them whenever they conflicted with his inclination of the moment. Sometimes his erratic behaviour irritated the unlucky Admiral and sometimes it greatly embarrassed him, as when Jérôme, now in command of a vessel, fired a shot across the bows of a peaceful British merchantman and made her Captain heave to in order to 'find out how things were now going between France and England'. In desperation the wretched Admiral finally ordered him to return to France but Jérôme, who was thoroughly enjoying himself, pointed out that no one could be really sure whether there was still peace with Britain and that if he was captured by the British Navy the First Consul would be liable to hold the Admiral responsible. Vallaret-Joyeuse was bound to admit that Jérôme had a point and agreed to the return journey being made on a neutral vessel, whereupon Jérôme, who was very anxious to visit the United States, took passage on an American vessel at Martinique and sailed away to Norfolk, Virginia, arriving in July, 1803.

As the brother of a man soon to become Emperor of the French he landed with a staff of four and was warmly received by the hospitable Virginians, but the French party did not stay long in Norfolk, setting out at once for Washington. Jérôme had urgent business. He not only had to find a neutral vessel to take him to France; he had to find the French Consul-General and borrow some money.

The French were extremely popular in America at this time. The colonists who had broken away from Britain and founded their own republic twenty-five years before had not forgotten the active assistance given to them in the struggle by men like Lafayette, and the bond forged between the two countries during the War of Independence was strong. In addition, everyone in Washington had now heard of the famous Napoleon and an opportunity to pay court to his brother was welcomed. Invitations poured in from all sides, hostesses competing with one another to entertain the youngest brother of the celebrated Napoleon. Pichon, the Consul-General, was co-operative and busied himself chartering a vessel at Philadelphia from where he hoped to send Jérôme with instructions to travel home incognito, for the British were now on the watch for him.

Jérôme agreed to everything Pichon advised but instead of hurrying to Philadelphia he went to Baltimore in response to the invitation of a sailor-of-fortune called Joshua Barney, whom he had met during his West Indian travels.

Within four days the horrified Pichon learned that Jérôme's identity was known all over Baltimore and it was therefore extremely likely that any vessel they chartered would be stopped by British patrols, a circumstance that Jérôme was not slow to point out, for he was captivated by American hospitality and was in no hurry to leave.

His good looks, good manners and free spending impressed everyone, and with Joshua Barney as his adjutant Jérôme made the most of his stay. After further delays – and a polite refusal on Jérôme's part to tour the Western States – it was decided that he should await the First Consul's instructions as to the exact manner of his return home. Before those instructions had crossed the Atlantic Jérôme had gone to considerable lengths to cement Franco-American relations. He had married the belle of Baltimore.

William Patterson, son of a Donegal farmer, was a respected and extremely prosperous merchant. From shipping-merchant's counting-house he had risen, by hard work and shrewdness, to a position of considerable importance in America. He had donated large sums of money to the revolutionary cause during the War of Independence and was on friendly terms with the President. His eldest daughter, Elizabeth, was the best match in Baltimore, for in addition to her father's wealth and social position she was a considerable beauty. She was dark, with fine eyes, excellent features and a good figure, her mouth suggesting a tenderness that she did not in fact possess. At the time of her meeting with Jérôme she was eighteen and she had received what passed for a good education although, as the wretched Pichon hastened to inform Talleyrand, 'like all young persons in this country her education was limited to very little'. The young people met at one of the parties arranged for Jérôme by his friend Barney and Jérôme was fascinated by her from the start. She encouraged him and as soon as it became known that an American girl had won the heart of the engaging young Buonaparte every patriot in Baltimore supported the match. Elizabeth's parents were delighted with such a prize and further encouragement came from the Spanish Consul-General, deputed by Jérôme to make a formal demand for Miss Patterson's hand. Everything conspired to hurry the match forward. Elizabeth, madly in love with the gay young Frenchman, declared 'I would rather be the wife of Jérôme Buonaparte for one hour than the wife of any other man for life' but when Pichon heard of the forthcoming marriage he was terrified and could see nothing emerging from it but disgrace for Jérôme and ruin for himself. At first he dismissed the rumours as ridiculous but confirmation arrived in late October when Jérôme himself called upon the Consul-General and announced that he was about to marry, adding that the wedding would take place in nine days.

Pichon at once set to work to persuade his troublesome guest that such an act would be madness. It was well known that the First Consul regarded the marriages of his brothers as his personal business. For Jérôme to marry the daughter of an American merchant without first having obtained official permission from France, would arouse such a storm from the other side of the Atlantic as would surely overwhelm the pair of them and perhaps result in Jérôme being forbidden to return to France. Jérôme remained unconcerned, pointing out that as a lieutenant he was technically over twenty-one and could marry whom he pleased, with or without his brother's consent. He left after inviting the dumbfounded Pichon to attend the forthcoming ceremony.

The moment the door had closed on the prospective groom the Consul-General began a minute examination of his country's laws on the subject, discovering that no Frenchman could marry without his father's or mother's consent until he was twenty-five. Having written to Jérôme informing him of this he followed up with a letter to the French representative at Baltimore and another to William Patterson, father of the bride. He then hurried round to the Spanish Consul-General and gave him a piece of his mind for seconding Jérôme on such a dangerous undertaking, and also extracting a promise from the Spaniard that he would not attend the wedding. He then tackled his least welcome task, the preparation of a full statement of facts for Napoleon.

From Pichon's viewpoint the storm-cloud lifted somewhat during the next few days. Patterson, after studying Pichon's letter, told Jérôme that he could not consent to the marriage at present and when Jérôme's letter of protest reached him, Pichon reflected that, however headstrong the young man might be, he could not go through with his plan without funds and was now penniless, having spent 16,000 dollars since his arrival in Virginia in July. In fact money seemed to be the key to the situation and it occurred to Pichon that he had only to withhold funds for the danger to pass. He had a lot to learn about Jérôme's talents as a borrower.

To Pichon's relief news came in early November that 'on mature reflection' Jérôme had decided to break off the match and that Elizabeth had gone to cool her ardour on the family estate in Virginia. His satisfaction on receiving this welcome news was increased by news that a French frigate had arrived in Baltimore, so he tried to coax Jérôme aboard and remove him altogether from the temptation to resume his foolhardy project. Jérôme was not so easily trapped. He told both Pichon and the Captain of the frigate that he was 'on a mission and had received no orders to leave from anybody', whereupon he took himself off to New York to attend yet another round of parties, suppers and balls given in his honour.

Notwithstanding Jérôme's refusal to take passage on the frigate, however, Pichon was persuaded that there was now no question of a marriage and accordingly advanced Jérôme a thousand dollars, with a promise of another nine to come if he continued to behave himself. What Pichon did not know was that the lovers had been in constant communication with each other during their brief separation and that Elizabeth had now persuaded her mother to bring her back from Virginia in time for the season. When Jérôme returned to Baltimore early in December the young couple enjoyed a rapturous reunion and at once set to work to melt Papa's heart. Plagued by his wife, entreated by his daughter and besieged by dozens of enthusiastic friends, Patterson soon gave way; this time Pichon did not receive an invitation to the postponed wedding. On Christmas Eve Jérôme Buonaparte and Elizabeth Patterson were married at the Patterson home in Baltimore, the ceremony being conducted by the Right Rev. John Carroll, Roman Catholic bishop of the city.

Many notables were present, including the mayor, and the groom cut a wonderful figure in purple satin laced and embroidered, with white, satin-lined skirts falling to the heels. His shoes had diamond buckles and his hair was powdered. The bride wore rather less, witnesses declaring that her wedding ensemble could have been stowed in one of her husband's pockets! There might well have been room for it, for inside was a receipt for another 4,000 dollars sent that same morning by the trusting Pichon.

After the wedding congratulations were exchanged all round and the happy couple left for a honeymoon on the Pattersons' estate outside the city. On January 3rd the distraught Pichon sent an account of events to Talleyrand. Much of the letter was taken up in attempts to clear himself of complicity.

All that week letters addressed to Paris were leaving the eastern seaboard of America. Bride and groom wrote to Joseph and his mother, Pichon wrote despairingly to Talleyrand, William Patterson wrote personally to Napoleon and sent his letter by the hand of his son Robert; other letters were despatched to the President of the United States and the Secretary of State, with enclosures for the First Consul. With the arrival of each letter Napoleon's rage increased, so that soon few dared to mention the matter to him and when John Patterson arrived in Paris, on March 11th, 1804, Talleyrand told him bluntly that Jérôme would be well advised to remain in the United States until his brother's anger had subsided. Napoleon had heard rumours of the engagement (and its cancellation) in January and had at once despatched orders for Jérôme to return home, but these did not reach America until May, so that the first news Napoleon received of the wedding was Pichon's report sent on January 4th. The family did not share

Napoleon's sense of outrage but were inclined to look upon the marriage with amusement. John Patterson, the bride's brother, had a reassuring interview with Lucien and both Joseph and Letizia gave what amounted to their blessing. Joseph even talked of investing money in America so that his brother would have access to family funds. As the days passed, however, Napoleon's attitude remained inflexible and knowing Jérôme he took the obvious step to bring the young man to heel. Pichon was forbidden to give him one more dollar and French captains were instructed to prohibit 'the young person with whom the First Consul's brother had formed an attachment' to set foot on board a French ship. Napoleon was on the point of making himself Emperor, and the Minister of Marine, through whom the instructions regarding Jérôme were issued, warned the bridegroom of the fate that had just befallen Lucien. In the course of a long, kindly letter he told Jérôme that his brother would forgive his error only if he returned home without his wife, but that if he was so misguided as to bring Elizabeth with him she would not be allowed to set foot on the soil of France!

Whilst awaiting news from France Jérôme and his wife continued their round of balls and receptions, the Pattersons forming a kind of miniature court around them and President Jefferson showing them kindness and interest. Renewed efforts were made by Pichon to get Jérôme on board a French ship unaccompanied by his wife but these were unsuccessful and it was not until several such attempts had failed that a vessel arrived captained by a man who had not yet received instructions regarding the ban on Elizabeth. Jérôme took advantage of this piece of luck and the young couple boarded the *Didon*, but British frigates were off the coast and they were unable to put to sea. By now it was August and news had arrived of Napoleon's assumption of the imperial title, together with a command that Jérôme should renounce his wife at once and return home by the first available ship. Jérôme's dilemma was cruel. So long as his brother had been First Consul there had remained a certain amount of elbow-room for manoeuvre, but now things had changed and it was with a touch of awe that the young man wrote to the Minister of Marine pleading for a more merciful alternative. Finally a brig was hired and in October a secret start was planned from Philadelphia, but Jérôme's astonishing luck was running out. The vessel ran on to a sandbank and Elizabeth, now pregnant, was almost drowned in rescue operations. All Jérôme's money was lost in this disaster and he and his party were left stranded and penniless at Delaware. Yet another attempt was made to leave on a warship, but the pestilential British Navy again intervened, anchoring a frigate alongside the French vessel in Chesapeake Bay.

Throughout all these tribulations Jérôme had never ceased to believe that the sight of Elizabeth would melt his brother's heart and at last, in a vessel owned by his father-in-law, he arranged a passage to Europe for himself, his wife and their little suite. This time the ship managed to evade British patrols but Elizabeth, poor girl, was a bad sailor and suffered torments in the Atlantic swell. The voyage must have tested her love, for apart from seasickness she was in a state of extreme nervous tension caused by the uncertainty of her reception.

They reached Lisbon on April 8th, 1805, close on two years after Jérôme had sailed gaily away from Nantes as a bachelor ensign. In the meantime Napoleon had published a decree denouncing 'the pretended marriage of Jérôme, a minor, contracted in a foreign country without his mother's consent' and imperial officials everywhere were instructed that no transcript of the ceremony was to appear on their registers. A subsequent decree announced that any children from this association would be regarded as illegitimate.

The situation looked ugly the moment Jérôme's vessel dropped anchor in Lisbon harbour. A French guard surrounded the ship and the French Consul-General came aboard and asked what he could do for 'Miss Patterson'. Miss Patterson's spirit triumphed over her seasickness and the insult and she claimed her rights as a member of the imperial family. The Consul-General was not impressed. She was forbidden to land anywhere in France, Spain, Portugal or Holland, he said, and orders for her husband were explicit. He was to proceed at once for Milan via Toulouse and 'the woman with whom he was living' was to be left behind.

Jérôme took the only course open to him in the circumstances.

He set off overland and told Elizabeth to travel round to Holland by sea, assuring her that she would be allowed to land the moment he had been able to make a personal plea to the Emperor. He was to see her once again during his life – casually, in a picture gallery in Florence, and on this occasion he was accompanied by his second wife. Neither of them spoke a word.

CHAPTER SIX

'Must I then isolate myself from everyone?
Must I rely upon myself alone?'

Napoleon, in 1804

THEY HAD BEEN bickering all their lives and intriguing, to some
degree, ever since he had placed them in positions of authority,
but whenever one of the clan was threatened the ranks had closed
and there had been family unity. An event just over the horizon
was to change all this, to destroy their sense of unity and strike at
family loyalties in a way that brought little credit to any of them
and bitter reproaches from the man who had made their fortunes,
so that he was to proclaim, in despair, 'Must I then isolate myself
from everyone? Must I rely upon myself alone?'

In the early summer of 1804 Napoleon took the step that he had
been contemplating for some years and made himself Emperor
of the French people. A title was at once invented for Letizia –
Madame Mère and each of his brothers, Lucien excepted, became
their Imperial Highnesses. The revolution was over; henceforth
everyone in France was to address him as 'Sire'. Alone among
them Lucien, an exile in Rome, remained aloof.

For a nation that had been shouting republican slogans for nearly
fifteen years France adapted herself to imperialism with a speed
that astonished her neighbours. The fraternal greeting 'citizen'
was heard no longer on the boulevards and rhetorical jargon of
the kind Lucien had employed in St Maximin became not merely
unfashionable but archaic. Fourteen eminent soldiers of the Republic were made Marshals of the Empire and not one of them
declined the honour. One hundred and thirty of the men who had

voted for the execution of their king in 1792 hurried to take office under an adventurer who had received a free education from the Bourbons. Curtseys were practised and books of etiquette studied as the entire social structure was turned upside down, but as initiator of all these changes Napoleon remained cynical: 'The Marshals, having grand titles of their own,' he told Roederer, 'can hardly make fun of mine!'

Joseph, became a grand elector, without many reservations, and Louis in the same way became Constable and Chief of the Imperial (once Consular) Guard. For Lucien, who still refused to abandon his wife and return home, there was nothing. Despite pleadings, threats and bribes Lucien preferred to remain outside the family circle.

Caroline's husband, Murat, already a Marshal, was made High Admiral of France. He had never served at sea but in view of the fact that not long ago French hussars had captured the Dutch fleet by riding across the ice in the Texel the title was not as unusual as it might have been. Caroline and Murat were riding high these days. They possessed a gold dinner-service more magnificent than anything in use at the Tuileries, but the two new titles secured by her husband did little to moderate Caroline's disappointment when she learned that, whilst her brothers were to be known as Imperial Highnesses, she and Elisa were to remain plain Madame Murat and Madame Bacchiochi. In a furious temper over this obvious omission she flew to Napoleon and expressed her indignation. He listened to her in silence but would give her no title. 'One would imagine that I was depriving them of the inheritance of the king, our father!' he remarked when she had left. Elisa, not so deeply immersed in her study of music, drama and poetry that she could sneer at honours, sided with Caroline, reminding Napoleon that Pauline was already a princess. Pauline, now living in Rome and quarrelling sporadically with her husband Borghese and his aristocratic family, was concerned less with titles than her prolonged absence from Paris. Napoleon had been told of her homesickness some time before and had written her a stiff letter, following it with another to Uncle Fesch, who was now Archbishop of Lyons and a cardinal. Fesch, it will be recalled, had also suffered from homesickness in the past but now he remonstrated with Pauline and supported his nephew's plea that she should practise Roman virtues. Since her widowhood had come to an end Pauline was conducting herself like a Roman matron, enjoying her daily bath in milk and engaging in a series of love affairs with courtiers, but despite all this she longed for Paris gossip, Paris shops and French lovers.

Napoleon was particularly busy and the complaints of the family, added to secret reports he received of their complicated domestic quarrels, must have been distracting to a man preoccupied with mounting an invasion of England and the re-establishment of a new social structure. From time to time he turned aside to reason with them and when reason failed he sometimes lost his temper, as when he learned that Joseph had instructed his daughter to continue to address her uncle as 'Consul'. 'Does he imagine that he has been made an Imperial Prince in order that he may hobnob with my enemies and walk the streets of Paris in a round hat and brown surtout?' he growled but he took no action against his eldest brother, for one mutineer in the family was more than enough. Instead he had a better idea, rekindling Joseph's youthful enthusiasm for the military life and encouraging him to become a soldier like Louis. So Joseph, already in receipt of two millions a year as an Imperial Prince, was added to the muster-rolls of the Grand Army as a colonel, but the nagging continued for Joseph, egged on by Elisa and Caroline, complained of Napoleon's tentative arrangements regarding the succession and demanded a promise that his brother would not have Josephine crowned at the forthcoming coronation in Nôtre Dame. Recognition of Josephine as Empress, Joseph said, would mean that any children of Louis and Hortense took precedence over all the other Buonaparte grandchildren. Napoleon was amazed at this piece of insolence and complained bitterly of his family's ingratitude to the courtiers, who had no choice but to listen. He pointed at the difference between his family and his step-children in their attitude towards him. Eugène and Hortense, he declared, were so loyal that they overlooked his occasional affairs with women, assuring their mother that her husband was still a comparatively young man and that these episodes signified nothing. He went on to mutter that his brothers and sisters irritated him by constant reference to the possibility of his death and added that, if it were not for the fact that he found happiness in his home life, he would be a very miserable man!

All this time the rift between the Buonapartes and the Beauharnais families grew wider, but brothers and sisters seemed to be losing ground for their continual sniping prompted Napoleon to defend the woman whose conduct had been irreproachable since his return from Egypt and who now seemed to appreciate his true worth. 'She is a good wife to me!' he declared, 'and she shall be crowned, even if it costs me two hundred thousand men!'

He kept his promise, but before the coronation took place there were further eruptions inside the family and this time they came from a source that caused Emperor and Empress a great deal of anguish. The marriage of Louis and Hortense was seen to be a miserable failure.

The honeymoon quarrel had been patched up, but the wounds inflicted by Hortense's giggles and Louis' quarrelsome disposition prevented the adjustment that usually succeeds the squabbles of newlyweds. No matter how hard she tried Hortense could never make contact with the real Louis behind the sullen, self-doubting young man she had married. There had never been love between them, but his bullying and nagging poisoned the relationship from the beginning. Within weeks of the marriage Louis was spending long periods away from home and returning unexpectedly in the hope of catching Hortense engaged in some folly or indiscretion. Her dependence upon her mother maddened him and he was convinced that she thought him an object of amusement. There were undoubtedly faults on both sides and anyone who reads Hortense's own account of this wretched period of her life will conclude that she suffered from what would now be diagnosed as a persecution complex, but most of the blame lay in Louis' disordered imagination. Hortense needed a husband capable of

restoring to her some degree of self-confidence, but of all the Buonapartes Louis himself stood most in need of confidence and suffered
from a depressive gloom that showed itself in a distrust of everyone
who approached him. His health, never good, was getting worse
and he was troubled by the after-effects of several heavy falls from
his horse during the Italian campaigns. He was obstinate but it
was the obstinacy of a weak, irresolute man, utterly unlike the
quiet and courageous obstinacy of his exiled brother Lucien. He
mooned through the first year of his marriage, nursing his rheumatism, watching the progress of alterations at his country estate
at Baillon, and making sudden descents on his wife whom he
accused of all kinds of imperfections so that she either wept or
took refuge with her mother. Her tears did nothing to melt her
husband's heart. 'Whenever I speak to her she bursts into tears!'
he complained to Napoleon, when the Emperor accused him of
harshness towards his wife. Finally he declared that he must go to
the Pyrenees to take a water cure for his rheumatism and that
Hortense, although she was pregnant, must accompany him. Napoleon and Josephine objected, pointing out that a long and exhausting carriage journey might be fatal to the unborn child, and
eventually Louis went off alone. Hortense, heaving a sigh of relief,
returned to the Tuileries where she shocked observers by appearing at balls and flaunting a figure that most young wives de-
cline to advertise.

Tongues began to wag. Soon gossips were saying that the First
Consul was taking an exceptionally keen interest in the child, was
even talking of adoption before it was born, and making it known
that if Hortense produced a son he would declare him his heir.
Was this significant? Had it a link with Josephine's failure to produce a child? Had the demands of state prompted the First Consul
to betray his wife and brother?

Perhaps no man in modern history has been the target of more
slander than Napoleon. Down to this day historians do more than
hint at the paternity of Napoleon Charles, yet no more substantial
proof has been offered for this than for Napoleon's alleged incest
with his sisters. It was not long, however, before the whispers
reached Louis, where they found a fertile soil in his morbid

imagination. He reappeared shortly before the child was born, an event which occurred suddenly on the night of October 10th, 1803, and when an old nurse exclaimed 'Voila, notre Dauphin!' he glowered at her and told her to hold her tongue. His temper had not been improved by Hortense's effort to humour him a day or so before the birth. Laughingly she informed him that if the child arrived on the predicted date – October 1st – it would make its appearance three days short of the nine months dating back to their wedding, in January. Hortense, of all people, should have known better than to expect Louis to appreciate this kind of joke, but would she have risked making a remark of this kind if Napoleon had in fact seduced her? Louis reacted as one would expect in the circumstances, thundering that if such a scandalous thing did in fact happen he would leave her at once. As usual she burst into tears and he stalked off, to be told by his brother that he was a surly fellow and did not deserve such a wife.

A few days after the birth of Napoleon Charles the First Consul approached his parents with an offer to adopt the child, but neither father nor mother took kindly to the suggestion and in the end Napoleon compromised, getting a law passed that authorised him to exercise full control of the boy's future when he reached the age of eighteen. Then he and Josephine set to work to mend the marriage and the young couple were packed off to Compiègne, where Louis' regiment was stationed. It was wasted effort. The quarrels persisted, tears followed complaints and prohibitions on the part of Louis, and Hortense tried to forget her private misery in a whirl of social gaiety. She was regarded as one of the best ballroom dancers in Paris and courtiers would stand on chairs to watch her steps. One night a young officer thus occupied so far forgot himself as to applaud and was at once reprimanded for his bad manners. The next day, accompanied by his mother, he called upon Hortense to apologise. The apology was accepted and he was received on subsequent occasions. His name was Auguste de Flahaut and there are good reasons for supposing him to be an illegitimate son of Talleyrand. Both he and his official parents had been on the prescribed list, but Josephine, who was always ready to help anyone in trouble, persuaded Napoleon to allow them to return home. Soon de Flahaut was calling frequently and then, without explanation, his visits ceased. Louis had given instructions that he was not to be welcomed and for once Louis' suspicions were well-founded. The prohibition, however, came much too late. Before the birth of her second child, Hortense was deeply in love with the young officer.

The only times Louis could be relied upon to show something approaching tenderness towards his wife were when he was on the point of becoming a father, but even then his good humour did not last long and he was soon torturing himself with new doubts and newly imagined attacks upon his dignity. Rumours regarding the paternity of his eldest child continued to torment him and shortly after the birth of his second son (born almost one year after the first) he told his wife that his most fervent wish was that the child should resemble him. Sometimes his suspicions drove his wife into a frenzy, as when he skulked about her day and night when she was ill with milk-fever but it would seem that he never discovered his wife's affections were now wholly de Flahaut's, that the lovers were corresponding, de Flahaut writing under his mother's signature, and that sometimes they met briefly in the Bois de Boulogne. What continued to obsess Louis was Napoleon's proprietary interest in his eldest child and he deeply resented the edict that all Buonaparte grandsons must be given the name Napoleon.

Both Louis' children were now officially recognised as heirs to the imperial throne and every mark of favour his brother showed Hortense Louis viewed with bitterness and mistrust. Yet there was no open break, nothing for instance approaching the rupture that had occurred between Napoleon and Lucien, and it is doubtful if, in fact, Louis really believed the scandalous rumours that continued to circulate. His attitude towards his wife, his mother-in-law and his brother had its origin in a sense of personal inadequacy and his occupation of a kind of no-man's-land between two bitterly hostile families. If he had possessed the courage of Lucien he would never have allowed himself to be trapped into such a marriage, and if he had been as feather-brained as Pauline or as calculating as Caroline he would have made the most of his position. As it was, being Louis, he drifted – moody, querulous, indecisive, looking for trouble and finding it, a prey to morbidity and sharply divided loyalties. Few men could have passed a more miserable time than did Louis in the weeks leading up to the most spectacular event Paris had witnessed in a generation.

The Coronation was scheduled to take place on December 2nd, 1804 and His Holiness the Pope had travelled from Rome for the occasion. Cheering crowds stood in the bitter cold to watch the imperial cavalcade pass on its way from the Tuileries to Nôtre Dame and eyewitnesses who recalled the splendours of Marie Antoinette, in the days before the Revolution, had no hesitation in claiming that Napoleon far outdid the Bourbons as a showman.

True to his promise Napoleon had given pride of place to his wife and her grace and dignity on this occasion did him the utmost credit. Aged forty-one she looked, according to Madame Junot, no more than twenty-five. Her gown of white satin, embroidered with silver and gold, was caught at the waist by a jewelled girdle and on her head was a pearl and diamond tiara. Diamonds sparkled at her ears and neck and her narrow corsage was sewn with diamonds. Behind her, supporting a train of white velvet embroidered with silver and gold, moved a quartette of gorgeously attired women, and Josephine might have been excused for pausing in her stately progress towards the high altar in order to throw an apprehensive glance over her shoulder. Her train-bearers were Joseph's wife Julie, her own daughter Hortense and her two most dangerous sisters-in-law, Elisa and Caroline Buonaparte.

The presence of Elisa and Caroline in the capacity of train-bearers signified another minor victory for Napoleon. They had both declared categorically that nothing would induce them to perform such a humiliating function. For nine years now the Buonapartes had been at war with the hated Creole, the woman who possessed not only the magnificent display of diamonds she wore but seven hundred dresses and two hundred and fifty hats, who had won the goodwill of the army and people as they would never win it and who now stood between the family and the source of illimitable wealth and absolute power. Napoleon listened to their reproaches in silence and then, in a calm voice, presented them with a straight choice. Either they attended the coronation as Josephine's train-bearers or they did not attend at all. Both sisters surrendered immediately.

There had been anxiety for Josephine two days before the ceremony, but this time it was of her own making and amounted to the taking of a shrewdly calculated risk on her part. She had informed the Pope that she was not married in the eyes of the Church, that the hurried civil ceremony in the Mairie of the eighth district in the night in March, 1796, had not been followed by a religious ceremony. In view of this she questioned her right to be crowned in Nôtre Dame the following day. His Holiness, who must have wondered why she had left her confession so late, hastily arranged a private religious wedding in the Tuileries and Napoleon, summoned to take his place as groom nine years after the original wedding, protested and grumbled but ultimately gave in with good grace. Uncle Fesch officiated in the presence of two witnesses and Josephine, outwardly demure but inwardly triumphant, returned to her apartment to study her Coronation toilette with the knowledge that it would now be very difficult indeed to dislodge her as wife and empress.

The night of the coronation Napoleon and Josephine dined alone and in a playful mood he insisted that she should sit at table wearing the little crown that he himself had placed upon her head earlier that day. It was a small gesture that signified much, perhaps a final victory over the family.

Letizia, Madame Mère, had been summoned to take part in the ceremony but she did not come, preferring to demonstrate to the world loyalty to her exiled son Lucien and the wife he refused to discard. Thinking that posterity might find his mother's absence significant Napoleon instructed David, his official painter, to include his mother's face among the relatives surrounding the throne in Nôtre Dame. It was about this time that somebody who could have known very little of the proud, unsmiling Corsican woman asked her if she was not astonished by the progress her sons and daughters had made in the world. 'It is all very well, so long as it lasts!' replied the old lady in her Italianate French.

The question of succession seemed now to be settled. Whenever he had time to spare from his official duties Napoleon liked to dandle Napoleon Charles, now aged two, upon his knee but Louis, the child's father, was not flattered. Backed by Joseph he had sworn that he would not stand meekly aside and see himself and Joseph disinherited by his own child. Napoleon did not press the point. His rages regarding brothers and sisters were less frequent now for he flattered himself that he had learned how to deal with them. He was confident that, if necessary, both Joseph and Louis could be brought to heel and he was not seriously worried about the irresponsible baby of the family, now staging his way along the dusty roads of Spain while his wife, the woman Patterson, went to Holland to await a summons to the imperial presence. Lucien was still a serious problem but even Lucien could be bribed after passing another year or two in exile. Pauline attracted scandals and generally behaved like the feather-brained girl she had always been, but with Pauline there was never a possibility of rebellion or intrigue, only folly and extravagance, and as Josephine's husband he was qualified to deal with both. As for Elisa, she would make periodic complaints about being neglected because she had married a stupid man but now that it was clear Bacchiochi would never make a soldier he could always be given a civil appointment where he could pass as important but do no harm to the Empire. Caroline and her theatrical husband Murat continued to irritate him, but war was coming and Murat would soon be fully occupied in the field and he had learned how to deal with Caroline when she became too demanding. Soon after the coronation she and her husband had seen him playing with little Napoleon Charles and when he said, 'Do you know, little one, that you are in danger of being king one day?' Murat had cried, 'What about my boy? What about Achille?' Napoleon had replied, with deliberate malice, 'Achille? Oh, I daresay little Achille will make a good soldier!'

In the meantime there was an unpleasant duty to be fulfilled.

Jérôme must be disciplined and persuaded, once and for all, to discard this bourgeois American girl he had shipped all the way from Baltimore. Napoleon wrote to his mother saying that 'the foolish boy had arrived in Lisbon with the woman he is living with' and instructions had been issued to refuse 'Miss Patterson' permission to land anywhere on French or friendly soil. 'If she attempts to evade these orders and appears anywhere else, she will be escorted to Amsterdam and put on board the first ship for America.' As for 'that young man', he was to travel direct to Turin via Perpignan, Toulouse and Grenoble and then report in Milan, where an ultimatum would be delivered by the Emperor in person. 'I shall show him no mercy,' Napoleon continued. 'If he shows no disposition to wipe out the dishonour with which he has stained my name by deserting the colours for a wretched woman, I shall utterly disown him and perhaps make an example of him to teach young officers the sanctity of military service and of the enormity of the crime they commit if they prefer a female to the flag!'

Near Truxillo, in Spain, Jérôme met some fellow-countrymen, one of them an old friend of the family. Laurette Permon, now Madame Junot, was accompanying her husband to Portugal on a mission when Junot arrived with the news that he had just met Jérôme Buonaparte passing through on his way to Milan. Junot, a kindhearted man, was deeply sorry for the boy and invited him to breakfast, but Laurette was distressed to find herself entertaining a very different person from the gay young man she had met at her mother's house in Paris. His lively expression, she noted, had changed to one of pensive melancholy and he was clearly undergoing a terrible struggle with his conscience. When Junot urged him to forget the girl and make his peace with the Emperor, Jérôme burst out, 'Even admitting that I am at fault, on whose head will punishment fall? Upon that of my poor, innocent wife! Surely my brother will not outrage the feelings of one of the most respectable families in America!' He then showed them a miniature of Elizabeth and Junot, who had recently fallen in and out of love with Pauline Buonaparte and was soon to fall victim to her sister Caroline, remarked upon the likeness of the girl to Jérôme's sisters. 'I only wish my brother would consent to see her,' added Jérôme. 'If he did I am convinced that her triumph would be as complete as that of Lucien's wife, Christine, whom the Emperor rejected but eventually liked as much as his other sisters-in-law.' Junot said nothing, knowing that the prospect of outraging the feelings of every respectable family in America would not deter the Emperor from rejecting a sister-in-law of whom he had not first approved. The days were gone when he could afford to make the best of a bad job, as in the case of Christine Boyer, and his attitude towards Lucien's second wife proved as much.

Jérôme reached Turin on April 24th. He must have hurried over the execrable Spanish roads for he covered the distance in fifteen days. From Turin he sent a pitiful appeal to his brother, then recently arrived in Italy pending his coronation as King of Italy, but Napoleon refused to receive him until he pledged himself ready to submit. For eleven days Jérôme considered the alternatives – unconditional surrender or exile and possibly arrest as a deserter. In the end, talking of 'mental reservations', he gave in and Napoleon allowed him to proceed to Alessandria. In a letter written to him from that town Napoleon said, ' . . . there are no faults in your conduct which a sincere repentance does not efface from my eyes. Your union with Miss Patterson is null in religion as in law. Write to her and tell her to return to America. I will grant her a pension of 60,000 francs during her life on condition that in no event she shall bear my name, to which she has no right, her marriage being non-existent. Your marriage being thus annulled of your own free will, I will restore to you my friendship and resume the feelings I have had towards you since your childhood.' On the same day Napoleon wrote to Elisa and also to the Minister of Marine, informing them both that Jérôme had acknowledged his fault and that Elizabeth was now disavowed.

The first words at the meeting of the brothers are supposed to have been Napoleon's: 'You Sir, are the first of your family to abandon your post shamefully. It will require many striking actions on your part to wipe that stain off your reputation. As for your love affair with your little girl, I ignore it!' Jérôme was then despatched on a naval mission to Genoa and within a few days Napoleon appointed him to command the 44-gun vessel *Pomone* in which he was to cruise offshore in squadron with four other vessels. The Patterson affair was over.

Jérôme's little girl, variously described as Madame Buonaparte, Miss Patterson, or 'that person', arrived at Amsterdam on May 1st three weeks after she had parted from Jérôme at Lisbon. She found Holland closed to her and the brig in which she sailed was ordered to stand off without communication with the shore. Guarded by two war vessels the brig and all on board her were virtual prisoners for the next eight days. Only when the American representative at Amsterdam intervened was it allowed to weigh anchor and leave for England.

Elizabeth was accompanied by her brother, an American woman friend called Anderson and a French doctor, and the forlorn party made the Dover Roads on May 19th. Nobody prevented her from landing and passports were at once sent down to the coast. She travelled on to London, taking great pains to avoid publicity and in June she took lodgings in Camberwell, then a Surrey suburb. It was here, at Park Place, on July 7th, that she gave birth to Jérôme's son, a child destined to become the founder of the American Buonapartes. Elizabeth still had faith in Jérôme's honour and had by no means given up hope of a reunion. When no letter arrived she assumed that he was being held prisoner by his terrible brother but as the weeks passed and news filtered across the Channel, reporting a reconciliation between the brothers, she accepted the inevitable and booked a passage home.

Her arrival there was a dismal anticlimax. As the Belle of Baltimore she had been the envy of every woman in America. Now, sent back like an unclaimed parcel, she was the object of pity and derision. There must have been times when she wished she had been drowned in the wreck off Delaware. For the rest of her long life she was to claim that she had been refused entry into the imperial circle for reasons of State, but in her heart was a bitterness that fed upon hurt pride and hatred, so that her friends and family watched her grow sour and intractable. She quarrelled with her father – who now declared that he had been against the match all along – and Patterson Senior complained of her unfilial conduct in his will. For sometime Jérôme continued to write to her and his early letters were full of protestations of undying devotion – 'My first thought on waking, as my last before going to sleep, is always for you and if I were not sure that I should have the happiness of rejoining my beloved wife I should not go on living . . .' About a year after their parting the letters ceased, although Napoleon continued to pay over the annul pension he had promised. Then, when Jérôme was installed as King of Westphalia, he wrote offering Elizabeth a principality with a pension of 200,000 francs a year if she would give him custody of their son. Elizabeth refused in a letter that does her credit. 'Although doubtless Westphalia is a large kingdom,' she wrote, 'it is not big enough for two queens!' The reply silenced Jérôme for another three years, after which he again wrote in affectionate terms declaring that 'all will be arranged sooner or later'. It was sooner than he expected. Four years later the Buonapartes were exiles and the greatest of them a prisoner on an Atlantic rock.

In middle age, when Elizabeth could look back upon the one adventure of her life with a certain amount of detachment, she recognised Jérôme for what he was, an impetuous, good-natured, irresponsible extrovert, but although Napoleon had broken up her marriage she was sufficiently objective to be able to admire his genius. More than forty years after she had been turned away from France she wrote: 'He hurled me back on what I hated most on earth, my Baltimore obscurity, but even that could not destroy the admiration I felt for his genius and glory. I have been an Imperial Buonaparte *quand même.*'

After Jérôme's abject surrender Napoleon made efforts to persuade the Pope to annul the wedding, claiming that it was void on legal and religious grounds. He backed the demand with a bribe of great value, a gold diadem ornamented with diamonds and rubies. What His Holiness did with the diadem is not recorded but he refused an annulment, stating that, after examining all precedents, he could find no good reason for declaring the marriage void. Napoleon fell back on the Gallican Church and in October, 1805, a decree of ecclesiastical nullity was published in Paris.

Elizabeth, for her part, obtained a divorce through the Maryland legislature.

For a matter of a hundred and forty-three years denigrators of Napoleon have been looking for proof of his essential brutality and coarseness of mind. They have quoted his abandonment of the plague victims at Jaffa, and the murder of the Duc D'Enghien, using both as examples of his immortality. These incidents, together with many others bearing the same hallmark of ruthlessness, can all be justified to a degree by military or political necessity, but there can be no such justification for his treatment of Elizabeth Patterson. The marriage, foolish though it undoubtedly was, was nonetheless legal. Jérôme got permission from his eldest brother and his mother, although not until after the event, and as the Pope pointed out when he rejected Napoleon's claim, the religious aspect of the marriage was perfectly regular, having been performed by the Bishop of Baltimore. It is difficult to understand why Napoleon behaved with such intolerance towards the young couple. Approval of the match would have at least won him goodwill in the States as well as striking a blow at protocol, which weakened the blood of every reigning house in Europe. Although he never accepted Lucien's second wife he had soon forgiven him for marrying Christine Boyer without first having obtained the approval of the self-appointed head of the family. Admittedly the Pattersons were bourgeois but were they more so than the soap-boiling Clarys of Marseilles, or the olive growing Buonapartes of Corsica? In later life Napoleon often discussed Jérôme's marriage but he never succeeded in justifying his merciless attitude towards it at the time, and one is left with the impression that it was not the marriage itself that roused him to such a pitch of fury but the fact that it had taken place during his brother's desertion from the Navy. Even if this was the case he was still arbitrary and unjust, for it was no fault of Elizabeth's that Jérôme had taken unauthorised leave in order to storm American hostesses rather than British ships of the line. He could have dismissed Jérôme from the Navy and let him kick his heels in America, or he could have recalled him, punished him and made the best of a situation that he could not, with justice, alter. For all that, it is Jérôme himself who emerges from this miserable affair with the maximum dishonour and his subsequent conduct as a king shows that Napoleon should have let him stay in America, disowned and dependent for money upon the generosity of his wife's family. Perhaps the Pattersons are to be congratulated on their escape. A year or so with Jérôme, denied access to French funds, would have landed William and all his sons in the bankruptcy court.

BOOK THREE

The Satraps

CHAPTER SEVEN

*'Soldiers, name your children after me and if one of them should
prove worthy of us I will make him my own son and adopt him
as my successor!'*

Napoleon's proclamation after
Austerlitz

LONGBOOTS WAS on the march again and it was with those words
he addressed his victorious legions after Austerlitz, a victory that
laid Europe at his feet. It was a curious promise from a man who
had gone to such lengths to keep the succession in the family and
had forcibly parted his youngest brother from the daughter of
a democratic American. But autumn 1805, was a heady season
and provoked heady proclamations. Under this kind of spur the
Grand Army, cheated of a descent upon the English coasts, turned
its back on the Channel and poured south-eastward across Europe
to roll up the Austrian army at Ulm and smash the new Russo-
Austrian coalition in Bohemia. And this was only the beginning.
Within eighteen months the Prussians had been overwhelmed at
Jena and Auerstadt and their army, the legacy of Frederick the
Great, had surrendered to a man. A check at Eylau followed but
Warsaw was occupied and by June, 1807 the Czar's armies were
decisively routed at Friedland. At Tilsit, on a moored raft, the
Emperor of the French and the Emperor of all the Russias discussed
how best to carve up the map and share a Continent. Friends,
allies and relatives of this astonishing man rubbed their hands in
anticipation of rewards: especially relatives.

The four campaigns had occupied about twenty-one months
and seemed likely to rain dukedoms, principalities, honours and
wealth on those close to the conqueror. With Jérôme brought to

heel only Lucien failed to benefit from these triumphs. Austerlitz had been fought exactly one year after Napoleon had crowned himself in Nôtre Dame and within two years of the victory Joseph, Louis and Jérôme were kings and Elisa and Caroline were Grand Duchesses. Pauline had been a Princess since 1803. Within one more year the Buonaparte family could boast of four crowned heads, for Murat, Caroline's gay hussar, also became a king. No wonder Madame Mère remarked: 'It's all very well, so long as it lasts!'

Joseph was the first to profit from the French triumph. At a critical moment in the campaign the Queen of Naples, distinguished for her hatred of Napoleon, threw open her ports to English shipping and Russian troops. She paid a high price for her indiscretion. The day after the battle Marshal Masséna, former cabin-boy, smuggler and fruit-seller, was sent down to Naples to proclaim that the Bourbon dynasty there had ceased to exist. On March 30th, 1806, Joseph and Julie were proclaimed King and Queen of the Two Sicilies.

Joseph's regiment had taken part in the great battle and had been mauled during the holding period of the engagement, but the loss of its eagles did very little to tarnish the splendour of the day and Napoleon was in a giving mood. Joseph, who had once refused the sovereignty of Lombardy, now abandoned the last of his republican principles and rode down into Italy, conscious of accepting his due. Always complacent, always inclined to accept whatever came along be it a kingdom or a notice of dismissal, Joseph longed for a quiet life and Naples, where the Bourbons had been unpopular, promised to provide one. Yet he did not leave Paris without certain misgivings. Basically his tastes were those of a country gentleman and he had enjoyed wandering about his estate and entertaining his numerous friends. When he first heard of his brother's plans for him he said, regretfully, 'I would rather be King of Mortefontaine.' It proved a prophetic utterance for Joseph's quiet days were over. More than ten years were to pass before he was to return to the semi-obscurity he preferred.

He retained all his French dignities, including that of Grand Elector, and now assumed the role of a dependent ally of France. Just how dependent he was soon to discover, for the moment he arrived in Naples Napoleon began to bombard him with instructions and advice. He was to pay a million francs annually to the French Treasury and his notion to found a local Legion of Honour, and call it 'The Order of St Januarius', was frowned upon as 'too ecclesiastical and too reminiscent of the banished Bourbons'. 'The mere name raises a smile,' wrote Napoleon, 'we ought to find something that inspires respect and gives rise to imitation.' Ten days later he was writing to Joseph on another subject. 'Don't allow anyone to be in sole command of your Guard. Nothing is more dangerous. I have told you before and I tell you again, that you trust your Neapolitans too much.' He went on to warn the new king of the dangers of employing any but French cooks and proposed devious sleeping arrangements in order to prevent unauthorised persons entering the King's room at night. Many times during those first few weeks as King and Queen of Naples, Joseph and his wife must have longed for the peace of Mortefontaine where they could eat everything put before them without wondering if the lethal skills of the Borgias were being revived for their benefit.

As soon as they heard of Joseph's promotion Elisa and Caroline began to scream with jealousy, but this time their demands had been anticipated. Elisa was given the principalities of Lucca and Piombino in Italy and Caroline's husband Murat was made Grand Duke of Berg and Cleves. Later the principality of Guastalla in Italy was made over to Pauline and before the year was out Louis was King of Holland. That same year Eugène, Josephine's soldier son, married Augusta, the daughter of the King of Bavaria. He was already a Viceroy, ruling Northern Italy on behalf of his stepfather. Whichever way one looked there was a Buonaparte or a Beauharnais in authority, and two of them were already wearing crowns.

The orgy of redistribution continued into 1807. No fewer than twenty hereditary duchies were distributed, either to marshals or to high officers of the French Court and as soon as Jérôme was safely married to a German princess, a kingdom was invented for him from territory torn from Hesse, Hanover, Brunswick and

Prussia. The new realm was known as Westphalia. It might aptly have been called Wonderland. All these readjustments were made in a matter of two years, but between the break-up of the army of invasion along the Channel coasts, and the second marriage of the youngest member of the family, a great deal had happened to individual members of the clan. None of it was heroic and much was scandalous.

Caroline, as the wife of a man who had played a useful part in the successful campaigns of 1805-7, was the first in line for rewards, for Murat had won more glory than any of the new marshals. It was he who had led the furious pursuit of the Prussians after Jena and he who first rode into Warsaw, where he dreamed of being crowned king of a reorganised Poland. At Eylau he saved the army, charging across the snow at the head of ninety squadrons of cavalry and changing a defeat into a stalemate. His close relationship with the Emperor, together with his vanity, clownish behaviour and taste for gorgeous uniforms made him an object of contempt in the eyes of hardbitten fighters like Lannes and Augereau. After Eylau the latter called him 'a dancing dog in pantomime dress', provoking a furious quarrel in Napoleon's presence, but Murat's love of display and personal courage endeared him to the lower ranks. Caroline was delighted with his success but this did not prevent her from indulging in an impassioned love affair with General Junot during his absence, Junot was one of Napoleon's closest comrades and Governor of Paris. Almost every night his carriage could be seen outside Caroline's house. She frequently received him alone and the two were seen together at every social function, Caroline acting coyly and Junot behaving like an infatuated schoolboy. Junot had asked for Pauline's hand in Italy but now he was more than consoled by the charms of her younger sister. His wife, formerly Laurette Permon, wept and longed for the return of the Emperor before the scandal led to a duel between Murat and Junot. Both were hot-tempered men and Laurette knew Caroline well enough to realise that the spectacle of two high-ranking officers fighting over her would not cause her a moment's anxiety. Luckily for everyone concerned the matter was soon resolved by Napoleon who, despite his prolonged absence from Paris, was very well informed about the affair. His first act on returning to Paris was to summon Junot and lecture him for two hours, sternly forbidding a duel and somehow convincing Murat that what had occurred was no more than a flirtation. Caroline took no part at all in these discussions, having forgotten Junot in the excitement of being made a Grand Duchess.

Jérôme played no part in the territorial triumphs of the Grand Army but he did succeed in collecting a little glory at sea. After his renunciation of Elizabeth Patterson he sailed away in command of five vessels and that same summer consoled himself for the loss of a wife by taking a mistress, an Italian beauty called Blanca Carrega. He was growing more experienced in the ways of the world and supplied the lady of his choice with a complaisant husband. When he became a king and had favours to distribute he rewarded them both for the kindness they had shown him during this difficult period.

In August, 1805, he was at Algiers, demanding of the Bey all the Italian and French slaves that he held as captives. For centuries the corsairs based on the Barbary Coast had plagued Mediterranean commerce but rivalry between the great powers had encouraged piracy to flourish and in every settlement around Algiers and Tunis were hundreds of Christian slaves. Some of them were skilled craftsmen and comparatively well-treated but a majority dragged out a miserable existence under their Islamic masters. The recalcitrant among them were humiliated, tortured and flogged and if they tried to escape and were recaptured they were usually flung from walls on to iron hooks known as 'scorpions'. Jérôme gave the Bey forty-eight hours to comply with his demand and well within the required time a total of 232 slaves came aboard his vessels, after which he returned in triumph to a civic reception in Genoa. There was a thanksgiving service at the Cathedral and afterwards the freed captives were entertained to a banquet on board ship, the day concluding with a ball in Jérôme's honour. Napoleon was delighted at this brisk display of duty and Jérôme was summoned to Paris to receive his brother's congratulations. He came at once and proceeded to pledge his credit with merchants, running up bills at a speed that would have astonished even

Josephine, but despite this he was given further promotion and command of the *Vétéran*, one of a squadron now despatched to the Cape of Good Hope to harass English shipping.

Napoleon's instructions to Willaumz, commander of this raiding force, were similar to those given to the admirals to whom Jérôme had been sent as a midshipman. 'Treat him with the firmness of a chief full of the sense of duty, combined with the consideration due to a personage destined to a rank which the Sovereign's will has not yet conferred on him,' ran the despatch. No special honour was to be paid to him for none, wrote Napoleon, was due! Willaumz read these instructions with tongue in cheek.

Before Jérôme could leave Paris he had to settle his debts and as Napoleon was absent from the capital he was obliged to turn to Joseph for the means to settle. Joseph, reluctantly loaned him another 80,000 francs and wrote to Napoleon asking for a refund. The reply was brief. 'If Jérôme cannot live on his allowance let him be imprisoned for debt.' The goodnatured Joseph never got his money back and unlike the million francs he had to send up from Naples every year this money came from his own pocket.

Freed of debt Jérôme hurried off to Brest where he was at once made second-in-command of the expedition. When he learned that the destination of the squadron was the Cape of Good Hope he tried hard to wriggle out of the assignment but was prevented from doing so by his commander's shrewd comment that a few months' arduous service now would pay a very good dividend in the future.

The squadron was turned back from the Cape owing to English strength in the area and sailed instead for Brazil and then the West Indies. Here Jérôme's vessel became separated from the others and he opened his sealed orders to find that a rendezvous had been ordered on the Newfoundland Bank. He did not follow these instructions but turned south again and fell in with a convoy of English merchant ships carrying timber and escorted by a single frigate. He captured and burned them (eleven in number according to him, six according to the British naval reports) but by now he was off the Azores and not far from home so, with his customary disregard for orders, he decided that it would be unwise to search for his squadron and steered for Brest.

He did not reach France without another dramatic adventure, for to get home he was obliged to run the gauntlet of four British ships of the line blockading the French coast. Half in mind to fight his way through to Lorient he had the good fortune to learn from a local sailor, serving aboard the *Vétéran*, that there was a passage into the harbour between the reefs. He gave the local sailor the helm and the *Vétéran* ran between the rocks and straight in under the guns of the fort, 'another example of Buonaparte luck' grumbled the British captain who reported the incident to London.

Again he was received like a hero and although the Minister of Marine criticised his conduct in abandoning his Commander, Napoleon sided with Jérôme, investing him with the Legion of Honour and promoting him to Rear-Admiral. Jérôme is probably the only sailor in naval history to attain that rank before his twenty-second birthday.

Napoleon now changed his plans as regards Jérôme's immediate future. It was time, he thought, to establish his younger brother's reputation as a general and with this end in view he took him with him on the Prussian campaign in the autumn of 1806, placing him in command of a mixed force of Bavarians and Württembergers. Jérôme had shown himself to be an impulsive and unreliable commander at sea and had proved the despair of commanders who expected him to submit to discipline, but he had more than his share of personal courage and the notion of being left behind to guard the rear did not appeal to him. He tried to get Napoleon to change his mind but his brother was not disposed to give him a forward position until he had proved his ability in the field. As it happened there was plenty to be done in Silesia and for the next few weeks the Rear-Admiral turned General was engaged in mopping up pockets of Prussian resistance bypassed by the Grand Army. He had no luck and acquired very little glory, but through no fault of his own. He was always in the wrong place at the wrong time and his relations with the veteran commanders charged with the responsibility of watching over him grew worse as the campaign proceeded. One such soldier was the notorious

Vandamme, a swaggering professional with a reputation for ruthless efficiency and Jérôme, who was still bombarding Napoleon for a command nearer the centre of operations, was soon quarrelling fiercely with his colleague. Unfortunately for the beginner Napoleon gave way to Jérôme's appeals when his brother was engaged in the siege of Glogau and directed him to hand over to Vandamme and move against the town of Kalisch. Jérôme obeyed and two days later Vandamme stormed Glogau. Hearing the news Jérôme cried out with rage and disappointment but by this time his brother was moving against the Russians on the Vistula and Jérôme wrote again, begging to be attached to the Grand Army and given another chance to make a reputation. Again the Emperor complied and Jérôme hurried to join his brother in Warsaw, leaving his rival Vandamme to conduct the siege of Breslau. By now the Rear-Admiral was learning the tricks of the trade and wrote to Vandamme forbidding him to enter Breslau if, as seemed likely, it capitulated. Vandamme was amazed at such an order. He had never liked associating with Jérôme and the partners had already quarrelled over the conduct of their troops in occupied territory. The Bavarians and Württembergers were a wild, undisciplined lot and their excesses were condoned by Vandamme, who was one of the few brutal soldiers serving in the Grand Army. He was a man who boasted that he feared neither God nor devil and his reputation in history, apart from that of being an able soldier in the field, rests on a remark he once made to the Czar Alexander. Captured during the campaign in Saxony, when the Empire was approaching dissolution, Vandamme was charged with his excesses in certain German towns. Undismayed by the accusation he reminded the Czar of the part played by that autocrat in the assassination of his own father, the Czar Paul. On receiving Jérôme's letter about the surrender of Breslau Vandamme remained outside the town when the garrison asked for terms, but he must have smiled when Jérôme, hurrying up from Poland, arrived too late to do anything but watch the defeated garrison march out and lay down their arms. Vandamme had Jérôme's measure by this time, and rank and file were laughing over his latest *bon mot*, made when Jérôme appeared in the trenches at Neiss just as a shot had spattered the staff-officers with earth. 'These devils of bullets,' remarked Vandamme maliciously, 'have no respect at all for strangers!'

After receiving the surrender of Breslau Jérôme was given the task of superintending the organisation of stores and supplies for the Grand Army in Poland and although he seems to have made a good quartermaster his thirst for a warrior's glory remained unsatisfied. He was soon immersed in campaigns of another kind and Napoleon (who never missed a whisper of scandal where his relations were involved) wrote complaining of Jérôme's excessive gallantry towards the fräuleins of the garrison town. His information was accurate. Jérôme was now involved in a passionate affair with an opera singer and, as in the case of the Italian lady Blanca Carrega, he was to introduce her into his Cassel harem when he became King of Westphalia a year later. Napoleon's letter carried a postscript reminding his brother that he was soon to marry a princess and should therefore try to behave like a prospective bridegroom. Jérôme took the hint and attacked Prussian forces attempting to relieve an invested town, but again he was too late. This time the cavalryman, Lefebvre-Desnouettes, defeated the enemy within hours of Jérôme's arrival at the front.

A curious assortment of hereditary rulers were unwilling contributors to Jérôme's new kingdom. Prussia, Brunswick and Hanover all yielded territory and so did the Prince of Orange, who contributed the Abbey of Cerney. In addition Napoleon appropriated to himself all the territory of the Duke of Brunswick-Wolfenbüttel (who had been killed at Jena) and then threw in various odds and ends, such as the Prussian fief of Stolberg and Hesse-Cassel's fief of Rietburg. Westphalia, in fact, was a hotchpotch of other people's property and its population of two million, some Catholics and some Protestants, writhed under the demands of increasingly excessive taxation and a harsh system of conscription. The problems of ruling such a kingdom, however, did not dismay Jérôme, who was delighted at the prospect of wearing a crown. He rejoined his triumphant brother in Dresden and in July, 1807, they both returned to Paris where, on August 22nd, Jérôme became a bridegroom again.

His new bride, Sophie Dorothea Frederika Catherine, was the daughter of Frederick of Württemberg and his senior by one year and eight months. In every respect she was a contrast to the high-spirited girl Jérôme had married in Baltimore four years before. The Pattersons had been rich and Catherine, although of ancient lineage, was so poor that she blushed for shame when compelled to stand beside such well-dressed women as Josephine and Caroline Murat. She had spent her childhood in Russia, moving west when her father and mother became estranged. Her mother, Augusta, died in childbirth at the age of twenty-four and there were rumours that either her husband or the Empress of Russia were responsible for the neglect that led to Augusta's early death. Whether or not this was so it is certainly a fact that her coffin remained unburied at Polangen, near Riga, for twenty-eight years, to be interred when her son heard about it whilst visiting Russia the year after Water-loo! Catherine's father, the Duke, was a man of violent tempera-ment with an unsavoury reputation but he was also a figure of fun, for his girth was enormous and wits said he occupied the largest bed in the world. Catherine had led a dismal life in Germany and welcomed the prospect of marrying a Buonaparte. This relief on her part survived years of married life to the most accomplished rake in Europe, so that the marriage can be said to have proved the most successful of the Buonaparte matches. Jérôme's new father-in-law, although recently elevated by French arms to the rank of King, was a snob and it is doubtful if he knew that the gentlemanly Marshal Bessières, who was sent to conduct the bride to Paris, had once earned his living as a hairdresser. It is from Madame Junot's pen that we learn a little about the appearance of the bride when she arrived in August. 'Not altogether pleasing,' declares this lady, and goes on to describe Catherine as 'a fine woman whose figure would have been more striking still if her neck had not been short!' Catherine was certainly not to be compared with the ravishing Elizabeth Patterson but Jérôme had learned to com-promise, and in referring to his readiness to marry again in com-pliance with his brother's wishes, Madame Junot adds, 'He wished to taste the sweets of power like the rest of his family and denied even before the cock crew!'

The Buonaparte clan assembled in Paris for the wedding, Pauline and her husband, Caroline in her new role as Duchess, and even Madame Mère, who had chosen to live with the exiled Lucien. Catherine made an excellent first impression on her mother-in-law and they remained on affectionate terms all their lives. After the wedding Jérôme chose a court from among his circle of cronies and with the approach of autumn the royal couple set out for their new kingdom, but before they could leave the inevitable financial crisis had to be resolved. Wherever he went Jérôme ran up huge bills that anchored him to the district where he had indulged himself, and this time Napoleon came to his assistance. Determined that Jérôme should begin royal life solvent he authorised the payment of debts amounting to three million francs from a Government sinking fund and, in addition, took the unusual step of allowing his brother to draw his salary as an Imperial Prince in advance.

For the first and only time in his life, Jérôme left Paris free of debt.

In early December the bride and groom crossed into their new realm and drove under triumphal arches and flags between crowds of enthusiastic, down-at-heel subjects. Had these Westphalians known what was in store for them in the immediate future their cheers might have been more restrained, but one can sympathise with their optimism. For years they had been driven into the ground by taxes and the ceaseless demands of successive national service decrees, and the arrival of the great Napoleon's brother and his German bride must have seemed to promise a happier era. They had no experience of being ruled by a king who cared only for beautiful things.

Lucien, stubborn and unrelenting, remained in exile but Napoleon now made another attempt to bring about a reconciliation. Joseph had had a meeting with Lucien in Modena, in March, 1807 and cleared the ground for a new approach by Napoleon, but when the brothers met in December of that year the rupture between them was not healed. Elisa had written to Lucien urging him to show

Napoleon 'unlimited deference' but her letter had little effect upon her brother's proud nature. He was the only man in Europe (save for the outspoken Marshals Lannes and Augereau) who dared to treat the epoch-maker as an equal or less than an equal. Within minutes they were quarrelling again. Exercising tremendous self-control Napoleon raised his price. If Lucien would repudiate his wife he could choose between the kingdom of Portugal, a new kingdom carved out of Italy, the hand of the Queen of Etruria (who was still awaiting a bridegroom) and a Duchy for Madame Lucien, with whom her husband might continue to live on condition that he regarded her as a mistress and did not appear with her in public. Lucien contemptuously rejected the terms. He would not, he said, repudiate a woman whom he loved and respected and he would not deprive his children of their mother. Above all, he would not imitate Joseph, Louis and Jérôme in resigning himself 'to the role of a prefect' and dance to the tune of an ex-republican general of artillery! Napoleon was enraged but he was also amazed. All his life he had been prepared to sacrifice personal relationships in pursuit of policy and the fact that his most talented brother should prefer domestic happiness to unlimited power genuinely distressed him. He pointed out how much Lucien's ennoblement could mean to his family but all he could extract from the stubborn man was a reluctant promise to send his daughter Charlotte to Paris to be groomed for marriage to the Prince of the Asturias, the heir to the Bourbon throne of Spain. In a letter to Joseph admitting his failure to win Lucien back to the fold Napoleon wrote: 'I did all I could to persuade him to employ his talents for me and for his country . . . his daughter must start without delay and he must send me a declaration placing her entirely at my disposal . . . my destinies must be accomplished.'

They were not accomplished, or not, at all events, through Lucien's daughter by the dead Christine, for Charlotte, now aged thirteen, had inherited her father's taste for irony and her precocity was to widen the breach between the brothers. Napoleon had already made up his mind to extend his influence to Spain and overthrow Godoy, a handsome guardsman who, as lover of the ugly Queen, was the virtual ruler of Spain. His aim was to

marry Lucien's daughter to Godoy's rival, the vicious but popular
Prince of the Asturias, and the scheme would probably have succeeded had it not been for Charlotte herself.

The girl was taken to live with her grandmother in Paris but
she was an extremely observant child and committed to paper all
she saw and heard about her royal relatives. Her letters to her
father were opened and Napoleon, once he had recovered from
the shock of reading the home truths they contained, took delight
in reading them aloud to the assembled Buonapartes. It is a pity
that Charlotte's letters do not appear to have been preserved and
all that is known about them is that they resulted in her being
returned to her father with the utmost despatch. No one was more
delighted with this twist of events than Lucien, who travelled
twenty leagues to meet her, exclaiming, 'My child, I committed
a great fault! But you are restored to me and the evil is repaired!'
It is the most human episode in the Buonaparte story.

Joseph and Jérôme were launched, Elisa and Caroline were fully
occupied with their state balls, amateur theatricals, duchies, titles
and the incomes that came with them, and Pauline, having all the
money she needed, could spend her days sitting for painters,
bathing in milk and entertaining a succession of lovers. Napoleon
had performed miracles for the family but Madame Mère, watchful
and unsmiling, continued to express distrust of the golden age
and to hoard her allowance like a threatened peasant. Her parsi-
mony, a great joke in the Paris salons, exasperated her son, but
when he remonstrated with her she told him, 'One day you will
need the money I am saving.' She had no patience with vain
display and the outward trappings of wealth and power. Her
natural simplicity, hardened by the bitter struggle to survive during
her youth and the period that followed Carlo's death, demanded
no more than security and she could see none in the world around
her, far less indeed than she had enjoyed in Corsica. If kings could
be crowned, she reasoned, they could just as easily be deposed.
The only permanent possession was soil, handed down from father
to son, and although her children now ruled over millions of acres

there was nothing permanent in their tenure. In spite of his impatience with what he regarded as avarice, Napoleon always treated her with respect. He would rave at and bully others but in his dealings with Letizia he was humble, as if, deep in his heart, he regarded his fantastic achievements as no more than her due. He had forgiven Jérôme at her request but even Letizia could not persuade him to re-admit Lucien to the family circle, so she held her tongue and saved most of the money he showered on her. The time would come when Lucien would be reconciled under circumstances she had anticipated from the beginning.

Things were going badly for Louis, soon to become King of Holland. His marriage was proving a disaster and his stubbornness another source of friction within the family. There had been renewed trouble over the question of succession soon after the Coronation, when Napoleon had sent for Louis and Hortense and re-opened the subject of adopting their elder son Napoleon Charles and crowning him King of Italy. Louis regarded the proposal as a personal insult and said that under no circumstances would he consent to a child of his receiving a rank more elevated than his own. Napoleon, faced with a flat refusal, stormed at his brother, calling him an ungrateful fool but Louis obstinancy was equal to the occasion and Napoleon became calmer, reasoning that the child could remain in France until he was of age and then maintain two separate establishments, one in Paris and one in Milan. It was no use, Louis refused to budge and Napoleon complained bitterly that neither brothers or sisters would share the tremendous burdens placed upon him, burdens that were the heavier because of his own childlessness. Hortense, who was present throughout this stormy interview, said nothing. 'What could I have said?' she afterwards related. 'In the end it was always my poor mother who was made to suffer for these scenes.'

Caroline was found a new role in the days of consolidation that followed the triple triumph of Austerlitz, Jena and Friedland. It was that of Imperial Procuress. Ever since his championship of Josephine at the time of the coronation, Caroline had been employing more indirect tactics in her attempts to undermine the marriage. She, Joseph and Elisa had exhausted themselves in endeavours to ruin the Creole by the spreading rumours and lies and by reminding Napoleon of his wife's extravagance and her past indiscretions. Now they suggested that he should disprove the claim that it was he and not she who was responsible for their barren marriage, a claim fostered by Josephine and one which seemed to have some basis for he had not yet fathered an illegitimate child, in spite of a string of mistresses in the last seven years. Madame Fourès, the pretty blonde with whom he had consorted in Egypt, had given substance to this story. When he complained to his intimates that 'the little fool did not know how to have a baby' she had exclaimed indignantly, 'It's not my fault, I can tell you that!' Since then there had been Grassini, the famous opera singer, and after Grassini the tragedienne, Mademoiselle Georges, but neither had conceived and Napoleon himself had been known to express doubts as regards his own virility. Caroline's plan was to parade beautiful women before her brother like slaves in an Oriental market. Sooner or later, she reasoned, one of them would make a lasting impression on him and perhaps, if the family were in luck, would bear him a child and convince the Emperor of the futility of remaining tied to Josephine.

In the early spring of 1806 Caroline's scheme succeeded. Among her ex-school friends who applied to her for a household post was a beautiful brunette called Eléonore Revel, née Denuelle de la Plaigne, the daughter of disreputable parents who had married her off to a scoundrel when she was seventeen. Within a few weeks of the wedding her husband was arrested on charges of forgery and sent to prison and the wretched Eléonore, facing destitution, applied for help from Madame Campan's most spectacular pupil, now Grand Duchess of Berg and Cleves. Caroline gave the girl a minor post and, having noted her beauty, lost no time in presenting her to Napoleon. Their liaison was extremely brief for Napoleon, heavily engaged elsewhere, tired of her almost at once, but at least she succeeded in ridding him of the fear that had been troubling him for years. As the year drew to a close and Napoleon, having crushed Prussia, was advancing against the Czar's army near Warsaw, a courier arrived from Paris with news that Eléonore Revel had borne him a son. He said little at the time but gave instructions that the boy was to be placed under the nurse of Caroline's child, Achille. Caroline was delighted and sent word to her husband Murat (credited by some as the father of the child) but it is doubtful whether the handsome innkeeper's son gave the matter another thought at that time; he was too busy wooing the Poles and riding about Warsaw in the most dazzling uniform ever seen in the city. For by this time Murat already saw himself as a king, ruler of a liberated Poland.

It was in that same year, 1806, when the Grand Army was grappling with the Russians in the bogs of Poland, that society in Paris surpassed the social standards set by Marie Antoinette during the final years of the old régime. The Revolution was over, its austerities and aspirations melting in the glitter of titles and social splendour, and it was Caroline who set the pace for the wives of soldiers, speculators and politicians who thronged the Imperial Court. All that winter there was a shortage of young men in the Paris ballrooms but the tempo of gaiety among wives, sisters and daughters of the veterans was not slowed by the absence of their menfolk in the field. There were any number of balls, fêtes, firework displays and musical entertainments and sometimes professional writers and musicians would be called in to supply roles for Caroline, Elisa and, on occasion, Pauline, who sometimes took part in these junketings but usually excused herself on the grounds of ill-health.

Pauline's health was a source of considerable bewilderment to her friends and relatives. Whenever an event demanded administrative effort on her part she adopted the whisper and patient smile of a permanent invalid and retired from the scene until everything was ready. Then she made an overnight recovery, devastated all the men among the audience with her beauty and richness of costume, and retired to a couch surrounded by lovers attracted by her dazzling performance. Always the most amiable of the sisters, she incurred but the minimum jealousy and even the women paid tribute to her attractions and tolerant nature. Her mode of life would have killed her had her health been as delicate as she pretended. On one occasion a special entertainment was prepared in which Pauline and Caroline were cast as leading characters in a musical comedy, Caroline as a thwarted lover and Pauline as a peasant bride. The piece, which was rehearsed for weeks, created a sensation in Paris, but artistically it was not a success, for Pauline could not sing and Caroline's acting would have disgraced a village drama group. Madame Junot declares that Pauline's singing was so tuneless that it was scarcely endurable whereas Caroline made a complete fool of herself 'by feigning agitation which came fretfully from pretty lips never intended for the passage of harmonious sounds!' Even when one makes allowance for the fact that General Junot, the critic's husband, was playing the part of Caroline's swain in the comedy and was hopelessly in love with the heroine, there can be little doubt that the Buonaparte girls lacked histrionic talent although their performances offstage sometimes reached a very high standard indeed. Elisa was persuaded to recognise her limitations as an actress and confine herself to more conventional roles. During the Consular days she and Lucien had been addicted to amateur theatricals, but on one occasion she played a tragic role to an audience including her brother and Bourienne reports that Napoleon laughed so heartily that tears ran down his cheeks. Napoleon was not a kindly critic and after the curtain fell he told his sister how much he had enjoyed 'her parody'!

After her elevation Elisa was able to give full play to the talents she did possess and ruled her principality of Lucca-Piombino so skilfully that Napoleon publicly congratulated her. In 1809 he added Tuscany to her domains but Elisa's husband, the self-effacing Felice, played a very minor part in his wife's sovereignty. When she took up her position in Italy, Napoleon made it plain that the gift was feudatory, an Imperial decree stating that any children succeeding Elisa would receive their investiture from the Emperor and could not marry without his consent. Felice, therefore, was no more than the Queen's husband and was told to walk several paces behind her on all State occasions. He was also allotted sleeping quarters on the far side of the palace and although given the title of Prince was compelled to swear a servile oath of fealty to his brother-in-law. This reversal of roles in the Bacchiochi household did not, however, ruin the marriage. Possibly Felice's acquiescence prevented a divorce and Elisa bore him a son and a daughter. In obedience to the Imperial edict the daughter was christened 'Napoleone'.

Having assigned to her husband a purely passive role Elisa now devoted herself to the task of reorganising her territories and in so doing showed energy and intelligence. She authorised public works, stimulated agriculture, patronised the arts and marshalled the quota of conscripts that was demanded of all who exercised authority under Napoleon. When Tuscany was added to her domains she cleared the country of brigands, and in this respect was more energetic than her brother Joseph in Naples, for among the letters Joseph received about this time was one from his brother ordering him to clamp down on local robbers.

Elisa had obviously inherited the Buonaparte talent for administration but Talleyrand, an excellent judge in these matters, regarded Caroline as the most intelligent of the Buonaparte girls and declared that she had the head of Cromwell on the shoulders of a pretty woman. Napoleon shared this opinion, saying that he was obliged to address his younger sister as if he was reading a proclamation. Later events were to prove that Caroline also possessed rare talents for intrigue and double-dealing, but at this period, on the tide of favours that followed Austerlitz, Jena and Friedland. She spent most of her time organising gay social events. In the two years that preceded her own elevation to a throne she was the leading hostess in Paris, and the Palais de l'Elysée, where she and Murat lived in France, was the scene of many brilliant spectacles. Napoleon encouraged these displays and ordered Caroline, Pauline and Hortense to give one ball each week during the winter seasons. Pauline protested that she was far too delicate to involve herself in the task of organising entertainments on such a scale (there were nearly two hundred guests at each ball), but Napoleon insisted and after Hortense's ball on Monday, and Pauline's on Wednesday, Caroline set to work to outdo her sister and sister-in-law on Friday. She usually succeeded, but the occasions were often enlivened by a sensational occurrence, as when she presented a quadrille danced by sixteen of the prettiest socialites of the capital, all wearing Tyrolean costumes. The quadrille was staged at a masquerade and when it was about to start Hortense, who was taking part, was summoned to a private room to pacify a lady who had turned up at the last moment and was insisting that she be included in the dance. Hortense was puzzled, particularly when presented to a short, plump woman wearing a mask. Feeling there must be some embarrassing mistake she hesitated, whereupon the fat lady bounced up, flung her arms about her and tried to kiss her. Servants rushed in in response to Hortense's shrieks and it was discovered that the volunteer was Camillo Borghese, Pauline's Italian husband, who was fond of practical jokes. Napoleon sometimes like to play the fool at these masquerades and once persuaded the painter Isabey to pass himself off as the Emperor whilst Napoleon himself, features masked, pretended to be one of the guests. Isabey's impersonation of Napoleon was excellent, but he had difficulty in concealing his hands which were very large, while Napoleon's were unusually small and graceful. There was an unpleasant moment for everybody at one of Caroline's balls when it was discovered that Hortense had invited an attractive but notorious young woman with whom Murat was having an affair. In her memoirs Hortense protests that she did this innocently, but it is far more likely that she issued the invitation as one more move in the Buonaparte-Beauharnais feud. Recognising the unfortunate woman among the guests Caroline made no effort to exercise the tact required of a hostess but shouted at the top of her voice, 'I demand that that woman leaves my house!' The remark reduced the unlucky guest to tears whereupon Josephine, always glad of a chance to snub the Buonapartes, enlisted the girl as one of the ladies of the Imperial household.

The dances and entertainments organised by Hortense were sociable events and everyone enjoyed them, but we do not hear much of Pauline's contributions except the occasion when she helped Caroline to stage a fête in honour of Josephine's birthday. It was decided to produce a play and Pauline favoured a presentation of *The Barber of Seville* while Caroline preferred a tragedy. For some time neither sister would give way and then a compromise was found and a comedy was presented in which both were given leading parts. It was about this time that Pauline, who adored posing as a model for painters and sculptors, was modelled in marble by the famous artist Canova, an occasion that gave rise to the remark for which she is famous. When shocked friends saw the finished work, and asked Pauline if she was 'not uncomfortable when posing almost nude before such a genius as Canova', she replied: 'Oh no, there was a fire in the room!' No remark does more to illustrate the character of Pauline, of whom someone said – on hearing that she had been given the territory of Guastalla to govern – 'It is small no doubt but even a molehill is too much for the Princess Borghese to administer!'

The relationship between Josephine's highly-strung daughter and Louis continued to deteriorate and Louis' elevation to the throne of Holland did nothing to improve it. Louis was reluctant to wear a puppet's crown and his wife hated the prospect of exchanging the society of her mother for isolation among the unfashionable Dutch.

Holland had suffered disastrously during the long war with England. Her maritime trade was at a standstill and her ports were closed by the Continental blockade. In addition Napoleon's Berlin Decrees, forbidding any nation within the orbit of France to trade with Britain, had ruined her internal economy. The highest authority in Holland was vested in the person of the Grand Pensioner, but the most powerful man in the country at this time was Admiral Verhuell, a patriot who realised the folly of defying Holland's powerful neighbour. In the cartographer's nightmare that followed Austerlitz, Napoleon had made up his mind to put an end to Holland's nominal independence and in March, 1806 he wrote to Talleyrand, 'I have seen Admiral Verhuell . . . Holland is without executive power and must have one. I will give her Louis. Instead of a Grand Pensioner she will have a king!'

Louis showed even less enthusiasm for a throne than he had for matrimony, but he was realistic enough to understand that a refusal would mean exile and that Napoleon would have no difficulty in finding a substitute. He made some kind of stand, however, and extracted a promise that Holland's independence would be guaranteed. With this worthless pledge in his pocket he and Hortense set out for The Hague on June 12th, 1806.

At Rotterdam Hortense had an extremely unpleasant experience. A mob of citizens, with no other idea in mind than that of giving the royal couple a warm welcome, took the horses from their traces and dragged the royal carriage through the streets amid scenes of riotous enthusiasm. To a girl whose most impressionable years had been spent in Paris during the Terror, a tumult of this kind seemed a prelude to the sort of upheaval that had ended in her father's execution and her mother's last-minute reprieve from the guillotine. She was almost hysterical with fright. 'This explosive joy' she afterwards wrote, 'so similar to fury, froze me with terror and I said to my husband, "This is how they received Marie Antoinette in France, with the same ardour they showed later in sacrificing her!" It was not the moment to recall such sad memories but everything was clouded by my state of mind.'

Hortense's state of mind was a good barometer. Her stay in Holland was to prove the most wretched period of an almost joyless life. Louis, despite his forebodings, began his reign with the best of intentions and made some honest and painstaking attempts to act imaginatively and efficiently, but from the first hour of his reign his brother's voice reached him from Paris or Warsaw or Berlin and complicated instructions, spiced with prohibitions and outbursts of Imperial wrath, arrived at The Hague almost daily. Louis' attempts to win the goodwill of the Dutch by the creation of local marshals and the institution of a noble order similar to the Legion of Honour, were received with derision and vetoed before they became public. Less than a year after his brother's arrival in Holland Napoleon was writing from Osterode: 'They tell me you have restored to the nobles in your states their titles and privileges. Is it possible that you are so shortsighted as not to see how fatal such a step would be to you, to your people, to France and to myself? You are as good as renouncing the French throne. A man ... who has robbed a nation of the fruit of fifteen years' fighting, toil and endeavour would be unworthy of such a position.

This cannot go on; my ambassador has instructions to inform you that unless you revoke this measure he is under orders to leave Holland and I have done with you!'

Louis could do nothing to please his brother and expressions of Imperial displeasure attended the most trivial of his measures. In January, 1807, when he had been ruling Holland for seven months, there was a national disaster at Leyden where some barges laden with explosives blew up in a canal, causing severe loss of life and wrecking eight hundred houses. Louis, moved by the townspeople's plight, opened a public subscription and travelled round the country collecting funds, but for some reason Napoleon saw in this kindly act a sacrifice of regal dignity and further vitriolic letters arrived, driving Louis to despair. There was more trouble over Louis' failure to supply the inevitable quota of soldiers for the Grand Army, and when the much-badgered king wrote pointing out that he had already supplied nearly half the required total Napoleon challenged his figures and complained bitterly of the quality of the Dutch conscripts who had arrived.

So it went on, an almost ceaseless exchange of excuses and recriminations and all the time, like a thread woven into the pattern of the Imperial policy for Holland, was censure regarding Louis' treatment of his wife. 'You treat your young wife as you would command a regiment,' wrote Napoleon, this time from Poland, where he was living with his Polish mistress, Marie Walewska. 'Allow her to dance as much as she likes; it is in keeping with her age. I have a wife who is forty years of age' (Josephine was forty-four at the time) 'and from the field of battle I write to her to go to balls, but you wish a young woman of twenty to live in a cloister or, like a nurse, to be always washing her children! Render the mother of your children happy . . . you should have a wife like sone of those I know in Paris. She would have played you false and you would have been at her feet.'

The natural result of this paternal advice was to send Louis hot-foot to his wife's boudoir, growling that Hortense had no right to complain of him behind his back. Hortense denied that she had complained, but he did not believe her and refused to accept her denials that she had betrayed him in the arms of a lover. It is very

difficult, at this distance, to decide whether Louis' suspicions regarding his wife's virtue were justified or the result of family gossip
aimed at discrediting Josephine through her daughter. In her memoirs Hortense declares over and over again that they were ground-
less, but reading between the lines it is at least clear that she enjoyed flirting with several young officers and even if she kept the
associations within reasonable limits her behaviour as Queen was
indiscreet. She was still secretly in love with de Flahaut and this
much is established by a curious interview that took place about
this time between Hortense and Caroline. Caroline pretended to
take her sister-in-law into her confidence and admitted that she
was in love with de Flahaut herself and had been told by him that
he was pledged to Hortense. Hortense was wounded by this revela-
tion and obviously looked upon the handsome young officer as
her own particular beau but it is doubtful if he was her lover at this
period, although he certainly became so later on when life with
Louis was no longer possible for a woman who valued her self-
respect.

Louis made several sincere attempts to mend the marriage but
his approaches were always hedged with scores of conditions and
pompous appeals for 'the truth regarding impropriety' on the part
of his wife. Hortense, although naturally timid and undeniably
brow-beaten by this difficult man, showed an obstinacy equal to
his and nothing came of his frantic appeals, not even when he sent
her a lengthy document setting forth a list of proposals that reads
like a peace treaty between two hostile nations. After the failure
of this outrageous attempt at a reconciliation Louis reverted to
spying on his wife and planted a French footman in her ante-
room with instructions to 'note down all that went on in his
wife's suite after dark, even the comings and goings of her female
attendants'.

In the meantime the relationship between the Emperor and his
puppet continued to deteriorate until they were close to breaking
point. Louis reasoned, no doubt, that if Napoleon could make
dukes and marshals of sergeant-majors, coopers and dyers' appren-
tices then he, as an independent sovereign, was entitled to create
a few Dutch marshals and restore to the Dutch nobles titles they

had enjoyed before the Revolution. He was soon reminded of something he should never have forgotten, that Napoleon had one set of rules for himself and another and very difficult set for everyone else, including wives, brothers, sisters, senators, satraps and generals in the field. In one respect only did he endeavour to help Louis, by cautioning Hortense to spend more of her time in Holland and not, as was her habit, long periods visiting her mother at Malmaison. On one occasion, when he had been successful in persuading Hortense to rejoin her husband, Louis nullified his endeavours by having a wall erected between his wife's apartments and his own. He also made it publicly known that this expressed his attitude to his wife's moral conduct. One might imagine that this action alone would have resulted in a permanent separation, but it did not, and not only because Napoleon had forbidden a divorce but because there remained in Louis an almost desperate determination to heal the wounds caused by his wife's neurotic sensitivity and his own suspicious nature. In his constant appeals to his wife one can recognise an element of self-torture, as when he appeared at her bedside in the middle of the night and cried, 'If you will only confess your frailties to me I will pardon you and we will start a new existence!'

The blow that fell upon the royal couple on May 5th, 1807, had nothing to do with these sordid squabbles, for on that date the six-year-old Napoleon Charles, first child of the marriage, died of croup. This additional sorrow came close to driving Hortense out of her mind and physical force had to be used to separate her from the dead child. In their mutual misery husband and wife found compassion for one another but Hortense was inconsolable, realising that in the death of this child lay the certainty of Josephine's divorce. Josephine, also dazed with grief, hurried to her daughter's side and Madame Junot, who saw her leave, says that fear of divorce was in every tear she shed for the young prince. Hortense, now in a state of nervous collapse, left Holland for an extended convalescence in the Pyrenees and after drifting about for a time, occasionally in the company of Louis but more often without him, she returned to Paris determined not only to live there but also to get a divorce.

She underestimated Napoleon's determination to keep her tied to his brother and under his influence yet another attempt was made to reconcile the wretched pair. On April 20th, almost a year after the death of the child upon whom the Beauharnais hopes were centred, Hortense gave birth to a third child at the Tuileries. It was a difficult birth and for a time she was seriously ill, but in the end she rejoined her husband in Holland where Louis, in Satanic humour, hinted that the boy was not in fact a Buonaparte. His jealousy regarding this child (who, more than forty years later, was to reign as Napoleon III) was publicised by his refusal to honour the birth with the traditional salute of 101 guns. For a time he refused to authorise the firing of any salute at all but Dutch officials eventually persuaded him to authorise the firing of twenty-one guns, the number accorded the birth of a royal daughter. De Flahaut, Admiral Verheull and a young official called Decazes are variously quoted as fathers of Napoleon III but there is not much doubt that these rumours were sponsored by Caroline, still angling for the recognition of her own son as heir to the Imperial throne.

Napoleon is said to have been much depressed by the sudden death of little Napoleon Charles, but if he was he concealed his feelings in public. On the day after he received the news in Poland, where he was on the point of winning a spectacular victory over the Russians, he appeared before a deputation with such a benign expression that Talleyrand suggested that he should, perhaps, try and show a little sorrow. 'I have no time to amuse myself feeling and regretting like other men!' he said shortly and wrote a brief letter to Josephine on the subject and another to Hortense. In the letter to the bereaved mother he said, 'Your grief pains me. I should like to see you show more courage. To live is to suffer and the honest man always struggles to remain master of himself.' He was clearly master of his own emotions for the letter ends, 'I gained a great victory on the 14th. I am quite well and love you very much. Adieu my daughter, I embrace you with all my heart.' This is not evidence of an unfeeling nature, for nobody could testify to Napoleon's essential kindness more than Hortense herself, but in the situation in which he now found himself, virtual master of Europe, it must have been almost impossible to isolate a personal sorrow, such as the death of a small child of the croup. Forty-eight hours before he dictated his letter of condolence he had watched thousands of men kill one another on the battlefield.

In March, 1808, having insisted on yet another patched-up peace between man and wife, Napoleon offered Louis the throne of Spain, pointing out that the Dutch climate did not seem to suit him and that it was unlikely Holland would ever recover from its ruins. Louis, to his credit, refused the offer. He had had more than enough of shadow sovereignty and he disapproved of the cynical farce staged by his brother to produce yet another empty throne. Napoleon did not press him. Years later he was to say, 'Louis' virtues have occasioned me more trouble than Lucien's vices.' Instead couriers were despatched to Joseph in sunny Naples and Joseph, less pedantic than his brother, accepted the offer. By so doing he attracted to himself more public odium than a man of his character deserved.

CHAPTER EIGHT

'No one has told Your Majesty the real truth.
The fact is not a single Spaniard is on my side'

Joseph writing to Napoleon in 1808

IN THE LATE SPRING of 1808 the throne of Spain was made available by a gigantic confidence trick – or by a series of confidence
tricks – culminating in a bluff almost without precedent in the
history of European power politics.

Relations with Spain had been getting steadily more complicated since Napoleon's assumption of power, in 1799. During the
intervening eight years she had been an unwilling ally in the never-
ending war against Britain. Almost all her ships, and at least a
thousand of her sailors, had been lost at Trafalgar and she was contributing, or was supposed to contribute, three-and-a-half millions
sterling each year to the cost of the war against Portugal, the last
remaining seaboard in Europe open to English commerce. The
internal state of Spain, however, made any alliance with France a
liability and as the years went by, and the government and finances
of the country became more and more chaotic, Napoleon's small
stock of patience was exhausted and he set about the task of converting yet another independent State into a satellite. This time he
went about it with a cynicism that astonished enemies and adherents.

In 1808 Spain was nominally ruled by the mild, impotent
Charles IV and his grotesque wife, Maria-Luisa, whose ugliness,
together with her uniquely sensual smirk, has been recorded by
Goya. The heir apparent, Ferdinand, Prince of the Asturias, was a
disreputable young man at that time feuding with the real ruler of
the country, a vain, bull-headed ex-guardsman who had gained

access to the corridors of power via the Queen's bed and was known as Prince of the Peace. His real name was Emmanuel Godoy and although the acknowledged lover of the repulsive Maria Luisa he was nonetheless secure in the affection and confidence of her husband.

The feud between Ferdinand, his parents and Godoy, smouldering a long time, had so far been confined to campaigns of slander and mutual recrimination. It was whispered that the King dare not eat anything that had passed through the hands of his son's adherents in the royal kitchen, but there had been no outbreak of violence up to the time the French columns began their advance on Madrid. As yet no state of war existed but the leisurely approach of Murat's army, supposedly paying a social call on their way to Portugal, stretched the nerves of the Madrilean mob to breaking point, and when Ferdinand was placed in custody on the pretext of having tried to poison his mother and father, the capital exploded and bloodthirsty mobs moved on the palaces of the Prince of the Peace. Terrified that what had happened not so long ago in Paris would now happen in Spain, the King and Queen announced their intention of quitting the country for their colonial possessions overseas but before any final decision could be made the mob had freed Ferdinand and gone in search of Godoy, vowing to hang him from the nearest tree. The Queen's lover took refuge in an attic where he rolled himself up in some matting and lay hidden for thirty-six hours while Ferdinand's supporters ransacked his property without finding him. Finally, driven from his hiding place by hunger and thirst, he was seized and brutally manhandled on his way back to the capital. His life was saved by the arrival of Murat's advance guard and the King's action in abdicating the throne in favour of his son. Murat had strict instructions to prevent royal bloodshed and persuade the rival fractions to lay their claims before the all-powerful and supposedly impartial Emperor of the French. Ferdinand was the first contender to be gulled by this invitation and hurried to Napoleon at Bayonne, close to the Franco-Spanish border. In the meantime French soldiers escorted the battered Godoy to the frontier and here he was joined by the indignant royal couple, also anxious to state their case. Napoleon

wined and dined them all and then pronounced the judgment of
Solomon. He could not, he said, recognise an abdication extracted
from Charles by threats of violence but it was plain that the King,
with or without Godoy's support, was unable to keep order in
Spain and conduct the war against Britain with the vigour it demanded. It was therefore in the interests of all, including the
rudderless Spanish people, that royal authority should pass to
someone who enjoyed the trust and support of France, and who
was more eligible than Joseph, his own dear brother, who had
been tidying up after the Bourbons in Naples? Charles and his
queen, preferring this solution to that of seeing their vicious son
on the throne, raised no serious objections, particularly as they
were guaranteed a generous annual allowance and a home in
France, and Godoy's nerve had been so badly shaken by his recent
experiences that he was happy to retire in comfort. Ferdinand,
however, made a violent scene, declaring that his pride would
never permit him to agree to such a despicable compromise.
Napoleon promptly offered an alternative. If he preferred he might
be shot instead and pass into Spanish history as a man who had
sacrificed his life rather than yield a crown stolen from his father.
Ferdinand's temper cooled at once and he was packed off to
Valençay in an almost conciliatory mood. He even suggested that
it might be a good idea if Napoleon revived his original notion of
marrying him off to one of the Emperor's nieces. So the Spanish
problem was solved in a matter of days, or so Napoleon believed
when he sent a courier to Joseph telling him to appoint a Council
of Regency, place Marshal Jourdan in command of his troops, and
join him at Bayonne where great events were imminent.

Joseph knew what was brewing. The previous year he had had
a long conversation with Napoleon on the subject of Spanish
affairs and he must also have been aware that, two months before
the Bayonne confidence trick, his brother had offered the Spanish
throne to Louis. The prospect of ruling Spain had now been
dangled before three Buonapartes in succession, for the subject
had been on the Imperial agenda during the abortive discussions
with Lucien, in 1807. Lucien had refused to pay the price for reinstatement within the family circle and Louis had had more than

enough of puppet sovereignty in Holland but Joseph was more pliable than either of them. Having proved a success in Naples he had gained confidence in himself as well as earning Napoleon's commendation.

It was not so long ago that Joseph had walked the streets of Paris 'in a brown surtout and round hat', talking nostalgically of the Republic one and indivisible but he had mellowed during the last two years and the prospect of exchanging the throne of a small State for that of a realm larger than France was tempting. He had got along reasonably well with the happy-go-lucky Neapolitans and was confident that he could acquit himself equally well in Spain. To his brother the Catholic faith was no more than an instrument of policy but to Joseph religion was a more serious matter. He has no bigot but he flattered himself that he had more sympathy with bigotry than had most Frenchmen who had witnessed the overthrow of religion in France. His amiability, and his wide experience in diplomacy, would be useful in convincing the Spanish that they would be far happier ruled by a benevolent foreigner than by a young scoundrel like Ferdinand, or a cuckolded cipher like Charles, or a lowborn upstart like Godoy, and he was probably correct in these assumptions. There was only one factor that Joseph, opening his despatches in Naples, failed to take into account and he cannot be blamed for the oversight. Someone with unlimited experience in politics had made the same miscalculation in assuming that a war against Spain (if, indeed, the Spanish were foolish enough to resent the substitution) would be one more war against a bumbling, archaic government. In taking this for granted Napoleon probably made the greatest single mistake of his career, inasmuch as he failed to take into account a variety of factors in which Spain differed from the former campaigning grounds in Italy, Germany, Poland and Egypt. To begin with the terrain offered appalling difficulties to the movement of men and munitions for there were not two good metalled roads in the country, but lack of roads was not the sole obstacle to a rapid conquest of Spain; even less tractable were the people themselves, steeped in centuries of cruelty, hardship and fanaticism, and united in a ferocious hatred of heretics, particularly heretics who had im-

prisoned His Holiness the Pope and had only recently reopened
their own churches. Spain had been execrably governed for genera-
tions and there seemed, to the onlooker, nothing left of the courage
and enterprise that had once made Spaniards masters of half the
world. The French were quickly to discover, that national pride
still glowed in the heart of every Spaniard and that priests would
have no difficulty in fanning the embers into a flame that would
scorch every Frenchman who set foot in the Peninsula. They were
to learn also that Spanish fanaticism, the legacy of war against the
Moors who had occupied Spain for hundreds of years, had produced a national character capable of converting half-starved
peasants and artisans into the most ruthless and mobile guerrilla
army that the French, for all their experience elsewhere, had ever
been called upon to fight. Ferdinand might be a suspected parri-
cide, Charles almost an imbecile, and Godoy a lowborn adventurer but at least all three were Spaniards and good Catholics,
whilst the French were foreigners and atheists and as such deserved no mercy in this life or the next. News of what had occurred
at Bayonne was not slow in reaching Madrid, where Murat and
his brilliant staff had been causing a considerable stir among a
population who delighted in public display and had no reason to
regard these colourful visitors with suspicion. The news spread
among the city crowds by travellers from the north-east was the
application of a torch to a powder-magazine. Without waiting
for a proclamation or an Imperial bulletin introducing their new
sovereign, King Joseph, the city erupted and the savagery shown
by the mob gave the French their first lesson in the kind of war to
which they were now committed. French soldiers strolling in the
sunny streets were surrounded, knifed, stoned or hacked to pieces,
and within hours Murat had a full-scale revolution on his hands.
Blazing anger at what had occurred was by no means confined to
the capital. Soon half the country was under arms as the revolt
spread like a grass fire from province to province. Inside a week
Asturias, Navarre, Old Castile, Galicia, Valencia, Murcia and
Aragon were aflame. French officers making the rounds of sentry
posts found their men garotted and stabbed, couriers were am-
bushed and crucified or boiled in oil, isolated detachments were

picked off by snipers firing blunderbusses loaded to the muzzle with nails and scrap-iron, and to the invaders' amazement even the ridiculous Spanish junta declared total war on the victors of Marengo, Austerlitz, Jena and Friedland.

Murat dealt swiftly and efficiently with the revolt in Madrid. In twelve hours he had cleared the streets, shot the ring-leaders and occupied all strategic points in the city. Then, regarding himself as the next king of Spain, he behaved with great moderation and despite a severe bout of colic caused by drinking too much Spanish wine he kept a tight grip on the city whilst awaiting reinforcements. Columns of conscripts and veterans were already pouring down from the Pyrenees and Murat shared his brother-in-law's contempt for Spanish valour. When despatches got through to the capital it was not the rumour of assembling Spanish armies that upset him so much as the news that he was not to be King of Spain after all and that Joseph was already on his way south. Murat, half-crazy with disappointment, was offered a choice of consolation prizes. He could accept Joseph's vacant throne in Naples or conquer himself a kingdom in Portugal and become king of Northern Lusitania. He was not long making up his mind. A British expeditionary force had already landed in Portugal and defeated General Junot, once the lover of Murat's wife, and under the terms of the armistice the French were shipped back to France in British transports. Sulkily Murat chose Naples and rode out of the Peninsula for good and in this respect at least he showed very good sense, for most of his fellow-marshals were to leave their splendid reputations on the battlefields of a war that was to last six years.

Joseph's abdication of the throne of Naples was made public in mid-July and on the 31st of that month the Neapolitans were told that their new King would be a Gascon innkeeper's son, who was also a Marshal of France, a brother-in-law of Napoleon, the Grand Duke of Berg and Cleves and a High Admiral. Caroline was delighted. For more than a year she had had to stand in the wings and give precedence to her plain sister-in-law Julie, a soap-boiler's daughter, who was a queen while she remained a Grand Duchess. Even Jérôme, the baby of the family, had been wearing a crown for months and Pauline, who was too lazy to organise a ball, had been a Princess since 1803. Caroline made up her mind that she would prove a queen the Neopolitans would never forget and the royal pair flung themselves into the task of making their Court the most splendid jewel in the Imperial diadem. In the process they made it the weakest link in the chain that Napoleon had forged around Europe, but that was unforeseeable at the time.

Joseph, an observant man, was not long assessing the measure of his popular support in Spain and his lessons began on his initial journey to the capital. When Napoleon had informed him that he was to replace the Bourbons in Madrid he had presented him to a group of tame Spanish grandees who were won over in advance to the Imperial plan, but during the new King's progress across north-western Spain it was obvious to even valets and drummer boys that there was substance in the Spanish comment of the time 'That Joseph might have put the crown of Spain in his pocket but he would never succeed in putting it on his head.' Joseph wrote plaintively to his brother: 'No one has told Your Majesty the real truth . . . the fact is not a single Spaniard is on my side. I haven't a single supporter here except those who accompany me!' This was confirmed the moment the new King entered his capital. Like a medieval seigneur he scattered largesse to silent crowds but his money was left lying where it fell. He formed his Court but in the mood of a man taking possession of a new house built under a smoking volcano, and within days the volcano erupted and news came in of popular revolts all over the country. Nor were they crushed as easily as Murat had crushed the Madrilean mob. General Dupont, hemmed in near Baylen, surrendered abjectly to the rabble army of Castanos with eighteen thousand men. The French army had not had such a disaster within living memory and a tidal wave of confidence rushed across the Peninsula and over the Pyrenees into captive Europe. Marshal Bessières, the former hairdresser, defeated the Spanish armies in the field but because of Dupont's cowardice he was obliged to retreat and Joseph had no desire to remain in his new capital without military support. Never a man of war, and already beginning to question his wisdom in exchanging Naples for Spain, the new king bolted for Vittoria. His Court bolted with him. The reign had lasted ten days.

Even if he shared his brother's misgivings about the wisdom of the Spanish adventure it was too late for Napoleon to withdraw. Europe was watching events in the Peninsula with interest and Napoleon realised that something would have to be done at once to bolster belief in French invincibility. Calling in veterans from Paris and Germany, together with such legendary fighters as Masséna, Soult, Ney, Lannes, Augereau, Mortier and Lefèbvre, he hurled the Grand Army over the frontiers and headed straight for Burgos, which was captured and sacked with an efficiency that caused Joseph renewed misgivings for the future. By the time the wretched Spanish levies had been scattered the frightful seige of Saragossa was under way and by now Joseph was quite sure that his brothers Lucien and Louis had been right to refuse the Spanish crown. Not only was he terrified of living among so many fanatical enemies, he was already beginning to doubt his brother's good faith, for Napoleon talked of annexing the north-western provinces to France and Joseph could see his realm beginning to shrink before he had unpacked. Lucien, writing of this moment years afterwards, declared that Joseph was so mortified by Napoleon's threat to dismember Spain that he resorted to witchcraft and peppered a portrait of his brother with close-range pistol shots. This reads like one of Lucien's rhetorical outbursts that had got him into trouble when he was a young republican in the south, but it is true that Joseph came out strongly on behalf of Spanish national rights and set to work, together with his amiable wife Julie, to win the confidence of his new subjects by every means at his disposal. Posing as a devout Catholic he championed the Church wherever he went but his good intentions were fatally undermined by Napoleon's act in closing two-thirds of the convents in Spain and then abolishing the Inquisition. Napoleon's presence in Madrid at this time must have been extremely embarrassing to Joseph, for it was Napoleon not the king who drafted all the decrees and proclamations and some of the latter have a familiar ring. 'Spaniards,' he announced, to a population largely illiterate, 'your destinies are in my hands! Let your King be certain of your love and confidence and you will be more powerful and happy than ever! I have broken the fetters which weighed upon the people; I have given you, instead of an absolute, a tempered and constitutional monarchy. It depends upon you whether this constitution shall become law. But if all my efforts prove useless and you do not respond to my confidence, it will only remain for me to treat you as conquered provinces and to find my brother another throne. I shall then place the crown of Spain upon my own head and I shall know how to make the wicked tremble!'

It was not only the wicked who trembled. French veterans, softened by pleasant billets in Italy and Southern Germany, were already learning to hate this land of trackless mountains, scorched plains, squalid, bug-infested villages and murderous natives who lost no opportunity of slitting a French throat or crushing an unwary straggler under a rock. The French might have been fighting heathen savages in the jungle and even the Egyptian veterans could not look back on experiences such as this. It was risking death to move fifty yards from an outpost or accept a drink from anyone but a French *cantinière*. Casualties mounted and wastage in the ranks was appalling. In Saragossa a civilian garrison notched their bullets to ensure the infliction of agonising wounds and blew up whole sections of the town rather than yield a yard of territory. Joseph might attend bull-fights, patronise the church, and go on spectacular royal progresses wherever the French could guard him but his goodwill was wasted on people whose hatred of the invader was now incorporated in the catechism taught the children by their priests. Very early in the struggle Napoleon had written Joseph from Bordeaux: 'Take care you don't destroy the spirit of the army by refusing to allow retaliation against the Spaniards. It is impossible to show consideration to brigands who murder my wounded and commit every kind of outrage.' And later, after the surrender of Saragossa, 'I have been reading an article on the capture of the town in the *Madrid Gazette*. The writer praises the defenders . . . no doubt to encourage those of Valencia and Seville! A singular policy indeed! I'll wager there is not a Frenchman who doesn't utterly despise the defenders of Saragossa . . . People who allow themselves to say such things are more dangerous than the rebels themselves!'

But soon Napoleon was obliged to regard Spain as a sideshow and leave Joseph to make what he could of the ever-deteriorating situation. Encouraged by the example of Spain, Austria now made another attempt to throw off the shackles and after chasing the impudent Sir John Moore half-way to the coast of Northern Spain Napoleon abandoned the pursuit to Soult and hurried across Europe to the Danube with the greater part of the Grand Army. He was never to return although the war dragged on for another six years. Joseph continued to rule but only within earshot of French cavalry trumpets.

It would be easy after examining the record of Joseph's first few months as King of All The Spains to dismiss him as a bumbling, well-intentioned, ineffectual ass but this would be an injustice. In the next few years – up to the very moment when he left Spain for good – he went some way to justifying himself as a man and a would-be ruler and if his task had not been so hopeless from start to finish his reign might have proved an important milestone in Spain's slow progress to tolerance and enlightenment. As it was he failed, and that dismally, but less because of his own earnest mistakes than a combination of factors that included bad luck, greed and selfishness on the part of his advisers, constant interference from Paris, and finally the bigotry of a majority of his subjects.

He was reinstated in Madrid in January, 1809 and spent most of that year and a large part of the next in attempts to pacify the country. When his policy of pacification failed, as it usually did, he tried hard to persuade his subjects that his intentions were those of a forward-looking administrator and not, as they insisted, those of a usurping tyrant.

At first the military situation improved although it still left a great deal to be desired. Various marshals, each exercising a semi-independent command, settled in various parts of the country

and were instructed to follow policies issued by the central government, but soldiers of fortune like Soult and Victor and Augereau,
all men who had risen to high command from the ranks, were not
likely to sacrifice ambition and personal enrichment for the sake
of a national policy and their rapacity and repeated failure to cooperate contributed in large measure to the long roll of French
disasters in the Peninsula. Nominally Joseph still exercised supreme authority but in a country like Spain, where the French
contingents were separated by vast distances, difficult terrain
and swarms of guerrilla fighters, cooperation would have been
difficult even if attempted with goodwill on the part of the
marshals. There was no goodwill, only daily exhibitions of avarice,
jealousy and selfishness and the result, as might be expected, was
chaos.

Matters were not improved by the activities of British and Portuguese forces under the skilful but excessively cautious Wellington.
The very presence of this small but well-equipped army was a
source of perpetual encouragement to the Spaniards. Defeated in
the open field over and over again the national forces were always
able to rally, recruit, regroup and strike again at isolated French
corps. If a military genius like Napoleon had unified the command
and brought the grasping, quarrelling marshals to heel there is no
doubt that Wellington would have been bundled into the sea,
but Napoleon was either busy elsewhere or leading a bourgeois
life with his new Austrian wife in Paris and when Masséna, the
greatest strategist among the marshals, was given enough men and
supreme command in the field it was too late, the British were too
well established and the Spaniards had learned the folly of fighting
pitched battles against highly disciplined troops. Sometimes Joseph
took the field and at Talavera, with Marshals Jourdan and Victor,
he inflicted heavy losses upon the invaders without, however,
beating them. Cadiz was never captured and in the clashes that
accompanied Wellington's parrying campaigns the French were
unable to face the devastating power of British volley-firing and
engagements usually resulted in mutual withdrawals.

In the sphere of civil administration Joseph was more successful
and was received in some areas with muted acclaim. He made it

known that his quarrel was with the British and Portuguese and not with his subjects and pledged himself to withdraw every Frenchman from Spain as soon as the enemy had been expelled. After that, he said, he would offer himself as a candidate for the throne but remain only if voted in by a majority of Spaniards. It was all useless. Napoleon, attempting to direct the war from Paris, remained out of touch with the constantly changing military situation and ignorant of the true temper of the Spaniards. When he divided the country into six military districts and allowed the marshals to exercise independent authority over the areas they controlled he struck a deathblow at his brother's policy of conciliation. Joseph went so far as to travel to Paris in the summer of 1811 and, like Louis before him, pleaded the cause of his unhappy subjects. He made some impression on his brother and returned with a promise of centralised authority, but decentralised military rule went on because there was no real alternative. Soult went on dreaming of becoming king of Northern Lusitania, Victor tried to win military glory in the criminal sacrifice of men, Augereau and Masséna accumulated loot and the less selfish marshals, men like Bessières and Suchet, administered their own provinces but refused to take Joseph seriously. All through the years 1809 and 1810 men and munitions poured into Spain and were instantly swallowed up in the mountains and plains of widely separated areas of administration. Guerrillas swarmed in every district, swooping on convoys, murdering and torturing despatch-riders and stragglers. Wellington built himself an impregnable fortress around Lisbon and his troops, supplied from the sea, grew fat whilst the encircling French starved, and still Joseph tried to combine moderate policies with the stream of contradictory orders that reached him from Paris in letters that had been dictated after a study of British newspapers, Napoleon's chief source of information about the embattled Peninsula.

In the early autumn of 1810 Masséna pushed Wellington over the mountains and into his entrenched position at Torres Vedras but he could not dislodge him, and after a miserable winter at the outposts, where French sentries exchanged jokes, newspapers and souvenirs with bored British sentries, the French withdrew into

Spain. Masséna was recalled in disgrace and the whole business
had to begin over again.

Harassed, betrayed and afraid the ever-hopeful King Joseph
struggled on, wondering how it would end, sometimes pleading
for supreme authority from his brother, sometimes begging for
closer cooperation from his subordinates. Nobody paid him much
attention and his wife Julie occupied herself ministering to the
poor. Thousands of young Frenchmen and thousands of Spaniards
died in a hopeless cause and across the Pyrenees the enemies of
France watched the struggle with satisfaction, reasoning that the
Corsican ogre would bleed to death through this open sore in his
heel.

Far away to the North, a thousand miles from the gates of Cadiz,
which would never open to King Joseph, another shadow-king
was drowning in troubled waters. King Louis of Holland had
refused to abandon his Dutch subjects in 1807, preferring to remain
and champion their cause against a man who had declared that
Holland could never rise from its ruins. It never did under Louis,
despite that stubborn young man's fight to keep himself and his
country independent of its neighbour.

Louis' difficulties were many, but chief among them was constant pressure from Paris to implement the Berlin Decrees and
prevent trade with England. The prohibition meant economic
ruin for the Dutch and to keep the country solvent Louis never
ceased to fight for concessions for his citizens. His obstinacy, and
his failure to understand the implications of his appeals upon
Imperial policy as a whole, maddened his brother and the correspondence between them became more and more acrimonious
until Napoleon, losing patience, threatened to send troops into
the country and annex Holland. Louis retaliated with a courage
and consistency that compels admiration. In December, 1809, he
was summoned to Paris to explain his conduct and the interview
resulted in one of the stormiest scenes in the history of the family.
Napoleon, who boasted that he never let his rage rise higher than
his chin, stormed at his brother like a cheated fishwife, accusing

him of violating treaties, disbanding naval contingents, disorganising armies and flirting with the arch-enemy, England. He ordered Louis to sign a treaty agreeing to seize and sell all American vessels in Dutch ports (America had replied to the Berlin Decrees by closing her ports to French vessels) and instructing him to maintain a fleet of fourteen ships and seven frigates together with a standing army of 25,000 men. As an afterthought he ordered his brother to suppress the Dutch nobility. The price of disobedience to these crippling orders would be the annexation of Holland and unification with France.

Louis signed but he must have known that compliance was impossible, that in the end his kingdom would be swallowed up whatever he did or did not do. He took the only course that remained open to him. On July 1st, a few months after his return to Amsterdam, he abdicated in favour of his elder son, Charles Napoleon Louis.

Napoleon flew into a terrible rage, declaring that he had been made to look a complete fool in the Chancelleries of Europe, but he had already made up his mind what to do about Holland and was not going to allow his policy to be changed by a quixotic gesture on the part of his stubborn brother. Six months earlier he had written to Louis setting out in great detail what he expected of him as King of Holland and indications of megalomania are apparent in the words and phrases of the outburst. 'What have the Dutch to complain of?' he asked. 'Were they not conquered by our arms? Do they not owe their independence to the chivalry of my peoples? Ought they not to bless the generosity of France which has consistently opened its canals and custom-houses to their commerce? Your Majesty has a mistaken idea of my character, based on false notions of my kindness and my feelings towards you!'

Whatever false notions Louis once harboured regarding his brother's feelings towards him had been erased long ago and on receipt of this decree he disassociated himself from his brother's policy. His abdication was at once declared void and within eight days union with France was a fact but even before Louis's act of desperation had been made public Napoleon had resolved to break with him altogether. In May, just over a month before the abdication, he had written, 'I am tired of protestations and fine phrases; it is time I was told plainly whether you wish to be the bane of Holland and to make your follies the ruin of the country ... I shall no longer keep an ambassador in Holland ... don't write to me any more of your usual fine phrases. You have given me nothing else now for three years; and every moment proves how false they are.' There was a twelve-word postscript to this letter. It read: 'I will never write to you again as long as I live!'

Void or not the abdication was a fact and Louis turned his back on thrones and courts and power politics, riding away to Dresden, then Töplitz in Bohemia, and finally to Graz, in Styria. 'He left his realm,' says one observer, like a man escaping from prison.' From henceforth he was to style himself Count of St Leu, finding what consolation he could in the pursuit of literature. He travelled wifeless, for Hortense had abandoned the long struggle to make the marriage work and had played no part in the final break between the brothers. She had troubles enough of her own. Six months before the abdication of her husband the fate that she and Josephine had feared for so long overtook them at last, when the Emperor discarded his wife and took another. At nine o'clock on December 15th, 1809, Josephine stood in the Imperial salon with her son Eugène and her daughter Hortense and heard the Arch-Chancellor announce the annulment of a marriage that had resisted the attacks of the Buonaparte family for fourteen years. Gathered in a group in the apartment were most of those who had done all they could to separate this man from the woman he respected above all others, including those he had professed to love. Three kings were present at that gathering, Louis, Jérôme and Murat, as were their wives, Hortense, Catherine and Caroline. Of the submissive brothers only Joseph was absent and as the assembled Buonapartes heard the pronouncement it may have struck them that their victory over this loyal, dignified woman signified little, for in standing aside for a nineteen-year-old girl she had won the sympathy of every Imperial subject outside the immediate family circle.

Few had ever seen Napoleon so moved, or heard him express

sentiments so clearly heartfelt as on this occasion. He spoke of Josephine as 'his most dear wife, his beloved wife, his truest and best friend and the ornament of his life' and for once he meant every word he uttered, so that it was obvious to everyone present that policy alone had nerved him to make this terrible decision. 'God knows how much this resolution has cost me,' he said, in announcing that the only reason for the divorce was the necessity for a legitimate heir, and added, 'Far from having any reason to complain of my wife I can only praise her love and tenderness and the admiration I feel for her in making such a sacrifice on behalf of myself and France.'

When he had finished speaking Josephine tried to read a prepared speech but her voice failed her and the acknowledgement was passed to another to be read aloud. Hortense, as might be expected, was sobbing openly and even the Buonapartes were awed by the solemnity of the proceedings. Among the silent spectators was Letizia, whose clannishness had encouraged her to support her children in the long campaign against Josephine, but there was no malice in her heart for the woman who had shared her son's rise to a position of supreme power in the world. Her contempt for the vanity of her children grew as the years passed and her sympathy now went out to a woman who could endure so much and keep her dignity. For dignity Josephine certainly had on this occasion and later; that same afternoon she descended the grand staircase of the Tuileries for the last time and passed through a throng of weeping courtiers, her carriage driving across the city in heavy rain. Some who watched her go said that Paris was weeping for her.

She retained her titles and an income of three million francs a year, as well as the splendid château of Malmaison and another in Navarre. Apart from a few irreconcilables like Caroline she left behind no enemies and when, some four years later, the Empire collapsed and Uhlans and Cossacks rode into Paris, it was to Josephine's home that Emperors and Kings came to pay their respects. So it might be said that although the family had won the long duel, honours remained with the vanquished.

*

Pauline was in the limelight again, this time as leader of Paris fashions, a role she assumed after the divorce of Josephine and Caroline's departure for Naples.

Pauline's marriage to the wealthy practical joker, Camille Borghese, had not been a conspicuous success and after a time man and wife had parted although a pretence of amity was maintained at the insistence of Napoleon. There had been quarrels, many of them, but none as bitter as the squabbles of Louis and Hortense, for neither Pauline nor her husband allowed emotional involvements to spoil the savour of life. They lived from day to day, an indolent, shallow, feckless pair and in most respects much alike. The pursuit of pleasure obsessed them completely and both were virtually uneducated. Camille's father, replying to a reproach once levelled at him on this account, had remarked carelessly, 'Camille will always know enough to be a subject of the Pope!', and Pauline constantly preoccupied with her figure and choice of clothes, had never given a single thought to the responsibilities of government. Perhaps this was why Napoleon spoiled her so outrageously. She was a splended ornament for his Court and made few demands upon him. She was frequently in debt but he often came to her rescue, treating her with far more indulgence than Louis or Jérôme. Pauline was now twenty-nine years old and generally regarded as the most beautiful woman of the Empire. Her taste in clothes and jewellery was bizarre but her generosity and good nature gained her far more real friends than her brothers and sisters. She was able to exploit her position as family favourite shamelessly but Napoleon was not so tolerant with her husband, as was proved in the matter of the famous Borghese art collection, one of the most valuable in Europe.

Wherever the French armies marched in the years between the first revolutionary triumphs and the collapse of the Empire in the spring of 1814, they exacted a substantial toll in money and art treasures from the countries they overran. Northern Italy had been stripped of its Leonardos, Correggios and Raphaels as long ago as 1796 but the Borghese family had managed to hold on to their private collection and Napoleon had difficulty in finding a pretext to rob a man who had held a command in his armies at Austerlitz and throughout the Polish campaign. Ultimately, however, he hit upon an approach and suddenly asked Camille the cash value of his exhibits. Camille, scenting trouble, replied that he had no intention of selling but his brother-in-law countered by saying that he was 'not asking to buy them but merely wanted to know what they were worth'. Prince Borghese then admitted he had been offered eighteen million francs for his collection and could have sold it to the English for a million sterling. Napoleon at once agreed to pay this sum. The method used in this remarkable transaction is typical of Napoleon's commercial technique. The vendor was given six millions in Government stock and the domains of Lucedio, in Piedmont (which had just been torn from its owner by force of arms) in lieu of another six millions. A further million was paid out by the purchaser towards the completion of Camille's residence in Paris and the balance of the purchase price was retained by Napoleon 'to be laid out at some future period for the benefit of the Prince!' It is not recorded what the Prince Borghese thought of this remarkable piece of book-keeping but he must have protested, for later on Pauline was able to extract a supplementary allowance from the Imperial Treasury in order to offset the balance of the transaction.

Ever since 1806 Pauline had been enjoying the revenues of the Duchy of Guastalla and in 1809 Napoleon, consideraing them insufficient to keep pace with Pauline's fantastic extravagance, augmented her income by adding other slices of territory. As a result of this Pauline now enjoyed an annual income of 80,000 francs in excess of that of her husband, who was one of the richest men in Europe. After leaving Camille to his own devices (he had been made Governor-General of Piedmont, Genoa and Palma) Pauline divided her time between the Tuileries and her magnificent château at Neuilly. She had never taken a very active part in the intrigues against Josephine and therefore derived no special satisfaction from the latter's divorce. She now came forward as champion of the Creole and was outspoken in her opposition to the marriage with Marie-Louise, so that it was Caroline and not Pauline who was chosen by the bridegroom to accompany the bride on her journey from Vienna to Paris in the spring of 1810.

Once the separation was over Napoleon became more cheerful and threw himself into preparations for the new alliance with a wholeheartedness that approached the ridiculous. He behaved, in fact, exactly like a lovesick young man who had surprisingly won an heiress. His bride's poverty (her personal jewels at the time of her marriage consisted of some hair rings, a few seed pearls and a necklace of coral) did not worry him since he had the keys of every treasure-house of Europe. What fascinated him was her ancient lineage, a line of ancestors that stretched all the way back to the twelfth century and linked her family with that of every reigning house in Europe.

Marie-Louise's education and preparation for marriage was what might be expected in a family where protocol had taken precedence over commonsense for hundreds of years. She had never been alone with a man other than her father and all references to the difference between the sexes had been snipped from her books with scissors. She had never owned a male pet of any kind and all her life she had been taught to regard the man she was marrying as a personal incarnation of the devil. When her father told her she was to be married to the ogre who had driven her family from Vienna twice in the last five years she was terrified but her obedience to Papa was instinctive and she made very little fuss. She was consoled no doubt by the long train of wagons that arrived in Vienna with an Arabian Nights trousseau. It included, among many other extremely valuable gifts, twelve dozen assorted chemises, twenty-four dozen handkerchiefs, twenty-four bed-jackets, thirty-six petticoats, eighty night-caps and a shawl valued at over 3,000 francs! Dresses costing 6,000 francs apiece, richly embroidered slippers, buckles, girdles and every kind of female adornment were there together with a fabulous amount of jewellery, one item alone being valued at 84,000 francs and a necklace and two pendants costing another million and a half.

Whilst the Habsburgs were goggling at this largesse the prospective bridegroom was showing an impatience that made his friends blush for him. He tried to learn to dance, with Hortense as his tutor, and embarked upon a frenzy of refurnishing and redecorating all the palaces and apartments that his bride was to inhabit. Jérôme's wife, Catherine of Westphalia, wrote to her father, 'Nobody had ever seen him like this,' and added that his antics were becoming the subject of dubious jokes throughout the Empire and beyond. Caroline had been sent to meet the bride at Braunau but Murat remained in Paris and when his brother-in-law's impatience was such that he could not wait for the official meeting at Compiègne, the King of Naples accompanied the groom on a furious ride to Soissons, in order to intercept the bridal cavalcade en route.

The weather was foul but both Napoleon and Murat had ridden through worse. Ineffectually disguised as junior officers they galloped through pouring rain as far as Courcelles where, sheltering in the church porch and both dripping wet, they saw the retinue enter the village. Napoleon was at once recognised by the Master of Horse. Flinging himself from his horse he pulled open the coach door and inside, looking as if she was about to be violated by highwaymen, sat the startled Marie-Louise with sister Caroline as chaperon. Caroline's long experience of her brother's unpredictability enabled her to conceal her astonishment and she introduced the bride, whereupon Napoleon planted a kiss on her cheek, climbed inside and the cavalcade resumed its interrupted journey to Compiègne.

That same evening, as they all sat at dinner, Napoleon asked Cardinal Fesch if he and the Austrian Princess were not in fact legally married. Told that according to civil law they were man and wife Napoleon wasted no further time, said goodnight to the startled company and carried the bride to her quarters, where he remained overnight. 'My friend,' he said to his valet in the morning, 'marry a German! They are the best of all women, sweet, gentle, fresh and innocent as roses!'

Four queens and two princesses walked in stately procession behind Marie-Louise at the religious ceremony that took place in the chapel of the Louvre a few days later. The occasion was the most impressive Paris had witnessed since the coronation in Nôtre Dame more than five years before. Since that day almost the whole of Europe had passed under the control of the gunner-cadet who

used kings and queens like an impulsive chess-player. Except
Lucien, still in disgrace, and Joseph, absorbed in the tricky business
of transferring crown from pocket to brow, every member of the
family was in attendance and to an ordinary onlooker, standing
in line as the bridal procession moved towards the altar, it must
have seemed that the dynasty this marriage was to perpetuate was
as firm as the rock of Gibraltar. Cynics like Talleyrand and Fouché
and pessimists like the impassive Madame Mère, might question
its permanence but there were no such doubts in the minds of the
hundreds of Imperial dignitaries present, all owing their exalted
positions in life to the bridegroom's blade. For here, it seemed,
was an empire founded on and maintained by personal achieve-
ment, owing nothing to the past but concentrating wholly upon
the immediate future. Yet it was the immediate future that worried
some of the gorgeously attired principals attending the bride.

Caroline of Naples, not actually a train-bearer but charged with
the duty of bearing a lighted taper to the altar, should have been
delighted to attend a ceremony that set the seal upon victory over
Josephine, but since escorting the bride over the frontier she had
had time to think and her reflections were not reassuring. Here
was a healthy nineteen-year-old girl replacing a forty-six-year-old
woman as potential mother of a legitimate heir. Should that child
make its appearance and should it, God forbid, prove to be a
healthy boy, then the door would close for ever on the advancement of little Achille Murat.

For Queen Hortense the occasion was even less happy. Her
mother had just been set aside to make way for the woman whose
train she now carried and in Holland Louis' throne was tottering.
As if this was not enough Hortense had just received news that her
lover, de Flahaut, was seriously ill. As she moved up the aisle in
the wake of the new Empress it must have seemed to her that
troubles would never cease.

Julie, Queen of Spain, was in a slightly happier frame of mind,
for at least she was back in France for a time and could eat a meal
without wondering whether it contained arsenic, the favourite
seasoning of her new subjects in Spain. Even so, Julie was a loyal
and devoted wife and it distressed her very much to reflect that

Joseph's life was in jeopardy every moment he remained in the Peninsula.

Catherine of Westphalia, Jérôme's wife, was another train-bearer and she had worries of a different kind. Two years of married life with Jérôme, reigning over a patchwork realm crushed by debt and conscription, was enough to worry anyone but Catherine laboured under an additional handicap; she was madly in love with the good for nothing she had married.

Elisa of Tuscany, the fourth train-bearer, resented her enforced attendance, finding it humiliating to bear the train of a chit of a girl who was as stupid as most hereditary princesses. Elisa had heard it said that the bride was proud of her ability to wiggle her ears; she and her sister Pauline would have given a good deal to box them. The Princess Borghese, who had never favoured the match, did not even try to conceal her contempt for the girl and quite soon she would be banished for failing to show the Empress proper respect.

So they brooded as they slow-marched behind the girl replacing Josephine and their misgivings were certainly shared by some of the fighting marshals, who had put on their best uniforms to attend the wedding. Josephine had enjoyed great popularity in the army and when things began to go wrong the men who had overturned half-a-dozen dynasties in the last fifteen years were to grumble, 'We've never had a day's luck since we lost the old lady!'

Among the official witnesses at the religious ceremony was Eugène Beauharnais. Josephine had begged him not to allow her divorce to check his brilliant and blameless career. He too had married a Princess and was now showing great ability as Viceroy of Italy. Eugène felt his mother's disgrace keenly but possessing more commonsense than all the Buonapartes put together he followed his mother's advice and neither then or later was his loyalty to Napoleon in question. But he must have felt some resentment when he saw his stepfather place the ring upon the gloved finger of Marie-Louise; maybe he recalled an occasion in Egypt twelve years before when, as aide-de-camp to General Buonaparte, he had served as outrider to the coach in which Napoleon's mistress, Madame Fourès, was driven about the streets of Cairo.

When the ceremony was over the guests were given little leisure to gossip for the Emperor's wedding-day expression clouded suddenly and courtiers saw in his frown a sure sign that something or someone had spoiled his day. Everyone watched him nervously and there was general relief when the storm broke upon the group of Italian cardinals, summoned to Paris for the wedding. Twenty-seven had been called but only fourteen had answered and Napoleon demanded to know what had happened to the missing thirteen, known from then on as 'The Black Cardinals'. He was told that their absence expressed the Pope's disapproval and disavowal of the recent divorce and when the act of pious defiance was explained to him his rage boiled over. With extreme difficulty he was dissuaded from throwing all the absentees into prison and even talked of having them shot, but as his rage cooled he contented himself with stripping the passive resisters of their offices and revenues, banishing them from Paris and forbidding them, on pain of severe penalties, to wear cardinal's robes in future.

Napoleon's rift with the Church had been growing wider every year. Towards the end of 1808 he had sent troops to Rome, hoping to intimidate His Holiness and compel a closer alliance between Church and State, but Pius VII was not easily frightened, not even when the Papal States were annexed to the kingdom of Italy in the following spring. That same year, 1809, the Pope found himself a State prisoner at Savona. The enemies of France professed to be shocked but, in fact, many were pleased at this turn of events. To oppose a man who had restored established religion to France was one thing, particularly when that man commanded the most mobile, the best-trained and the most confident army of all time, but it made opposition easier when the arch-enemy of the old order could be lampooned as 'the Anti-Christ', and the repercussions of this propaganda were soon felt by King Joseph, floundering in Catholic Spain.

The renewed quarrel with the Pope had serious repercussions elsewhere. Ever since Napoleon's final break with Lucien the family rebel had been living quietly in Rome, enjoying the protection of the Holy Father and leading the life (outwardly at least) of a private citizen preoccupied with literature and the arts. On the arrest of the Pope, and with his brother's troops swarming into the Holy City, Lucien's position became untenable. It was no secret to the French that Lucien, grateful for the asylum offered him by Pius, had repaid his debt by encouraging Papal resistance to Napoleon's demands. When His Holiness had been forcibly removed to France there would have been bloodshed had it not been for the promptness with which the kidnapping had been carried out by General Radet, the French Commandant in the city. With his patron under lock and key at Savona Lucien thought it wise to move to Tusculum, where he interested himself in archaeology. General Miollis, who replaced Radet as commandant, was not so tactful as his predecessor and kept Lucien under such close observation that the rebel made up his mind to remove himself and his family out of reach of his brother. There was no such place in Europe so Lucien decided to emigrate to America and applied to the local police for the necessary passports. Somewhat to his surprise he got them and upon application to Murat, King of Naples, Lucien was given passage on an American vessel due to sail from the port of Civitavecchia.

Everyone, it seemed, was anxious to expedite Lucien's voluntary exile but Lucien, piqued by the general eagerness to see him gone, now seemed in no hurry to leave and began his vast packing operations in a very leisurely manner. Ever since his profitable transactions as a negotiator in Paris and later as a diplomat and peacemaker in Spain, Lucien had been accumulating money and valuables. Pauline and Jérôme knew how to spend money but Lucien knew how to make it and was now a very wealthy man, not only in cash but in kind. Day after day crated masterpieces, gold and silver plate, all kinds of household goods and a large collection of Etruscan archaeological finds were carted to the loading bays of Civitavecchia and when it was obvious that the chartered vessel could not take so much freight Lucien made his selection and sent the balance back to Rome where it was deposited with Torlogna, the principal banker in the city. Among the goods that he did take aboard was a large portrait of Pope Pius VII. 'He has been a hospitable friend to me,' Lucien told everyone, 'and I must not forget him.' It seemed unlikely that he would, since in his pocket was a letter signed by Pius recommending Lucien to anyone likely to contribute to the family's happiness abroad. It was a valuable passport but in the event it proved of little value to the exiles.

The American vessel weighed anchor on August 10th, 1810, but things rarely went well for Lucien. Almost before the coast was cleared a tremendous sea whipped up and the Captain ran for shelter in Cagliari, Sardinia. Unfortunately for the emigrants Sardinia was at that time under the control of the British Navy and when Mr Hill, the British envoy, learned the identity of his unwilling guests he instructed Sardinian officials to inform 'Monsieur Buonaparte' that he could now regard himself as a prisoner of His Britannic Majesty, King George; the same applied to every member of his family and the ship's company, notwithstanding the fact that they were mostly Americans.

To make matters worse Lucien's wife was ill, but in view of the local attitude he did not dare risk a parley ashore. After fourteen harrowing days he told the captain to proceed on the journey, hoping that the British would not molest a neutral vessel. He was wrong. Two British frigates, seeing the Yankee making ready to sail, had slipped out of the harbour the previous evening and one of them, commanded by a Captain Barry, approached and fired a warning shot across the bows. The action so infuriated the American captain that he prepared to resist, declaring that he would pistol the first Englishman who stepped aboard his ship. Lucien told him that resistance was useless and that a merchant vessel, crowded with civilians, could make no headway against two fully-armed frigates. When Captain Barry came aboard by longboat the indignant captain consented to take his passengers to Malta and set sail escorted by warships.

Captain Barry, jubilant at securing such a valuable prize, nevertheless proved a courteous captor and Lucien, reflecting on his record of long-term defiance towards his brother, was confident that matters would be satisfactorily settled at Malta and that he and his family would be allowed to proceed on their journey. He underestimated his own importance as a hostage and British generosity. General Oakes, the British Governor of Malta, proved to be a martinet foreshadowing Napoleon's St Helena gaoler, the crusty

Sir Hudson Lowe. Overjoyed at finding a member of the Buonaparte family his prisoner, Oakes went out of his way to be officious
and overbearing, insisting that Lucien be quarantined and refusing
permission for Madame Buonaparte and the children to find more
comfortable quarters than the Lazaretto. When the quarantine
was over Lucien was transferred to Fort Riccazoli, a medieval
building lacking furniture of any kind, and here he was obliged to
provide chairs and bedding at his own expense. Friendly naval
officers sympathised with him and it may have been on their insistence that he was later moved to the more comfortable castle of
St Anthony, the former residence of the Grand Master of the
Knights of Malta during the great days of the Order. Here he
passed the time telling his children stories of the Knights' long
struggle against the Turk and when the children were in bed he
found consolation in poetry and began to write an epic on Charlemagne.

It was not until the end of December that instructions arrived
from London for Lucien and his family to be taken to England. In
vain he begged to be allowed to go alone, leaving his wife and
children in Malta until he had had a chance to plead his cause to
the Prince Regent. Then, as now, the official mind stuck to the
letter of the law and man, wife, children and servants were bundled
aboard a frigate for a midwinter voyage in the worst possible
weather. Captain Warren, yet another British martinet, had been
warned to give the French coast a very wide berth and the vessel's
sweep headed it straight into Atlantic gales prolonging what
should have been a fortnight's voyage by another month. Finally,
after a desperately miserable six weeks at sea, the fugitives reached
Plymouth, but even here Captain Warren refused to anchor and
risked the vessel and everyone aboard her by riding out a gale
overnight.

The following morning the prisoners landed and were received
by a Mr Mackenzie, who said that 'he was authorised to offer
them asylum'. The news must have come as a relief to the exhausted Madame Buonaparte and her children but Lucien, who
had defied the Master of Europe for years, did not accept the
situation without protest. After thanking the State Messenger for

his 'welcome assurance' he made his position very clear, declaring, 'I have been made prisoner illegally and I protest against everything which myself and my family have undergone since we quitted the port of Cagliari! I demand to be allowed to resume my journey and beyond that, Sir, I refuse all the offers of your government for I can accept nothing from a nation which is the enemy of mine, nor from a government that makes war upon my brother!' It was a remarkable ultimatum from a man who, since 1804, had declined to be bribed, bullied or flattered by the man in whose name he now challenged the British Empire, but it was Lucien running true to form. His wife, family and chosen friends could always lead him but neither the Grand Army nor the invincible British Fleet could drive him over a single inch of land or water.

Lucien was not to continue his journey to America and he and his family remained in England until the Empire collapsed. For the next four-and-a-half years Lucien was as far removed from his brother's authority as if he had settled in Cathay.

CHAPTER NINE

'It is a far cry from the profession of a soldier to that of a courtier!'

Napoleon writing to Jérôme
in 1809

SHORTLY BEFORE LUCIEN placed himself out of reach of his all-powerful brother both Elisa and the family favourite Pauline had incurred the displeasure of the King of Kings. Elisa's offence was trivial; Pauline's resulted in banishment from the one field where she was of some use to her brother, the Paris salons.

In the spring of 1809 word reached Napoleon that Elisa, the one member of the family whom he could trust to behave with circumspection, was opening a gambling saloon in Florence. Napoleon's vices did not include gambling. When he played a game of chance he invariably cheated and having enjoyed beating his competitors he returned his winnings with one of his pale smiles. He wrote to Elisa: 'My Sister: Take care that no one starts a gambling saloon in Florence! I don't allow them at Turin or anywhere in the Empire. They set a bad example and ruin family life. The only place where I tolerate them is in Paris, partly because in this huge city it would be impossible to suppress them, and partly because they are made use of by the police. But my intention is that they shall not exist in any other part of my Empire.' We hear no more of Elisa's efforts to anticipate Monte Carlo.

As for Pauline, she fell into deep disgrace after an undignified incident during the presentation of Marie-Louise in Brussels. Ever since the departure of Josephine and Napoleon's granting of permission to leave Italy and reside in Paris once more, Pauline had been enjoying herself, but her brother's marriage to an unsophisticated girl of nineteen changed the atmosphere of the Imperial

Court overnight. It lost its air of gaiety and extravagance and Napoleon, always prone to set examples of one sort or another, was now seen in the unlikely role of a self-made bourgeois married to a worthy wife and only interested in raising a family.

Pauline detested the Austrian and at the Brussels presentation went so far as to make an urchin gesture behind the back of the Empress, but she should have learned by now that her brother had eyes in the back of his head. The courtiers who saw the gesture giggled. Napoleon, who also saw it, summoned Pauline, rebuked her for her lack of manners and banished her from Court on the spot.

Pauline packed her hundred and one ball-dresses and returned to Rome, where she persuaded her semi-estranged husband to give her one of his splendid palaces as a social base. Here she relaxed throughout the remaining years of the Empire and enjoyed herself in her own fashion. She had as much money as she could spend, dozens of male admirers, and a horror of shouldering responsibilities like those thrust upon brother Joseph in Spain, or eagerly canvassed by Caroline in Naples. She sat for portrait painters, changed her ensemble half-a-dozen times a day, bathed each day in milk and occasionally took a lover, sometimes two.

Jérôme, King of Westphalia, took over his kingdom in December 1807. To travel free of debt he had had to borrow from his Imperial brother's sinking fund but for once in his life he borrowed in expectation of being able to settle within the foreseeable future. After all, he was now a king with direct access to a National Treasury. There would be no more embarrassing interviews with stingy relations, an end to his waiting to catch Joseph, Josephine or his tight-fisted mother in a giving mood. Orders had preceded his arrival to hold the funds of the State Treasury at his disposal from December 1st and with the prospect of a substantial income Jérôme hoped to cut a dash and win a reputation as a sovereign famous for prodigality, display and generosity towards old and tried friends, of which there were several in his train. A terrible disappointment awaited him. Almost as soon as he arrived in his

Lilliputian capital, Cassel, Monsieur Daru, Intendant-General of the Grand Army in Berlin, demanded of Westphalia the astronomical sum of 35,600,000 francs which he said was owing out of the 49,000,000 due to France as her share of maintaining the army billeted in Germany. To make quite sure of this contribution Daru, a keen man of business, had secured possession of all the revenues of the country before the new King set foot in his capital. All that awaited Jérôme there was a sheaf of unpaid bills.

The new King at once appealed to Napoleon, pointing out that without revenue he was not only prevented from administering his realm but could not repay the Emperor the 1,800,000 francs Napoleon had lent him from the sinking fund. Unfortunately for Jérôme, Daru had also written to the Emperor and with far happier results, for Napoleon came down heavily on the side of the Intendant-General, reminding his brother that in any case half of the revenues of Westphalia were earmarked for Grand Army expenses. Jérôme asked what was to happen to the remaining half, but in matters of finance Napoleon could be pitiless and the only reply was a brief letter refusing to accept Jérôme's inability to repay the sinking fund loan and adding that 'it would be a bad beginning for your reign and would suit your credit ill if you started off by not paying your debts.'

What was Jérôme to make of this? From the very beginning of his reign his position was desperate. All funds were closed to him, the national income was ten months in arrears with a deficit of six million francs (three millions excess over the estimated cost of Grand Army expenses) and he could not raise new taxes without beginning his reign under a cloud of controversy and national resentment. To make things even more difficult for him Napoleon now began to torment him with a series of carping letters attacking his extravagance. Not that letters of this sort ever made much impression upon Jérôme but he must have found it galling to receive pious exhortations to strict economy when, in fact, he had hardly a penny-piece to spend. His predecessor in Cassel had been so poor that his meanness had become a national joke. All the palaces and official buildings were in a state of disrepair and Daru, the

Intendant-General, stubbornly refused to hand over a single month's revenue to enable Jérôme to establish himself.

The first eighteen months of Jérôme's reign in Westphalia is a story of shifts and evasions on his part and menacing demands and threats on the part of Napoleon and Imperial officials. Jérôme's long experience of living well at the expense of others stood him in good stead but never, not even in his bleakest periods at sea and abroad, had he experienced anything like this, where his income was virtually nil and so much was expected of him. Making allowances for his extravagant nature one cannot but sympathise with his position and he was soon floundering in a morass of debt. In addition to the demands of Daru, and the frightful cost of maintaining French veterans on German soil, he was facing relentless pressure from Paris for immediate repayment of the 1,800,000 francs he had borrowed, and as time went on Napoleon's letters became more and more abusive. Not even Lucien and Louis had had to withstand such sustained attacks from the seat of power but unlike them Jérôme possessed the sanguine temperament that is essential to the life-long borrower and, all things considered, he remained cheerful. His replies to Paris, underlining the idiocy of the demands made upon him, were partially successful and he managed to reduce the Grand Army bill to seven millions. He also kept the sinking fund debt collectors at bay by payment of interest at rates of seven to eight per cent. What saved him from disaster, however, was his association with Isaac Jacobson, an extremely wealthy Jew who loaned him considerable sums of money in exchange for the removal of disabilities formerly imposed upon Jews in Westphalia. Under Jérôme the Jews became full citizens and with Jacobson's help the King managed to keep more or less solvent while he tried to raise a national loan.

The Westphalian free Parliament, first of its kind in Germany, approved the raising of such a loan in Holland and aimed at a sum of twenty millions. Unluckily for Westphalia, France herself was at the that time floating a loan in impoverished Holland and in October, 1808, when Jérôme had been ruling for less than a year, the loan was offered the people of Westphalia, everyone possessing more than five hundred francs being urged to contribute.

Napoleon, hearing about this while negotiating at Bayonne, wrote Jérôme one of the most vitriolic letters he had ever composed, not excluding those he was then dashing off to Louis in Holland. 'You have allowed bills to be dishonoured' thundered the Emperor, 'and that is not the act of a man of honour! I never allow anyone to fail me! Sell your plate and diamonds. Cease indulging in foolish extravagances which make you the laughing-stock of Europe and will end by rousing the indignation of your subjects. Sell your furniture, your horses and your jewels to pay your debts. Honour comes first of all! It ill becomes you not to pay your debts, when people see the presents you give and the unexampled luxury you live in, so disgusting your subjects. You are young and inconsiderate and you never pay any attention to money matters, above all at a time when your subjects are suffering the effects of a war.'

Jérôme's reply to this sermon is a masterpiece of irony thinly disguised in terms of humility as befitted a professional sponger. 'What can I reply, Sire?' he asks, 'when your Majesty tells me that I do not act like a man of honour? Beyond a doubt I am truly unhappy in that I cannot die after reading the words. If I have not paid the 1,800,000 francs which I owe the sinking fund it is because I have not the money *and did not think that Your Majesty's intention was that I should pay ruinous interest to get rid of my debts to you!*'

The national loan was a fiasco and the economy of Westphalia slithered from crisis to crisis like a rudderless ship with a drunken crew. Expedient after expedient was tried but there could be no real solution whilst half the country's revenues continued to be siphoned off by the Grand Army and Jérôme was determined to live and behave like a miniature Louis XIV. He tried every possible way to raise money and set his finances in order; the one thing he would not do was to reduce his standard of living to the level where people might mistake him for a Burgomaster.

Part of the friction between Jérôme and Napoleon at this time had nothing to with money but concerned Jérôme's loyalty to old friends, some of whom, scenting good pickings, had followed him to Cassel. Chief among the hangers-on was his boon companion of the American adventure, the handsome Le Camus, whom

Jérôme made Count of Fürstenstein and Minister for Foreign Affairs. Like his patron Le Camus was a born opportunist. He brought with him to Westphalia three pretty sisters and a brother. Two of the sisters soon made advantageous marriages and the brother, employed as a diplomat, was sent on a mission to America to tie the loose ends of the Patterson affair.

Jérôme's behaviour towards his friends, and particularly towards Le Camus, is reminiscent of the weaknesses displayed by certain Plantagenet kings towards their chosen favourites. His curious and rather touching loyalty frequently got him into fresh difficulties and when Napoleon heard that Le Camus had been made a Count, with an income of 40,000 francs a year, he exploded. 'I have marshals who have won ten battles and are covered with scars and who have no such reward as you are giving Le Camus!' he raved, but Le Camus held on to his income and secured his future by marrying an aristocratic bride. He found the greatest difficulty in pronouncing the German title Jérôme had bestowed upon him. Le Camus must have had an engaging personality and a lively sense of humour for he is reported to have joined heartily in laughter provoked by his mispronunciation.

Part of Le Camus' attraction for Jérôme was his usefulness in providing a steady supply of royal concubines. Although married to a woman who was deeply in love with him, Jérôme did not forego the traditional pleasures of power and while courtiers complained that Cassel was very dull (some of the Frenchmen who had followed Jérôme to Westphalia soon left, disgusted with the lack of diversion) life in Cassel was never dull for him. Among his mistresses were the Breslau actress he had met during the 1806 campaign, the opera singer he had courted in Italy, and several ladies of his wife's household. One of the latter was discharged on the grounds that she was far too friendly with the King and when Le Camus delayed her departure she had to be whisked out of the country by the police. Between them Jérôme and Le Camus hatched a plot to prevent this happening to the lady from Breslau, who was hastily married to the King's valet. They were the victims of their own strategy; shortly after the wedding the valet resigned his post, left for Paris and took his wife with him.

Queen Catherine's unsuspicious nature was the subject of frequent comment in the reports of Napoleon's spies in Cassel but it is doubtful if, in fact, she was as naïve as they supposed. Her childhood had been dull and spartan and she very much enjoyed being a queen, even the queen of a bankrupt State, and Jérôme, although consistently unfaithful, never treated her like his brother Louis treated Hortense, and in some respects the marriage was a great success. At all events this oddly assorted couple remained on affectionate terms all their lives.

Every time he had a little cash in hand Jérôme did his best to relieve the tedium of life for his subjects by staging a spectacular social event, like the opening of the 1809 carnival season. Nine hundred guests attended this party, at which Jérôme and Catherine were received by garlanded shepherds and shepherdesses who approached the royal dais under an arch of shepherds' crooks. At a similar party there was a wonderful fireworks display provided by one of Jérôme's aides and the chief of police. King, Queen and subjects enjoyed the spectacle very much but the following morning the hosts were reminded that fireworks were strictly forbidden in Westphalia and that there were heavy fines for firing them. It would be interesting to know whether the money from the fines went into the national coffers or into Jérôme's pocket.

In the spring of 1809, when Jérôme had been reigning for about eighteen months, war broke out with Austria again and Westphalia, together with the whole of French-occupied Germany, was placed on a war footing. The Tugendbund, a murderous secret society flourishing in Prussia, was active in Westphalia and two attempts were made by German patriots to invade the country whilst Napoleon was busy beating the Habsburgs on the Danube. One plot involved the kidnapping of Jérôme by officers of his household, but for all his mad extravagance Jérôme was not unpopular and the plot was foiled, the King sending his wife Catherine to Paris for safety and himself taking command of the Tenth Corps, which was billeted in the area.

As a general Jérôme was no more successful than as a sailor or financier. When Jérôme went to war he did not believe in denying himself the creature comforts he enjoyed at home and he set out on a campaign with an attendant retinue, including cooks, valets and corps of diplomats. He took his time moving about the field of operations and after reoccupying Dresden he ordered a *Te Deum* and attended the opera before evacuating the city in disobedience to his brother's commands. He would have been a great success as a commander of field armies in the more leisurely eighteenth century, but his brother had introduced new military methods and Jérôme was sadly behind the times. His orders, as commander of the Tenth Corps, were to watch Austrian moves against his own country, Saxony and southern Germany as a whole. Napoleon, fully occupied in the Danube area, had sent him a carefully worked out plan aimed at sandwiching an Austrian army between the Westphalians and a corps commanded by General Junot, the soldier who had sympathised with Jérôme during his journey across Spain at the time of the Elizabeth Patterson affair. Jérôme, however, had plenty of ideas of his own and they were usually in direct contradiction to those of his brother. Hearing that the English were contemplating a descent on Holland he marched his corps north instead of making the pincer movement planned for him. As a direct result of this Junot had to beat a hasty retreat and only an armistice saved Jérôme and his army from annihilation.

Napoleon was furious. To owe his treasury millions and spend money like water was bad enough; to risk disaster in the field by disobeying orders was a great deal worse and the Emperor's wrath came down on Jérôme's head like boiling oil. He had already written expressing his contempt for Jérôme's method of making war and had urged him to 'stop making himself ridiculous, send his diplomatic corps back to Cassel, go without baggage and suite, have no table but his own, make war like a soldier in need of glory and reputation and, in God's name, learn sense enough to talk and write as you ought!' but this letter was mild compared with the one dispatched by Napoleon when he learned of Jérôme's fatuous march to the north. It is the longest letter ever sent to Jérôme by his brother and is a classic of its kind. After underlining the terrible risks Jérôme had taken by disobeying orders he went on, 'I am sorry for your sake that you give so little proof of talent, or even of good sense in military matters. It is a far cry from the profession of a soldier to that of a courtier. I was hardly as old as you when I had conquered all Italy and beaten Austrian armies three times as numerous as mine. But I had no flatterers and no Diplomatic Body in my train. I make war like a soldier and there is no other way of making it. I did not set myself up as an Emperor's brother, nor as a king. I did everything that needed doing to beat the enemy . . . if therefore you intend to continue as you have begun, following your fancy and not carrying out my orders, you may stop in your seraglio! You are a spoilt young fellow, although you are full of fine, natural qualities. I very much fear it is hopeless to expect anything of you.'

On military matters it was indeed hopeless to expect anything of Jérôme. Napoleon was more justified in this particular censure than in criticising Jérôme's financial failures. Jérôme lost his command of the Tenth Corps and afterwards had to content himself with an army of six thousand Westphalian recruits, but the war against Austria was over and Napoleon had already made up his mind to marry an Austrian archduchess in the hope of securing Austria as a permanent ally. Jérôme returned to Cassel where he was rejoined by his adoring Catherine. There were more parties, more mistresses and possibly more fireworks that produced a little ready money in the way of fines. Financial worries continued to multiply, but as far as the King of Westphalia was concerned shortage of money was a daemon that had attached itself to him since boyhood and was to follow him until the end of his days. He temporarily abandoned the pursuit of military glory and devoted all his energy to the less exacting task of cutting a figure at court.

CHAPTER TEN

'I do not believe that any man in the world is more unfortunate in his family than I am!'

Napoleon commenting on
his relatives, 1810

BY NEW YEAR'S DAY 1811, the huge, sprawling pyramid was complete. On March 20th of that year the final touch was added. About eight in the morning, after three days of fearful anxiety, the Princess who could wiggle her ears gave birth to a healthy male child. At last, after eleven years of supreme power and fifteen as the most talked of man in the world, Napoleon Buonaparte had a legitimate heir. The succession had been secured, the dynasty founded. From now on the family was no more than an expensive luxury, yet brothers and sisters, their marriages, their progeny, their extravagance, quarrels and ceaseless intrigues continued to harass the man who could never rid himself of the responsibilities he had assumed when Carlo Buonaparte had died more than twenty years before.

When the twenty-second cannon shot told Parisians that the sex of the Imperial child was male, Napoleon reached the pinnacle of power. Never before had so much territory and influence been so rapidly acquired; few would have believed that it would slip from this man's grasp in thirty-seven months.

Apart from the war in Spain the huge Empire was at peace. French troops stood on the shores of the Baltic and on the Mediterranean. Most hereditary houses in Europe acknowledged Napoleon as master and several owed their continued existence to his bounty. The political map of Europe had been carved and recarved to provide kingdoms, dukedoms and fiefs for his relations by blood and marriage and for the most distinguished among his comrades-in-arms. His sisters and their husbands ruled central and southern Italy. Northern Italy was controlled by the son of his divorced wife. Holland and the Low Countries had been absorbed by France. Most of the Spanish peninsula was occupied by his legions. Central Europe was ruled by a group of quiescent ciphers, including among their number his youngest brother. Gold-laced marshals, the sons of lawyers, coopers, brewers and private soldiers, stood by to see that puppets remained puppets. The Czar of all the Russias, the only one among all his rivals who possessed the power to challenge his overlordship, was his friend and admirer. Anyone might have been forgiven for supposing that the heirs of Carlo Buonaparte, who had once importuned for free places at the educational establishments of the Bourbons, were as sure of their patrimony as the Romanoffs in Petrograd and the Hanoverians in Windsor. The small scrap of humanity whose birth at the Tuileries had been witnessed by more than a hundred dignitaries ensured as much; or so almost everyone believed.

Of the family King Joseph was still embroiled in Spain, ex-King Louis was sulking in Austria, Lucien was a prisoner in England, King Jérôme was devising means to raise and spend money in Westphalia. Of the Buonaparte girls Elisa was building roads and reviewing her miniature army in Tuscany, Pauline was taking baths and choosing gowns in Rome, Caroline was quarrelling with her husband in Naples. Alone among them Madame Mère pondered the future in the French capital, living frugally, hoarding money and wondering how and when it would end and whether, when it did, it would be possible to reclaim her olive patch in Corsica.

News of the birth of the King of Rome reached Joseph in Madrid on March 29th and it did little to encourage him. Three years as nominal King of Spain had given him a distaste of monarchal responsibilities. He had ruled as a king for two years before he set foot in this dreadful country, but the crown of Naples had been far easier to wear. He was harassed and desperately miserable, for the situation in which he found himself was not only humiliating but distressing to an essentially tolerant man. Spain was still divided into military districts and in each area swaggering adventurers like Marshal Soult and Marshal Victor, or astute soldier-statesmen like Marshal Masséna and Marshal Suchet, treated the King with less respect than they showed active guerrilla chiefs like Mina and Empecidado. They ruled efficiently despotically, according to their natures, but one and all they levied revenues, shot or pardoned rebels, looted churches, burned villages, ennobled collaborators and generally behaved as if there was no such person as King Joseph ruling in Spain.

Reviewing this situation Joseph, basically an earnest, worthy man, almost wept with frustration and wrote letter after letter to his brother in Paris, pointing out that something must be done to improve this anarchical state of affairs. Couriers from Paris (those that actually arrived in Madrid and did not have their throats cut en route) brought him little satisfaction. Napoleon seemed to have forgotten Spain and when he thought about it at all he showed more confidence in professional soldiers like Suchet than in his brother Joseph. He promised, laconically, to review the position and perhaps introduce new measures when possible, but his promises were never made good. In March, after Masséna had recoiled from Torres Vedras with an army of half-starved men, Joseph wrote to his brother, 'I should deserve my lot if I sought to prolong it,' and then talked of imitating Louis and abdicating in an attempt to shame the man who had involved him in this appalling mess. By July he had changed his mind and chosen another course, posting off to Paris with the intention of making a direct plea to the Emperor and either getting satisfaction or re-signing on the spot.

He neither resigned nor gained the slightest satisfaction, for Napoleon was no longer the dynamic warrior-lawyer of the Italian and central European campaigns. He was enjoying, for the first time in his life, the slippered ease of a successful man of business who had decided, since remarriage, to leave the management of his complicated affairs to well-paid subordinates.

The two brothers met at Rambouillet and all Napoleon would talk about was his son, and how fortunate it was that Joseph had arrived in time for the christening. Joseph was so indignant that he refused to attend unless his brother would promise to withdraw arbitrary powers from the marshals in Spain and restore to him some semblance of authority. Napoleon humoured him, being in a conciliatory mood. Britain, he said, already recognised Joseph as the rightful King of Spain and would withdraw her armies from Portugal the moment the Spaniards accepted him as sovereign prince. Then France would recognise the independence of Portugal and fighting in Spain would be confined to the bull-ring. Joseph made very little of this, reasoning that if universal recognition was dependent upon the goodwill of Spaniards then he would be dead long before the House of Buonaparte was firmly on the throne. Glumly he returned to the Peninsula where, as he had anticipated, things had taken a turn or two for the worse during his absence. Wellington, reinforced, well supplied from the sea and supported by a Portuguese army commanded by British veterans, came over the mountains and pounced on the key fortresses of Badajoz and Ciudad Rodrigo. Soult and Victor continued to sit outside Cadiz with no hope at all of taking the city. Suchet and Macdonald had established themselves in the east and the province of Navarre was aflame. Marshal Marmont, Napoleon's oldest friend, came down to replace Masséna as supreme military commander in the Peninsula but he paid as little attention to Joseph as any of his predecessors. Then, to make matters worse, Napoleon began to withdraw veteran troops from Spain to swell the ranks of the huge army he was gathering for his advance into Russia. Marshals and men went gladly, happy to leave a country where large armies starved and small armies were cut to pieces. Their pleasure in leaving Spain would have been moderated by knowledge of what was in store for them in Russia.

In the summer of 1812, when the Grand Army was gathering for the Russian adventure, Wellington attacked Marmont at Salamanca and defeated him, so that once again King and Court had to evacuate the capital. They were back again by November, for Wellington was a gambler who only backed certainties. Even before the second flight and return Joseph had abandoned hope of winning the goodwill of his subjects and in the absence of his wife, who went to take the waters at Vichy, he let slip the reins of government and consoled himself with mistresses. In March of that year he had written to his brother, 'Sire, events have deceived my hopes. I have no longer a hope of being of any service. I pray Your Majesty then to permit me to place in your hands my right to the throne of Spain, which you deigned to transmit to me four years ago. In accepting this crown I had no object in view but the welfare of this vast monarchy. It has not been in my power to accomplish it. I pray Your Majesty to receive me as one of your subjects and to believe that you will never have a more faithful servant than the friend whom Nature gave you.'

His plea was rejected. Instead, partly as a sop to pride and partly to trap him in a situation from which he could not resign without being called a coward, he was made Commander-in-Chief of all the forces left in Spain. The honour was to bring him more disappointments. Wellington's victory at Salamanca was only the first of them.

Of the four brothers Lucien was undoubtedly the luckiest, the happiest and certainly the most fortunately placed in the year 1811. Having no throne to lose and possessing ample private means he settled down as an English country gentleman and made his home the rendezvous of savants, astronomers and provincial squires with literary and artistic tastes. Lucien was no longer a prisoner in the real sense of the word and his captors treated him with great respect. After his proud refusal to be numbered among his brother's enemies he was taken to Ludlow Castle and made the responsibility of the Lord Lieutenant of Salop. He was given permission to travel within a two-mile circuit of the castle and whilst at Ludlow he resisted the blandishments of Englishmen who saw in his record as a rebel a potential valuable ally. Lucien made his position perfectly clear to those who tried to enlist his support against Napoleon. He was not, he told them, Napoleon's servant but he had no wish to be included among the enemies of his native land. All he asked was to be left alone to pursue his many cultural interests and his detention in a medieval fortress that had once been the home of the ill-fated children of Edward IV did not depress him. After a time his gaolers relented and he was allowed to leave the castle and buy the estate of Thorngrove, on the road to Worcester, and here he turned his home into a salon and a studio and became a favourite with the local gentry for miles around. The estate, purchased from a French emigrant, cost him 18,000 guineas but he could easily afford it and started embellishing it with some of the family portraits and Etruscan treasures that he had brought with him from Italy. He and his wife were ideally happy and children arrived regularly, nine in all, as well as the two daughters by his first wife, Christine. He took a keen interest in astronomy and bought a huge telescope for 50,000 francs, installing it in his private observatory. He finished his long epic poem on Charlemagne, then a drama, and finally a couple of comedies which were performed in his private theatre before an audience of two hundred neighbours. His wife and the older children took part in these plays and Lucien watched, reflecting perhaps that there was more satisfaction to be gained from these modest entertainments than from his brother's masked balls at St Cloud. He took a keen interest in his children's education and with the family talent for administration he drew up a scheme for the week's studies every Sunday morning. Sunday evenings were devoted to concerts at which children and guests performed. All things considered Lucien's was a very agreeable existence and among his visitors at this time were the Duke of Norfolk and the daughter of Herschel, the famous astronomer. As far as Lucien could foresee he was here for the remainder of his life. The war between Britain and France had already been going on (with one brief truce) since 1793, and there seemed no prospect of it ending. He must have mellowed a good deal during his years of exile in Rome for he made friends with squires who would have been horrified by his republican speeches in the past. Such speeches as he composed at Thorngrove he put into the mouths of his characters.

In Töplitz, the Austrian town to which he had gone shortly after his flight from Holland, Louis continued to defy his persecutor. It was now evident to observers why he had left his throne so hurriedly. His aim had been to embarrass Napoleon before every court in Europe and in this he had succeeded, for the Emperor was thunderstruck by the news that Louis had renounced the authority he had been forbidden to exercise. For a man who valued his political judgment above that of all his advisers Napoleon showed a curious weakness in one respect. He could never face up to criticism on his treatment of blood relations and now, afraid that his enemies all over Europe would see in Louis' abdication an act of desperation, he announced that his brother's withdrawal from the royal circle was due to mental instability and general ill health. In order to lend credulity to this fiction he relaxed his attitude toward the truant and even granted him a pension of two million francs, but at the same time he brought heavy pressure to bear upon Hortense to get her husband back to France.

His demands placed Hortense in a very difficult position. Under no circumstances whatever did she wish to resume her life as Louis' wife and regarded his absence abroad as a boon. Obliged to make a pretence at persuading him to come back, however, she made a few feeble efforts and was delighted when her emissary returned with news of her husband's refusal to return. His abdication, both as sovereign and husband, left her free to live in France and renew her long association with the handsome de Flahaut.

In her tedious memoirs Hortense goes to great lengths to persuade readers that de Flahaut was very persistent and that she virtuously resisted his advances for years, but there is no doubt that she gave the young man every encouragement and after Louis' desertion felt free to take him as a lover.

In the meantime Napoleon had lost no time in taking charge of Louis' six-year-old son who had been abandoned in Holland when his father fled to Austria. Welcoming the bewildered child to the Tuileries he said: 'I will be your father and you will lose nothing by the exchange.' The child, in spite of his tender age, was made Duke of Berg and Cleves in succession to Murat, who had relinquished this title on becoming King of Naples, in 1808.

Hortense remained a favourite of her stepfather and was given the honour of holding the infant King of Rome at the christening ceremony in Nôtre Dame. It was a duty she did not relish, for she had not been inside the cathedral since her own eldest child had been buried there after his death in 1807. She made much of this morbid fear and irritated Napoleon by refusing to take part in the christening ceremony, but in the end she let herself be persuaded, once again incurring the jealousy of Caroline, who said that no matter how artfully she modelled herself upon Hortense she was never able to evade disparaging comparisons by the Emperor. Jérôme, it will be recalled, had a similar grudge against Hortense's brother Eugène, with whom he was often and unfavourably compared. Napoleon sometimes went out of his way to ferment these jealousies.

Louis, in spite of a pressing invitation, did not attend the christening and in his absence Hortense had to bear the cost of the carriages ordered on her behalf. She paid the bill with great cheerfulness, regarding Louis' absence as worth the price of a couple of carriages. About this time Louis wrote a pathetic letter to his Uncle Fesch, who acted as a clearing house for Buonaparte feuds. 'Tell me if you think I will be allowed to live in tranquillity and obscurity, for that is all I desire,' he said, but Uncle Fesch could give him no such assurance for Napoleon continued to publicise the idea that poor Louis had lost his wits; sometimes it seemed true, for Louis forbade his wife to accept an increase in Imperial revenue on their country estate at St Leu, and what Buonaparte in his senses had ever rejected an offer of money? Hortense ignored his instructions and herself accepted the gift; after all she had those christening carriages to pay for.

When news reached Napoleon that Louis was trying to buy land in Corsica and return to the island homeland as a private gentleman he was very worried and again urged Hortense to use what influence she had to bring the ex-king back to Paris. Hortense tried again, with as little success, and it became obvious that Louis was going to prove as embarrassing in exile as brother Lucien. It was at this time that Napoleon declared, and not for the first time, that he was cursed with relations whose sole object in life seemed to be to shame and humiliate him. 'I do not believe any man in the world is more unfortunate in his family than me' he complained, after dictating a letter to his father-in-law, Francis of

Austria, asking him to expel Louis from his territory and convince him that it was the duty of every member of the Imperial family to live in France. Francis, who had just given his eldest daughter to a man whom most Austrians regarded as Beelzebub, relayed the message to Louis in a watered down form but he had no more success than Hortense. Louis merely left Töplitz and moved to Graz where, like all Buonapartes with nothing better to do, he devoted himself to the pursuit of literature. Here, for the next two years, he remained, wrapped in a shroud of resentment, deaf to pleas and bribes from Paris.

Jérôme in Westphalia, Joseph in Spain, Lucien in exile in England, Louis in voluntary exile in Austria; the four brothers of Napoleon made news of a sort in the year 1811, but it was not the kind of news the head of the Buonaparte family liked to read in the newspapers he scanned in the Tuileries. His sisters were doing rather better. Shocking rumours reached him from time to time, mailed by the spies he maintained in and around his sisters' establishments, but at least Elisa, Pauline and Caroline confined themselves to local and domestic scandals.

Elisa troubled him the least, although he would have preferred her to show more respect for her husband and hold her tongue about their marital relationship. Pauline continued to get herself talked about but there was no hope at all of her improving and by now he had forgiven her behaviour at Brussels and permitted her, on such occasions as her presence promised to be useful, to take part in organising balls and fêtes at the Imperial Court. Both she and Caroline played roles in the big social event of February, 1812, when the last of the famous Court quadrilles was staged in the Tuileries theatre, this time taking the form of an allegorical entertainment portraying the annexation of Rome. Every seat was occupied and the two princesses appeared, Pauline as Rome and Caroline as France, wearing little silver helmets and carrying shields that glittered with diamonds. Surrounding each principal was a group of the most beautiful women of the court, each dressed as a naiad or as Isis, with attendant chamberlains and equerries in the costumes of zephyrs and Apollos. When the show was over Hortense and the Empress opened the ball with French country dancing and the Emperor moved round the ballroom making his usual blunt remarks to guests but passing no comment at all on the allegory. He had plenty to say about it on the following day, however, when Hortense and Caroline called on him and found him in a tetchy mood. He told them that the choice of subject for their allegory was unfortunate and that what had been presented with the object of flattering him had irritated him. 'Whilst Rome is obedient to France she is far from content' he said, 'and the notion of representing her as happily resigned to subjection is ridiculous!' He added that, in his opinion, the piece of nonsense had been conceived in order that Pauline and Caroline could look beautiful in spectacular costumes and that they would have done far better to pursue this objective without dabbling in politics. Having roused Caroline to fury he turned on Hortense and criticised her for dressing her little son as a Polish lancer. 'Such a costume might start a rumour that I intend to make your boy King of Poland,' he growled, 'and that would involve us in war with Russia!' Caroline, nursing a new grievance, returned to Naples where she resumed her private guerrilla war with Murat. Antagonism between them had been growing ever since they came to Naples. Reduced to simple terms they quarrelled about which of them was to rule the kingdom.

Murat had gone to Naples with the best intentions. Not for him the mild administration of a Joseph, the playful poverty of a Jérôme, or the obstinacy of a grouser like Louis. Unlike Napoleon's brothers he had earned his crown in the field, risking death a thousand times and, in his own estimation, doing more to make Napoleon Buonaparte master of Europe than any other man in the Grand Army. His reward, he felt, should be complete independence so long as he maintained an alliance with France based upon a friendship between two sovereigns.

He had now ruled Naples for years and was beginning to realise that he had misjudged the strength of the opposition at home and abroad. He discovered that he was subject to the same pressures that had sent Lucien and Louis into exile, had made Jérôme a despairing bankrupt and was reducing Joseph to a nervous wreck. His every attempt to act as an independent ruler was thwarted by an edict from Paris, telling him how to raise troops and money, what campaigns to mount against the Neapolitan Bourbons and the English in Sicily, what laws to draft and how to apply them when drafted, and whenever he questioned any of these instructions Napoleon's roar of rage reached him over the nine hundred miles that separated their capitals. As an innovator Murat had a good deal more to recommend him than his predecessors, and he flung himself into the work of reorganising the kingdom from top to bottom. He abolished the feudal system, divided up the land, stimulated agriculture, built excellent roads like the Strada di Posilipo and Campo di Marte, drained marshland, opened colleges and tried to stimulate his subjects' interest in astronomy. The Neapolitans looked with amazement at this furious activity, appalled at so much energy being generated by one man and that a happy-go-lucky chap who cantered about in a sky-blue tunic, pink riding breeches and a cocked hat crowned with plumes and heron's feathers. It was when Murat tried to prove to his subjects that from now on they were quite independent of Paris that he ran into real trouble. He announced, for instance, that every member of the armed forces must be a natural-born or nationalised Neapolitan wearing a Neapolitan uniform of Murat's own design, and this decree brought a furious letter from Paris. 'All Frenchmen are citizens of Naples anyway!' thundered Napoleon, reminding the author of the proclamation that he owed everything he possessed to the courage of French soldiers, and if he ever forgot it the same men would soon make nonsense of his pretentions by stripping him of his rank and escorting him back to the barracks from which he had emerged.

Murat's anger on receiving this rebuke was so great he tore off his French decorations and threw them on the ground. But he had to obey, in spite of his boasts that he had no intention of becoming 'a second Bacchiochi' or a lackey of France. Yet a lackey he remained, for when he set out to drive the English out of Sicily his own generals would not obey him but acted on secret orders from Paris, and the expedition came to nothing. Murat cursed the

Buonapartes, using language that was almost treasonable and accusing his wife of siding with her brother to humiliate him. He was wrong and he was right; Caroline was not interested in promoting Napoleon's policies inside her frontiers but neither was she the kind of wife who could be relied upon to show her husband loyalty. There was no room in Caroline's heart for loyalty of any sort. The touchstone of her character was self-interest, ruthlessly and relentlessly pursued, and she had her own ideas about the correct way to safeguard the future of the throne of Naples. Alone among the younger Buonapartes she suspected that Napoleon's empire might not endure and that one day she would wake up to find herself poor again. Yet she had none of Letizia's thrift and tried other ways of buttressing her future against adversity. She set to work to woo the Neapolitans and improve relations with Austria, foreseeing that when the crash came she would be the one reigning Buonaparte to hold insurance. In pursuance of this policy she bribed her husband's ministers for secret information and sent her footman down to the waterfront to keep appointments with bribed officials. She also maintained a network of personal spies in and about the royal apartments so that the Court of Naples had a four-tier structure of professional informers. By the year 1811 almost every State employee in the city was on somebody's private payroll. On the ground-floor, so to speak, were Napoleon's secret agents and immediately above them those paid by Murat. Above these again was a group of ministers and flunkeys paid on results by the Queen, and overlapping into all three sections were international agents in the pay of Metternich, the Austrian Chancellor, and the British cabinet! Some of these observant gentlemen were double-agents so that even men with Talleyrand's talent for sifting information must have been baffled by the contents of the satchels of Neapolitan couriers. When her husband's smouldering quarrel with Napoleon flared up in 1811 Caroline visited Paris with the avowed intention of mending the relationship between husband and brother but once she had the ear of the Emperor she used her opportunity to widen the breach. On her return there were renewed quarrels between the royal pair and Murat kept out of her way as much as possible. His favourite pastime at this period was the systematic hunting down of brigands with which the realm was infested and their numbers multiplied after recruits were landed by British naval units anxious to increase Murat's difficulties. Hunt-the-Brigand became a national sport and droves of bandits were rounded up by the royal posses, but despite his regal status Murat never lost his barrack-room sense of humour: on one such hunt a captured brigand told Murat that he could have shot the king dead in an ambush the previous day but had declined to take a mean advantage of him and now found himself the victim of his own restraint. Murat, having checked the story and found it true, pardoned the man and gave him honest employment.

King Jérôme was having trouble with bandits of a different kind. His territory had been carved out of various hereditary fiefs and the original owners had by no means abandoned hope of repossessing themselves by force. One such victim, the Duke of Brunswick, took advantage of Austria's new bid for freedom in 1809 and found himself at the head of 2,000 men, but he had been abandoned by his ally and Napoleon did not take him seriously until he swooped on Brunswick and captured it. The townsfolk did not rise, as he had hoped, so the Duke dodged Jérôme's General Rewbell and made his way to the coast, ultimately reaching England by way of Heligoland. Jérôme was furious with Rewbell for his failure to catch the Duke and when Rewbell asked for permission to sack Brunswick in order to indemnify his troops Jérôme dismissed him from the Westphalian service. Rewbell accepted his dismissal philosophically, reasoning perhaps that there was no future in serving a king who neither paid his soldiers nor permitted them to make up arrears of pay by pillage. Jérôme was still unable to make ends meet and in another attempt to raise some ready money he indulged in a little smuggling, contravening the Imperial decrees that prohibited trade with England and conniving at the entry into Westphalia of three hundred cartloads of British goods. When his brother found out about the deal he wrote the usual blistering letter but Jérôme replied that unless he received financial aid from France his country could not survive another two months, and that he might as well abdicate and be done with it. The threat worked and Imperial pressure was relaxed for a time. Napoleon did not want a third fugitive in the family.

Shortage of money dogged Jérôme all his life but it never prevented him from making the most of what he could borrow. A succession of carnivals, balls and royal sleigh-rides continued to enliven the poverty-stricken Court at Cassel. At some of the winter revels the King changed his disguise half-a-dozen times in an evening and danced to the click of castanets whilst Queen Catherine, who must have relished all this fun and laughter after her depressing life in Württemberg, appeared disguised as an old Jewess, an American Squaw or a Black Forest peasant, surrounded by Court beauties dressed as ancient hags. Jérôme was a great believer in keeping up appearances. Whenever he and his suite went abroad, or paid a State visit to the Tuileries, the Westphalians were always considered the best dressed of the assembled company. Westphalian chamberlains wore mantles of scarlet velvet with collars of cloth of gold, white satin sashes with gold-fringed tassels and plumed hats, while their king wore a suit of gold-embroidered white satin and sported a diamond clasp in his feathered hat. Jérôme, himself a rake, showed commendable tolerance for the weaknesses of others, as when he learned that his mistress, Blanche Carrega, had betrayed him with a cavalryman called Marbreuil. The circumstances of the discovery, however, must have caused Jérôme some satisfaction for Blanche, who was prolific with her favours, was caught by Marbreuil in the arms of a soldier employed at the War Office. In a fury of jealousy Marbreuil gave both of them a sound thrashing with his riding whip and it was the cries of the injured Blanche that brought her indiscretion to Jérôme's notice. He soothed her and sent Marbreuil to join the Westphalian Legion in Spain and expelled the rival lover from his dominions, but Blanche was allowed to remain at Court. It was not long before she was unfaithful again, this time with Queen Catherine's brother, the Prince of Württemberg, but again Jérôme forgave her and begged her to mend her ways. In the meantime Marbreuil had returned with a wound, a captaincy and the Legion of Honour, but service in Spain had failed to improve his temper and he made another violent scene in public and was banished. He obtained his revenge years later when, with the Empire collapsing under allied assaults, he demonstrated his sympathy with the Bourbons by tying Napoleon's Legion of Honour insignia to his horse's tail.

Blanche Carrega's scandals soon became so notorious that even Jérôme could not afford to keep her at Court and she was sent to Switzerland where she lived on a handsome allowance paid her by the Prince of Württemberg. Jérôme consoled himself elsewhere and was sometimes seen to disappear from a ball at midnight in the company of one of his wife's ladies-in-waiting, reappearing the following day with a plausible explanation for his temporary absence.

The days of masked balls, sleigh rides and the eternal shifts to find money for occupying troops and the administration of the country were passing, however, and not only for Jérôme. In six years he had accumulated a national deficit of over fourteen million francs and supplied Napoleon with nearly half-a-million recruits from a total population of two millions. Russia was defaulting on her Tilsit agreements and trading openly with the English and there were other causes for a rupture between the two despots who had agreed in 1807 to share Europe between them. All over the Continent men were marching and another clash between Russia and France could not be delayed for long. By May 1812, Napoleon had assembled a huge army in the Dresden area and Jérôme was given another chance to win military glory when he was made co-commander of the right centre, with an army group numbering sixty thousand men. It was by far the most important military appointment he had ever held and the only thing that qualified his satisfaction was the appointment of the humourless, bald-headed Marshal Davout as his partner. Davout was known as the Iron Marshal – and with very good reason. He was a first-class soldier and completely incorruptible and Jérôme had reason to dislike him. Not long before, Davout had been sent to West-phalia to make sure of the King's contributions towards the cost of the French army and had turned a deaf ear to all Jérôme's excuses. He was Napoleon's man and allowed nothing to come between him and duty. He forced Jérôme to honour an agreement to repair Magdeburg fortress at a cost of three million francs and during his stay had proved an exceptionally hard taskmaster. Why Napoleon, the great psychologist, allowed these two men to share a command is hard to understand, but he did and trouble was not long in coming. Within two months of taking up his command Jérôme was in disgrace again and remained out of favour until the Hundred Days.

BOOK FOUR

The Survivors

CHAPTER ELEVEN

Gentlemen, I see clearly that you have no relish for this war . . .

Napoleon at a Council of War in 1812

IN THE LIGHT of what has happened in the Western World since 1945 and the apparent permanence of the cold war between the two blocs on either side of the Iron Curtain, it is interesting to look back over a century and a half of Russia's relationships with the rest of Europe and see what Napoleon had to say at St Helena on the subject of the campaign that precipitated his downfall.

'That war,' he said, and for once he was speaking in all sincerity, 'should have been the most popular in modern times. It was a war of good sense and true interests, a war for the security and repose of all. It was purely pacific and preservative, entirely European and Continental. Its success would have established a balance of power and would have introduced new combinations, by which the dangers of the time present would have been succeeded by future tranquillity. In this case ambition had no share in my views. In raising Poland, which was the keystone of the whole arch, I would have permitted the King of Prussia or an Archduke of Austria, or any other to occupy the throne. I had no wish to obtain any new acquisition and I reserved to myself only the glory of doing good and the blessing of posterity.'

There were those about him, a majority, who were more interested in their firesides than in the good opinion of posterity. The fighting marshals were tired. They had been at war, more or less continuously, since their youth and unlike Jérôme they had no need to win military reputations. At a council of war with Murat, the Chief of Staff Berthier, and General Rapp shortly before the Russian campaign opened Napoleon noted the reluctance of these men to risk all they had won in a new adventure. He observed, 'I clearly see you have no relish for this war. The King of Naples has reluctantly quitted the fine climate of his own kingdom, Berthier desires nothing better than to hunt on his estates at Grosbois and Rapp is impatient to inhabit his mansion at Paris.' Of the three men Rapp was the most outspoken. He cheerfully admitted that Napoleon spoke the truth.

Murat had received his summons with dismay. He was enjoying himself in Naples and was reluctant to leave Caroline at home with responsibility for governing his kingdom. The prospects of acquiring fresh glory in the good cavalry country between Warsaw and Moscow were encouraging but Murat was over forty now and even he had had enough of soldiering. Of Napoleon's close relatives only Murat and Jérôme accompanied the half-million men who crossed into Russia on the evening of June 22nd, 1812. Murat, commanding the twelfth corps, headed the advance, a prancing, pantomimic figure in a gorgeous uniform waving a gold wand. The Cossacks were much impressed by him and he was a legend among them before the long columns had trudged as far as Smolensk. Davout, with Jérôme's eighth corps on his immediate right, commanded the first corps and among the other veterans present were Ney, Macdonald and Victor, all failures from Spain, the gallant Oudinot, who was to receive several more wounds to add to his final tally of thirty-four in the wars of the Empire, and such experienced warriors as Lefèbvre, Mortier and Bessières of the Guard. It was the most impressive array seen in Europe since the Persians had marched on Greece in ancient times.

Things went fairly well at first although rations soon ran short and thousands of horses died through eating unripe rye. The Grand Army succeeded in dividing the Russian defenders and General Bagration, retreating eastward, was in great danger of being caught and crushed between the pincers of Davout and Jérôme, respectively pursuing from north and south. And so he would have been if Jérôme had bustled instead of wasting nearly a week at Grodno and allowing the Russians time to slip away. Napoleon, learning why the enemy had escaped, was furious with his brother but it was not his miscalculation that brought disaster to the King of Westphalia in search of glory. When he did decide to move (and there seems to be some excuse for his delay owing to the exhausted condition of his men) he wrote to the irritable Davout as an equal, proposing certain co-ordinations between their corps. Davout replied saying that he would issue any orders that were necessary and that Jérôme was to regard himself as a subordinate commander.

It is difficult to discover whether in fact Napoleon had issued confidential instructions to this effect. Probably he had, recalling Jérôme's poor performance as a soldier in Saxony six years before or his irresponsible career as a sailor. At all events Jérôme took umbrage and to make things worse he put his grievance in writing and sent it to the Emperor, after which he withdrew to Warsaw to await a decision. This ridiculous gesture amounted to resigning his command in the face of the enemy and all the irritation that Napoleon had felt for his younger brother in the past was nothing compared to his fury at such defiance. He swore aloud that never again would he entrust his wretched brother with a command of any sort and Davout, smiling grimly, pushed on with the advance to cross swords with Murat who was exhausting the cavalry and exasperating the infantry by galloping after the retreating Russians as though he was conducting a peacetime review.

Jérôme, now officially dismissed, returned to Cassel. Had he known it he was well quit of a campaign that was to bring credit to no one but Ney as leader of a shattered rearguard. It was July when Jérôme threw up his command; within five months only a remnant of that magnificent army survived to return to the billets of central Europe. All the rest, more than four hundred thousand of them, were dead or prisoners of war.

It is not within the scope of this narrative to retail the well-known story of Napoleon's disastrous Russian campaign. The seven main characters of this chronicle played no part in it if one excludes Jérôme's brief and inglorious spell as co-leader of the right centre. Throughout the five months that elapsed while the Grand Army crawled towards Moscow, poked about among its smouldering ruins for loot and then dragged itself back to East Prussia, Napoleon's four brothers and three sisters were remote from the scene of operations. Elisa, Pauline and Caroline spent the time in Italy where Pauline pursued her uninterrupted round of pleasures, and Elisa and Caroline supervised the administration of their realms. Jérôme plunged into a whirl of public and private entertainment in Westphalia, and Lucien and Louis continued their literary pursuits, the one surrounded by a circle of admirers at Thorngrove, the other a lonely exile in Graz. Only Joseph's exertions were comparable in any way to those of the man facing disaster in the east and Joseph had already come to terms with the hopelessness of his task. Unlike his brother he could contemplate with pleasure the prospect of retirement from the demands of State.

News of the French disasters in Russia were slow to reach the mountain fastnesses of Spanish guerrillas and the scattered garrisons of British and Portuguese troops in the eastern half of the Spanish peninsula. Rumours crossed the sierras from time to time, stories of a severe check to the French advance at Borodino and of crippling losses sustained by an army far from its sources of supply and recruitment. There was a particularly persistent rumour that Moscow had been burned to the ground by gaolbirds and finally came whispers of the wholesale destruction of the famous army and its pursuit across the plains by the Cossacks of the Czar. No real news came out of Russia, however, until Napoleon issued his famous bulletin in which he frankly admitted the magnitude of the disaster. This was not made public in France until December and therefore did not reach Joseph in Madrid until some three weeks later.

News had travelled in the opposite direction much faster, a hard-riding courier delivering Spanish despatches to Napoleon outside Moscow only twenty-six days after they had been written in Madrid. The despatches asked for the dismissal of Marshal Soult because of his persistent refusal to cooperate with the King and Court. Napoleon, as familiar with Soult's longing for a throne as with Joseph's incapacity to administer anything larger than a country estate, gave no answer; he had other and far more pressing problems to solve.

Napoleon, preceded by a prancing, overdressed King of Naples,

entered Moscow on September 15th. He left it, with 115,000 men
and countless camp-followers, on October 19th. In the forty-six
days between the evacuation and his abandonment of the army
his command had dwindled to a few thousand semi-invalids, held
together by a single invincible, Marshal Michel Ney, formerly a
barrel-cooper's apprentice, later a trooper in a hussar regiment,
later still Prince of the Moscowa. There was little or no glory
gained in those forty-six days by the greatest captain of the age
and none at all for his gaudy brother-in-law, the King of Naples.
Alone among the senior officers of an army that had enjoyed
fabulous success over a period of eighteen years, Ney left Russian
soil unbeaten and undaunted. By the time Ney had crossed the
bridge over the Neimen Napoleon was well started on his record-
breaking journey from Smorgoni to Paris, a sleigh and carriage
ride achieved over mid-winter roads in twelve days. He was
followed almost at once by Murat, to whom he had handed over
supreme command. With less compunction than the least of his
starving troopers the King of Naples had turned his back on the
rabble for the South, there to trim his sails for the coming storm.
For it was clear even to such a thick-headed man as Joachim Murat
that his wife had been right after all and that their crown was not
necessarily in pawn to French bayonets if they kept cool heads and
pulled together instead of in opposite directions. With this inglorious thought in mind the royal deserter covered the distance
between the Neimen and Naples almost as fast as his master had
made the journey from Smorgoni to Paris. Left behind to do what
he could for the famished, frostbitten survivors was Eugène Beauharnais, Viceroy of Italy and son of the discarded Josephine.
Eugène did not run for Italy. Instead he stuck to his post and behaved in every way like a responsible commander. So Napoleon
too had been right when, sixteen years previously, he had recommended Eugène to the shiftless Jérôme as 'a perfect model of what
a young man ought to be'.

There was nothing particularly catastrophic about the collapse of
the Napoleon Empire. As has been implied, it was not accomplished

overnight. From the days of the Great Retreat to the last act
when the surviving marshals confronted their Master at Fontainebleau, the process of disintegration occupied about eighteen
months but perhaps the most terrifying aspect of the eclipse was
the inevitability with which the end stole down upon Imperial
office-holders, upon all, that is, but the Emperor himself. Between
December, 1812 and April 1814, every officer in the Grand Army
and every soldier in the garrisons between Elbe and the Douro,
was looking over his shoulder at the approach of doom. It might
take a year, or two, or five, but it would happen just the same and
nothing could avert dissolution. Madame Mère had known this
for long enough and Caroline, the most politically astute member
of the family, had suspected that it might occur within her lifetime, but now everybody knew it and there was a kind of desperate
fatalism in the way the family drew together, demonstrating a
loyalty that had been lacking in happier days. Only Caroline persisted in her toruous diplomacy, dragging her half-willing, half-
resisting husband behind her; among the others there was no sign
of treachery but rather the distraction of a board of directors at
the approach of bankruptcy, or the panic of a family awakened in
the small hours and told their home is on fire. Their patron and
provider might look to them for sympathy but nothing more.

Jérôme, dancing, whoring, play-acting and borrowing in his tinsel
capital at Cassel, was the first of the Buonapartes to learn the full
truth about the Russian disaster. Situated as he was, much nearer
the mainstream of fugitives than his brothers or sisters, he was
aware of the facts shortly before Napoleon passed through Warsaw on his way home. At once Jérôme's better nature revealed
itself. Caroline might use this opportunity to nag her weathercock
husband into changing sides but Jérôme, in almost every respect a
worthless, selfish, egocentric fool, emerged from this and subsequent crises as worthier to wear a crown than any of his brothers
or sisters. The moment he heard that Napoleon had abandoned
the army at Smorgoni he sent couriers to intercept him but Napoleon refused to break his journey. He had no time for his younger

brother's advice or sympathy. It was essential that he should reach Paris before the full extent of his disaster became public. Westphalia, as an ally, was expendable.

Ever since he had thrown up his command and returned to his capital Jérôme had been acting like a disgraced son hiding shame in a whirl of pleasure. He had engaged the attention of half-a-dozen new mistresses, plunged his country deeper into debt, forged ahead with plans for building an opera house at Cassel and dipped into the local army chest to engage an expensive company of players to appear there at the opening night. Now the party was over, or almost over. New Year had always been a time of gaiety in Cassel, with a round of masked balls, banquets, plays and carnivals in which King, Queen and courtiers played leading roles. There were very few parties during the carnival season of 1813, for everyone in Cassel knew that even if France survived, Westphalia could not endure. The Cossacks, and behind them the armies of the Czar, were moving westward and Cassel lay in their path. Napoleon, working eighteen hours a day at the Tuileries in a titanic effort to raise and equip a new army to replace the hundreds of thousands lost in Russia, wrote urgently to Jérôme to push on with the fortification of Magdeburg and then hold it at all costs. For the first and only time in their relationship the Emperor sent Jérôme a large sum of money before it was demanded and without troubling his head about security. But it was far too late for such improvisations. Westphalia had been drained dry of men and there was hardly enough money in the country to lay the foundations of a glacis or a curtain wall at Magdeburg. On March 4th, less than three months after the remnants of the Old Guard had dragged themselves into winter billets, the Cossacks rode into Berlin and Prussia prepared to throw off the mask of neutrality; six days later Jérôme sent Queen Catherine to Paris for safety.

So far times were perilous but not desperate. Jérôme, in sending his wife to safety, had misjudged his brother's ability to rally and so, in most respects, did his enemies, now gathering on the Saxon plains. They were numerous and they were increasing every day. The Czar's armies came trudging out of Russia and Poland and the Prussia of Frederick the Great, whipped into a frenzy of nationalism by years of humiliation, began to bully the prince-lings whose lands buttressed France. Down in Italy Murat and his wife plotted and schemed with the hesitant Emperor of Austria whose daughter had secured Napoleon's dynasty. England still dominated the seas and maintained a permanent blockade. France was emptied of young men and the bourgeois were beginning to talk nostalgically of the vanished Bourbons. And Spain, as usual, was in a turmoil, with the cautious Wellington creeping slowly across the peninsula and Joseph, in obedience to instructions from Paris, falling back from Madrid to the line of the Duoro. Yet all was far from being lost. The gunner-cadet who had manipulated kings and princes for years retained all his power to shock and dismay and with his new army of boys, captained by men like Ney, Oudinot, Mortier and Marmont, he pounced on the allies at Bautzen and Lutzen, mauling them so severely that at first it looked as if the work of destroying him would have to begin all over again. There were, however, a number of serious flaws in the apparent recovery. The French were desperately short of cavalry and were thus denied the opportunity to pursue the enemy after beating them. There was also the problem of making good losses sustained in battle, a wastage that the allies could repair day by day and Napoleon could not, in spite of his demands on the dwindling army in Spain and the German garrison towns. Thirdly, and most important, there was the longing of the senior officers for peace, a longing expressed before the Grand Army had set out on its march to Moscow and now emphasised by cynical comments like that of Augereau, who, at the crisis of a battle, said that he refused to die for a German suburb and calmly yielded ground.

Throughout May 1813, the Grand Army appeared to be showing its usual form. All the fighting marshals were in the field, including Murat, now obliged to risk everything on the results of a new campaign. This was the second time in twelve months that he had been compelled to leave Naples and he came very unwillingly indeed. He now had a fresh grievance against Napoleon who had published a bulletin in the *Moniteur* criticising Murat's desertion of the Moscow survivors as cowardice and warmly praising the man who had taken his place. He wrote to Murat in January,

1813, 'I am not going to tell you how displeased I am with your conduct which has been diametrically opposed to your duties. It is due to your weak character, as usual. You are a good soldier on the battlefield but off it you have no energy and no character. Take warning by an act of treachery, which I attribute to fear and give your best wits to my service. I am counting upon you ... the title of King has turned your head; if you want to keep it behave yourself and be careful what you say.'

Murat was so furious on receiving this reproof that he was half inclined to follow Caroline's advice and proclaim openly against his benefactor. Far away in Sweden ex-marshal Bernadotte, now a Crown Prince, had already declared war on France and Bernadotte was Joseph's brother-in-law. But something still prevented Murat from making the final decision. Perhaps it was the weakness of character that Napoleon had mentioned or perhaps it was something worthier, the dregs of loyalty to a comrade who was being betrayed by his own sister. Whatever the cause Murat temporised, continuing negotiations with Austria but riding off to the north to take command of the depleted cavalry of the Grand Army. En route he met a courier from Vienna with despatches for Naples but the messages were in cipher and Murat had to send them on to be decoded. It was an ironic decision; the despatches contained acceptance by Austria of his own and Caroline's offer to abandon Napoleon if the allies would guarantee their survival as king and queen of the Two Sicilies. By early autumn of that year Austria had followed the Russians, Prussians and Swedes into the field and Murat, who, with a little more luck or a little more nagging, might have joined them, found himself leading brilliant cavalry charges against the armies of his would-be sponsor. 'You see those men in flat-topped shakos?' said a sergeant of infantry to a seventeen-year-old conscript at the commencement of an action against the Austrians, 'They have run away from us fifty times since 1794?' They ran away again when Murat, momentarily forgetting all about his treachery in the joy of battle, led one of his spectacular cavalry charges that helped to win the battle of Dresden.

*

It was at Dresden that Napoleon received news of a fresh disaster in Spain. After obeying his instructions to fall back on Valladolid Joseph, in a rare mood of optimism, decided to stand and engage Wellington in a pitched battle at Vittoria, fought on June 21st, 1813. It was an extremely unwise decision for the British had the advantage of numbers and ground, and it resulted in the worst defeat the French had suffered in the Peninsula. Marshal Jourdan, who occupied the position of Joseph's chief military adviser, warned him of the likely result before a shot was fired, but Joseph was insistent. Within a couple of hours the French were overwhelmed and Joseph was galloping for the frontier. Jourdan, who had acquired philosophy in Spain, said: 'Well, you've had your battle and it seems to be a lost one!' Not only had the battle been lost but much else beside for so precipitate was Joseph's flight that he abandoned plate, private papers, a valuable collection of Spanish pictures and military pay chests containing twenty-seven million francs. It was fortunate for him that the British were expert looters for in the scramble for the contents of the royal train the enemy gave him a start, and he needed the respite for he was an extremely poor horseman. Years ago, when the unbeaten French armies were in camp at Boulogne awaiting the signal to invade England, Napoleon had decided that brother Joseph should train as a soldier and in preparation for the career Joseph had taken riding lessons. Picking himself up after a heavy fall from his horse in flight from Vittoria he may have reflected that his training at the Riding School had been inadequate.

Two thousand Spanish families who had accepted Joseph's sovereignty preceded him across the Pyrenees into France. The 'Josephinos' as they were called by their contemptuous countrymen did not wait to see whether the King would win his battle. As the nineteenth century equivalent of World War II quislings they would have been garrotted had they been caught by the partisans. After their departure only one section of the Spanish nation acknowledged French overlordship and that was the south-east where Marshal Suchet had established himself. Joseph's headlong flight made Suchet's withdrawal imperative. By October the British were at the French frontier and

he reign of Joseph, King of All the Spains, had passed into
aistory.

One man in Europe refused to accept this fact and he was the
author of all the confusion that had reigned in the peninsula since
he famous confidence trick at Bayonne, in 1808. Reading the
despatches informing him of the defeat at Vittoria, Napoleon sent
for Marshal Soult, he who had dreamed of a Spanish or a Portuguese
throne for so long and so unsuccessfully. Soult was told to leave
and hold the line of the Pyrenees for as long as possible. He left
the same day and once there acquitted himself brilliantly in the
long-drawn out rearguard action that continued into the following
spring. The British beat him in the end but not before he had
earned among them a reputation that was to stand him in good
stead in his old age.

The early victories of Napoleon in Germany resulted in an
armistice that was to prove fatal to the cause of the Empire. By
October of that year, with the British hammering at the south-
western frontier of France and the Coalition outnumbering the
Grand Army by more than three to one, the French were brought
to battle again. On October 16th – 19th was fought the four-day
battle of Leipzig, known as the Battle of the Nations. It was the
largest and bloodiest engagement of the war and ended in a disaster
that wiped out the French victories earlier in the year. When he
learned of it Louis, who had spent the summer composing epic
verses in Graz, left Austria for Switzerland and wrote a conciliatory
letter to his brother suggesting that now might be a good time for
him to return to Holland as King and help to restore Buonaparte
fortunes by keeping the Dutch loyal to the Empire. In making
this proposal Louis miscalculated in two ways. He underestimated
his brother's belief in his own invincibility and failed to take into
account the injury he had inflicted upon Napoleon's pride when
he bolted from The Hague in 1810. 'I would rather return Holland
to the Prince of Orange than send Louis back there,' Napoleon
said after studying his brother's offer and to his mother, who was
now intervening on behalf of her exiled son, he wrote a long letter
putting on record his feelings for the young man who had shared
his billets long before either of them dreamed of becoming kings.

Underlining his determination to retain Holland as part of the French Empire he commented bitterly on Louis' past behaviour, reminding Madame Mère that he had overwhelmed Louis with kindness when he was a boy and had been repaid with ingratitude and disloyalty. Louis would be forgiven, however, 'if he came forward as a French prince in support of the throne at a moment of peril'. He recommended, however, that if Louis did return to the fold he should not reside in Paris. 'Let him live quietly and un-obtrusively in some out of the way place,' he wrote. 'He used to like Switzerland. Why did he ever leave it?' In the event it was a pointless re-opening of old wounds for the Dutch, notwithstanding Louis' championship of them when they were on the point of being swallowed by France, decided that it would be safer to invite the Prince of Orange to occupy the vacant throne.

Soon after the defeat at Leipzig Murat made his excuses and bowed himself out of the Grand Army for good, returning to Naples to see what could be salvaged from the wreck and whether, in fact, the Emperor of Austria would appreciate the delicate situation in which a brother-in-law of Napoleon had found himself during the recent campaign. On his way home he passed through Switzerland where he happened to meet Louis, to whom he gave some brotherly advice on the wisdom of deserting Napoleon while there was still time. Louis was a surly, obstinate man, who, time and again, had proclaimed his hatred of Napoleon but angry words are one thing and treachery is quite another. Like Jérôme in Westphalia and Lucien in England Louis was loyal to the clan and indignantly rejected Murat's advice. Hortense was notified of Louis' possible return to France by her mother, who wrote her a warning letter from Malmaison. Always tactful and restrained in her behaviour Josephine praised Louis' attempt to mend his quarrel with Napoleon but hinted that his return might make fresh trouble for Hortense, and she ended her letter on a curious note: 'Courage, my daughter, a pure mind like yours always ends by triumphing.' It is strange that Josephine, so wise in the ways of the world, could bring herself to write in these terms to a daughter who regarded her husband's absence as a blessing.

*

Joseph and Julie were now back in the home they should never have left, Mortefontaine, the chateau Joseph had bought in the earliest days of his brother's success. For him it was full circle and although his pride had suffered, and he was dismayed by the future, he had few regrets about leaving Spain. His beautiful home was a rendezvous of uprooted royalty and fugitive dignitaries. Catherine, until recently the reigning queen of Westphalia, was there despite the fact that her father was about to lend his not inconsiderable weight to the advancing allies; the Grand Inquisitor of Spain was there, hoping for better times and finding it convenient to forget that Joseph had abolished the Inquisition. So, oddly enough, was Julie's sister Désirée, who might have married Napoleon but had married Marshal Bernadotte, now Crown Prince of Sweden and commanding one of the four armies about to advance into France. Désirée was the only one among them who could hope to pluck a crown from the chaos around them for there was talk of replacing Napoleon by her hook-nosed husband after the allies had marched down the Champs Elysées.

On January 1st, 1814, Louis took the plunge and entered France without Imperial sanction. He was in close touch with his mother whose remark, 'Pourvou que cela doure!', did not seem so unreasonable these days. Madame Mère was also in correspondence with Elisa in Italy and with Caroline, now a potential enemy.

Fouché, one-time chief of Napoleon's police, was staying with Elisa and doing his best to persuade her and Bacchiochi to adopt the course Caroline and Murat had taken. 'The only thing that could save us all would be the Emperor's death,' he told her but Elisa, to her credit, showed no inclination to emulate her sister in Naples. Instead she wrote her mother chatty letters asking for social news in Paris, letters that might easily have been written by Pauline but seem a little frivolous over Elisa's signature. Not much is heard of Pauline during these days but she was to come forward when her brother stood in most need of comfort.

Napoleon, watching the Empire shrink like an orange squeezed had recently come to a new conclusion about his family. He thought of them all as worthless, especially Joseph, his senior. He told Roederer, 'I fancied I needed my brothers for the dynasty but it is safe without them. It has been brought into being in the heart of a storm by the nature of things. Joseph cannot forget that he is the firstborn. Was there anything more absurd? If he were talking of our father's vineyard that would be another story. His interests are in women, houses, furniture. He likes to go out rabbit-shooting and to play blind man's buff with the girls.' His distrust of Joseph had increased when he read reports about the kind of company his brother kept at Mortefontaine and the talk that circulated there on winter evenings. He knew that Joseph was incapable of intrigue but now that things were going from bad to worse Joseph began to patronise him with brotherly advice of the kind that Louis and Jérôme had given him in the past and were to offer again before the clock struck twelve. Joseph, like the marshals, had had more than enough of war and saw, or thought he saw, some prospect of saving what was left of the Empire by accepting terms offered by the allies. It was hopeless, however, to insist that soon there would be no bargaining counters left.

Napoleon had seen too many battles lost and won to believe that there was no chance of a sudden reversal of fortune in his favour. It was the Emperor himself who was playing blind-man's-buff now, for he was facing five armies led by two emperors, a king, a crown prince and a haughty Irishman who thought of his incomparable infantrymen as the scum of the earth. The manpower of Russia, Austria, Prussia and Sweden were already on the Rhine and down in the south-west Soult was fighting the battle of his life against the British, Portuguese and Spanish who had crossed over on to French soil. In the last weeks of 1813 France was defended by seventeen-year-old French boys, most of whom had never been taught how to load a musket.

In December and early January, 1814, Napoleon did some quick thinking about his family. Louis was allowed to come to Paris, on condition that he came as a French Prince and not as an exiled king. The number of exiled kings in the Paris area was increasing and the king-maker found their presence embarrassing, particularly when they begged him to accept ridiculous proposals for France to withdraw to her natural frontiers, the Rhine, the Alps and the Pyrenees. Having told Louis to mind his own business and think about his own numerous failures, Napoleon set about untying the Spanish knot and here he had an advantage in that Ferdinand, who had once been elected King by real Spaniards, was still a detainee at Valençay. Napoleon suggested that he should return to Spain as King with French approval and that friendship between the two countries should be cemented by a marriage between Ferdinand and Joseph's thirteen-year-old daughter. Only one important condition was attached to this remarkable proposition, an amnesty for all Spaniards who had supported Joseph during his five-year reign.

Joseph was not consulted during these discussions. Napoleon was less and less inclined to take his brothers and sisters into account and in any case Joseph was now under a kind of house arrest and was not allowed to visit Paris without special permission. Galled by these restrictions Joseph sent the likeable Julie to reason with her brother-in-law but Julie failed and finally it was Hortense's lover, de Flahaut, who was sent to bring Joseph to the Tuileries to be told of Ferdinand's reinstatement. It was either a dying spark of ambition or a notion to repay Napoleon for his recent behaviour that caused Joseph to raise violent objections to the arrangement. It was necessary that his formal abdication be obtained before matters could proceed but to everyone's annoyance, Joseph began to raise all kinds of objections to the project, implying that, technically at all events, he was still King of Spain and might not want to abdicate after all. For a man who did not rule over a single inch of Spanish territory and had recently been bundled out of such provinces as he held by armed force it seems odd that he should have taken such a stand, but he did and Napoleon had the greatest difficulty in bringing him round. On January 7th, 1814, shortly before he left for the front, Napoleon sent him an irritable letter explaining his various reasons for reinstating Ferdinand and when Joseph countered with fresh arguments he wrote again, this time demanding a public avowal of his brother's loyalty to Marie-Louise as Regent. 'Perhaps you can't do this,' he sneered, 'perhaps you haven't enough sense! In that case return to the provinces as inconspicuously as you can. If my life is spared you will live there undisturbed. If I die you will be arrested, perhaps put to death.

You will be useless to myself, to my family, to your daughters and to France and you will be out of my way. Choose quickly and decide which you will do.'

In the end, as always, Joseph submitted but it required the combined pressure of his mother, his wife, and, in the final instance, his brother Louis, to persuade him that such a course was essential. He then agreed to cooperate but only on the understanding that he retained his royal title and would always be known as King Joseph.

In the meantime Joseph's brother-in-law, the renegade Bernadotte, had freed Holland. Ex-King Louis, who had recently taken to advising everyone else what to do, began to reconsider his own position and he too decided to hold out for his title, in spite of the fact that the Dutch would have nothing to do with him.

Word came from Jérôme at Cologne, clamouring to return to France and swell the ranks of dethroned Buonapartes in and near Paris. All was lost in Westphalia and the carriage of the Elector of Hesse had been dragged in triumph through the streets of Cassel within a week of Jérôme's departure. Jérôme's exit had not been as undignified as Joseph's, for at least a few of his subjects had tried to defend the capital. Cossacks had appeared outside Cassel on September 27th, 1813, and Jérôme had slipped away early the next morning, accompanied by his bodyguard. There was no popular uprising (doubtless Westphalians thought they might as well be pillaged by Cossacks as by Jérôme) but on October 13th, shortly before the great battle of Leipsig, one of Jérôme's generals recaptured the city. As a reward he was made a Count with a pension of six thousand francs a year although his chances of drawing it were as remote as his sovereign's chance of borrowing enough to pay it. When news of the disaster at Leipzig reached Cassel all pretence of holding Westphalia for France was abandoned and Jérôme and his supporters, now deserting by the hundred, moved over the border into Berg, the last German state to fly the French flag.

In the final number of the *Moniteur Westphalien* Jérôme announced that his absence from Cassel was temporary and that 'he had confidence in his subjects conducting themselves with the same devotion and the same calm for which they have always been distinguished'. Nobody was taken in by this nonsense and all who favoured the French cause followed the Court to Cologne where, as usual, Jérôme found himself in dire financial straits and was compelled to sell his plate and uniforms. Not all his uniforms, however, for although in flight from a country that had rejected him Jérôme clung to the outward trappings of royalty. Westphalian guards in their theatrical gold-laced tunics were posted around the private house he occupied as headquarters. An eye-witness who met the fugitive Court at this time says it reminded him of a troupe of provincial actors playing a tragedy to an indifferent audience.

Offers were now made to Jérôme to come to terms with the coalition of his brother's enemies but these he rejected, hoping against hope that Napoleon would see at last reason and accept the generous peace offers made to him by the allies before they invaded French soil. It was some time before he could bring himself to quit Germany altogether, feeling that as long as one Buonaparte remained east of the frontier all was not quite lost, but in the end he had to go and wrote to Napoleon suggesting a meeting at Mayence.

For Napoleon Jérôme's letter was the final straw. Joseph had come trailing into France from Spain with a hundred thousand armed men in pursuit. Louis, who had refused to come to Paris and receive forgiveness for his abdication in 1810, now arrived from Austria and considered himself qualified to give advice on the wisdom of coming to terms with the enemy. And now here was Jérôme, the third dethroned king, proposing a meeting to consider the means of regaining a kingdom that would be redistributed among its original owners as soon as the Allies had time to redraw the map. Napoleon cursed his family one and all and wrote forbidding his youngest brother to approach the capital and declining to meet him in Mayence.

Most men in Jérôme's situation would have been depressed by this rejection but not everyone possessed the resilience of the youngest Buonaparte. Rebuffed by the Emperor, and seeing no prospects at all of remounting a throne in Westphalia or anywhere else, Jérôme decided to return to France and settle as a country gentleman like brother Joseph, and with this aim in view dashed off a letter to Catherine telling her to buy and refurnish a handsome château at Stains and get it ready for immediate occupation. News of Jérôme's decision increased Napoleon's rage. All his life, he complained, he had been hampered by relatives who refused to face reality and, forgetting for a moment that he himself was continuing to act like a world-conqueror when in fact he was no more than a cornered adventurer, he dictated a furious letter to Cambacères expressing amazement that, 'when all private individuals are sacrificing themselves in their country's defence a king who loses his throne should be so tactless as to choose this moment to give the impression that he thought only of private interests!' He then forbad Jérôme to go within miles of his new château and told Catherine that she was not to spend a sou on getting it ready. Jérôme was ordered to proceed to Aix-la-Chapelle, where he was to reside if he still wished to remain in France.

Jérôme now displayed the same quiet obstinacy as Joseph and Louis in adversity. He would not go to Aix-la-Chapelle, he said, and he would go ahead with the renovation of his château, and as though to demonstrate to the family that Napoleon's authority was over he set off on a visit to his mother in Paris, after which he took up residence in Compiègne whilst his château was being renovated.

Napoleon accepted the situation. What else could he do? He was on the point of defending north-eastern France against the attack of four well-equipped armies and to oppose them he had with him some sixty thousand men, half of them conscripts without experience in the field. On New Year's Day, 1814, the Allies crossed the Rhine and began to march on Paris.

There was no longer any doubt about the policy of Caroline and Murat, but negotiations with the Allies had taxed their wits during the past few weeks and recent events had shaken their nerve. Austria was extremely unwilling to see the House of Bourbon restored to the throne of Naples but the British made all kinds of objections to a treaty of alliance with Napoleon's brother-in-law and sister. The secret discussions went on and on, Murat tortured by conscience and Caroline torn between fear that her husband would back down on her and anxiety whether Britain would succeed in persuading Austria to break off negotiations. In the end her skill and patience were rewarded and on January 11th, 1814, ten days after the Allies had crossed into France, a treaty was approved by the British Government recognising an alliance between the Emperor's father-in-law and brother-in-law. For Caroline it was triumph after months of intrigue but Murat was still terrified of the prospect of Napoleon defeating his enemies in the north and marching to Italy to call him to account. To do him justice it was not death as a traitor that frightened Murat so much as public exposure of his ingratitude to the man to whom he owed everything. Madame Récamier, who visited the Court of Naples about this time, describes a curious scene she witnessed between Caroline and Murat in which the latter's misgivings are described in vivid detail. Caroline expressed her fears that Murat would lack resolution to go through with the business and pointed out that the people of Naples, like everyone else in Europe, were longing for peace and were behind her in turning her back on the Emperor. Madame Récamier's visit took place on January 16th, less than a week after the treaty had been ratified by the British, and on the following day, when she returned to the palace, she found the royal couple having one of their domestic quarrels. 'Murat's hair was disordered and his eyes were rolling like those of a man in a fit' she relates, 'whereas Caroline was pale and extremely agitated. As I entered the room the Queen whirled on her partner and shouted: "In the name of Heaven and for the sake of your own glory, remain here! Do not show yourself in this state!" and then said to me, "I am going to give a few orders and will return immediately."'

No sooner had his wife left the room than the man who had led ninety squadrons of cavalry across the snow against the Russians at Eylau flung himself at Madame Récamier's feet and taking her hands cried: 'Tell me, tell me the truth! It is certain that you must think I have behaved basely. Is it not so, is it now?' and went on to accuse himself as Murat the renegade, finally bursting into tears and covering his face with his hands.

Madame Récamier, who had no love for Napoleon, was badly shaken by this scene but when Murat appealed to her again and again to justify his action she told him bluntly that in her view this was no time to desert a man to whom he owed so much. Murat, for answer, pointed through the window and across the celebrated bay where the visitor saw a squadron of British ships anchored, but further lamentation by the penitent was checked by the return of the Queen who glanced contemptuously at her husband and snapped, 'In the name of Heaven, Murat, be silent or at least lower your voice! In the next room there are a hundred ears listening to you. Have you lost all self-command?' Then, in a low voice, she returned to the endless task of injecting him with fresh confidence, telling him that if necessary she would face Napoleon alone and defend her right to retain the crown he had given her. To Madame Récamier's astonishment this approach had an almost magical effect on the pitiful man who pulled himself together and hurried from the room. Later that same day she saw him on horseback among the crowds and he appeared perfectly calm as he received the acclamations of Neapolitan fishermen.

Caroline's last words to her friend provided the real key to their relationship as man and wife. Parting from Madame Récamier she said, with a shrug, 'You see? I am obliged to have courage for him as well as myself!'

CHAPTER TWELVE

*I will be master of France everywhere, so long as I have breath in
my body*

Napoleon to Joseph, March 1814

TWENTY-ONE YEARS had passed since Paris was last threatened
with invasion. In those days, the days of Danton and the September
massacres, almost every able-bodied man in France had rushed
into the citizen armies and marched off to the north-east carrying
a weapon forged at one of the improvised smithies set up in the
streets. A mob orator, with a brisk line in republican rhetoric,
could recruit a company of bystanders in ten minutes. Men went
into battle wearing civilian clothes and singing the 'Marseillaise'
and the armies of the kings were thrown back across the frontiers
in wild confusion. And so they might have been again if those
same volunteers had been alive to face the invasion of 1814. Twenty
years added to their age would have made little difference to the
rank and file under the leadership of the man who had won fifty
battles and no nation, at any time in its history, possessed a more
gifted cadre of senior officers. Here, to some extent, lay the trouble.
Almost every survivor of the republican armies was a colonel, a
general or a marshal and the great majority of the men with whom
they had marched in the old days was dead. Their bones lay in
places as widely separated as Seville, Moscow, Hamburg and the
mud cities along the River Nile. The survivors, veterans like Ney,
Oudinot, Mortier and Marmont, were still capable of inspiring
the rank and file to perform prodigies of courage and miracles of
improvisation but even among the senior officers there were serious
gaps, for Lannes, Duroc, Bessières and Poniatowski were dead,
Bernadotte was with the Allies, Murat was a traitor and, at Lyons

189

with the reserve army, the duellist-dancing-master Augereau, stalled orders to march with a string of excuses. The group round Napoleon himself fought on, doggedly and loyally but with no illusions about the inevitable outcome, for the men they now led were boys who had been in their cradles when Napoleon swept into Milan in 1796 and won the war in less than forty days. Napoleon might write to the hesitant Augereau, 'I have annihilated 80,000 of the enemy with conscript battalions which had no cartridge pouches, wooden shoes and uniforms in rags . . . if you are still the Augereau of Castiglione you may keep your command but if your sixty years lie heavy on you give it up . . .' but Augereau could reply, with unanswerable logic, 'Where are the men of Castiglione?'

The curtain was almost down and had anyone but Napoleon been playing the leading role the play would have been over long ago and everyone would have gone home to bed.

In the end he had been obliged to trust Joseph, for apart from those he needed in the field there was no one of comparable rank whom he could trust. Joseph, as Lieutenant-General of France and Governor of Paris, was now facing a situation more desperate than any he had faced in Spain. There the stakes had been relatively small but here they included every title, every honour, every sou and every stick of furniture to which the family could lay claim: in short the Empire itself, or what was left of it.

Yet even now, in this extremity, Joseph continued to receive letters of advice from his brother, just as he had in Naples and Madrid. It must have seemed to Joseph that his brother was moving in a hypnotic trance for the tone of his letters were those of a man on the eve of tremendous triumphs and he described with relish the broken and exhausted state of his opponents. What is more he demanded of Joseph that he should broadcast these fantasies in the form of officially inspired rumours. 'Give it out that the enemy is in difficulties and has asked for an armistice,' he ordered, 'and say that this is absurd because it would deprive me of the advantages my manoeuvres have won! Don't print this but see that everyone talks about it!' Joseph, who had even less illusions than the marshals about the hopelessness of the situation, neither printed nor talked about his brother's latest letters. He simply sat and stared at them like a ruined man holding a sheaf of writs. Then a final letter arrived for him in which Napoleon measured his own confidence against that of the men around him and added, as a footnote, 'I am master today, every bit as much as at Austerlitz! Don't let anyone in Paris flatter the National Guard!' Nobody did; Parisians who were not already sewing white cockades in readiness for the return of the Bourbons were praying that Joseph would not make good his boast to defend the city, for this might encourage the Russians to treat Paris as Moscow had been treated eighteen months ago.

They need not have worried. Joseph had never been a contender for military glory and after ordering Julie to fly west and take their children with her he followed closely on her heels heading at full gallop for Rambouillet, then Chartres. A day or so later he had mild qualms about his withdrawal and made a half-hearted attempt to rejoin the Emperor at Fontainebleau but the road between the brothers was now packed with enemy columns who had entered Paris on April 1st and he changed his mind, retiring with the Empress to Blois, on the Loire.

The marshals had decided to stop pretending that the tide could be arrested and turned. After a brief conference a deputation consisting of the old republican Lefèbvre and Ney walked in upon Napoleon and Chief of Staff Berthier and declared that the Emperor must make what terms he could and that this ruinous war must end at once. When Napoleon replied that he would take command of the troops Ney told him gruffly that the men would obey their leaders and Berthier, who had worked beside Napoleon for eighteen years, did not add a single word to the discussion. Napoleon accepted the inevitable and two of the marshals were despatched to Paris to announce that he was willing to abdicate in favour of his son. But it was too late even for this. Marmont, Napoleon's oldest friend, had already led his troops through the allied lines to Versailles and it was plain to all that even the rank and file of the Grand Army were now ready to exchange Napoleon for peace.

The news of the surrender of Paris and the treachery of Marmont stunned the Emperor into signing an almost unconditional abdication. That same night he swallowed poison but it only made him vomit. It was not a serious attempt at suicide. He had renounced the throne and accepted defeat because, for the time being at least, there was no alternative, but deep in his heart he still believed that some miraculous turn of fortune would soon make him master of Europe again. Why else should he have inserted in his deed of abdication a condition that each of his brothers and sisters should receive an annual pension of the equivalent of twenty thousand sterling?

At Blois all was confusion. Nothing but rumour penetrated the lines and Joseph, now joined by Jérôme, made a conscientious attempt to carry out the letter of his last instructions from Fontainebleau and persuade the Empress and her child to fly south of the Loire. She rejected the idea, preferring to throw herself on the mercy of her father, so they all set out for Orleans where they were met by a representative of the provisional government with reliable news of the abdication. The Commissioner was not so much interested in Napoleon's family as in the fortune in cash and diamonds that the fugitive Court had with them. They surrendered it, together with the famous Regent diamond and the infant King of Rome, and having done this there did not seem to be anything else that anybody could do, for news arrived that Napoleon was going into exile and that Francis, Emperor of Austria, was taking his daughter and three-year-old son into protective custody. So Madame Mère's gloomiest prophecies had been fulfilled at last and Empire, titles, thrones and riches had disappeared in a cloud of gunsmoke.

The Emperor took leave of his Guard and set out for the tiny kingdom of Elba on April 20th. By then the family had scattered, each ex-king or princess having made for the place that promised the maximum security and comfort, for although they had been dependent upon their brother's bounty for more than twenty years, and although they had looked to him for everything they had, each was secretly resolved to make the best of what could not be altered.

Looking back on the French débacle of 1814, one is tempted to compare it with what occurred under somewhat similar circumstances in 1870 and 1940. The autocrats of Europe entered Paris in 1814 as conquerors of a country that had dominated them since the French triumphs of '93 and '94. In the two decades that followed the rise of Napoleon the peoples of Spain, Holland, Italy and Germany had been subjected to the merciless exactions of French tax collectors backed by the bayonets of the Army, and Russia, although never really occupied, had suffered terribly from the invasion of her territory and the destruction of Moscow. In view of this it would not have been surprising if the coalition had entered France resolved to make her pay dearly for a generation of oppression and visit upon the Buonaparte family the vengeance Bismarck exacted in 1871 when he boasted that he would leave the French nothing but their eyes to cry with. Nothing like this happened. Napoleon himself was treated with respect and his brothers and sisters were in no way penalised for their part in the twenty years' spree at Europe's expense. All that was required of them was an undertaking to stay out of France and refrain from meddling in politics.

The same forbearance was not exhibited by some of the Emperor's former subjects and the record of his progress to his island kingdom is an object lesson in the fickleness of popular favour. In the ranks of the army there were still those who were prepared to die for him but the civilians, particularly those in the south, had other views. On several occasions during the journey he came near to being lynched by parents and wives who had lost fathers, sons and brothers in his campaigns and had it not been for his frequent disguises and the vigilance of escorting Russian, Austrian and British officers, he would not have reached the Mediterranean alive. In one town he saw himself hanged in effigy and in another, disguised as an Austrian officer, he discussed the possibility of his own assassination with a girl serving at a wayside inn.

Nobody ever impugned Napoleon Buonaparte's courage on the field of battle but all his life he had shown a horror of mobs and it was a badly shaken man who, after several sleepless nights on the road, arrived in the vicinity of Nice on April 26th.

Here was one member of the family to greet and comfort him. Pauline had been spending the winter on the coast, where she had rented a small country house and was attended by the minimum of staff. News of her brother's treatment on the road had preceded him and the ugly mood of the populace could be judged from Pauline's balcony under which people discussed the prospect of giving the tyrant a rousing welcome. Presently he arrived and Pauline, running to greet the pale, corpulent man descending from the carriage, drew back in astonishment when she recognised the Austrian uniform he was wearing as his latest disguise. For a moment the Corsican pride that characterised all Buonapartes, even a pleasure-loving harlot like Pauline, prevented her from rushing to embrace him and she said, sharply, 'Put on a French uniform before I kiss you!' He understood her scruples at once and withdrew to change, reappearing presently in the uniform of the Old Guard. She flung her arms around him and the bond that had always existed between these two brought him more comfort and reassurance than had any personal encounter of the last few weeks. He stayed by her side a day and a half and because nobody could remain despondent in Pauline's company he recaptured some of his jauntiness and even walked among the crowds in her courtyard, to the alarm of allied officers charged with his safety. They had no cause to fear assassination. The gunner-cadet who had wooed countless diplomats had not lost his touch and soon they were eating out of his hand. An old soldier who had accosted him was recognised as a veteran of the Egyptian campaign. In a few moments the mood of the crowd became curious and then so friendly that the officers of his escort coaxed him inside on the pretence that Pauline wanted to speak with him alone. Then, rested and refreshed, with his head high, he embarked for Elba, leaving France less than a day's journey from the spot where, twenty-one years before, the Buonapartes had come ashore in rags and claimed the Government's subsistence allowance doled out to refugees.

When news of Napoleon's journey south reached Joseph he and Julie left at once for Switzerland. Switzerland and Florence were the two favourite refuges of Buonapartes and Joseph, who seems never to have suffered from Jérôme's financial strictures, bought an estate at Prangins, near Lausanne. Here, with that ability to relax that was the unique characteristic of the eldest Buonaparte, he settled down to admire the splendid views of the Alps and write amiable letters of advice to brothers, sisters and old friends. There is something very droll about Joseph's sudden assumption of the role of family adviser. For years he had been drowning in a flood of advice and censure. Every courier riding to Italy and Spain had brought him pages and pages of closely-written instructions on what to do, what not to do and how to conduct himself as ambassador or king. Even when he was a young man contemplating a switch from church to army his meddling brother had dominated him, and once Napoleon had become head of the State the flow of advice and criticism never ceased. Now all was changed. Joseph was a country gentleman once more and well placed to make personal contact with every loyal Buonapartist, whilst his brother was stranded on an island surrounded by the spies of five nations. Napoleon was not slow to see the advantage of the situation and during the ten months he remained on Elba he used Joseph as a clearing-house, Joseph entering upon the task with enormous zest. He wrote to Napoleon about everything that was happening or was likely to happen on the mainland and Napoleon treated his information with a seriousness that must have been gratifying. In a letter written in July the exile discussed the conduct of his brother-in-law Murat, still sitting gingerly upon the very edge of the Neapolitan throne. 'Send someone to him with all speed,' he wrote, 'and write to him frankly on the iniquity of his conduct. Write also to the Queen on her ingratitude which nothing can justify and which revolts even the Allies.' Joseph complied and the composition of such a letter probably gave him satisfaction. Another subject upon which Joseph wrote long letters was that of various assassination plots against the Emperor's life, and these were not all frivolous, for there were men on the fringe of the political scene who would have given a good deal to see Napoleon dead. There were also numbers of adventurers ready to work for the plotters if they were paid in cash and guaranteed against arrest. One such man was our old friend Maubreuil who had used the horsewhip on his mistress and her lover in Westphalia some years before. Maubreuil came into prominence again during the first days of the Restoration by trailing his Legion of Honour badge at his horse's tail and also as the perpetrator of a cowardly attack upon Jérôme's wife, Catherine, when he and a band of ruffians made off with her cash and jewels. Evidently he enjoyed protection in high places for when Catherine complained to Louis XVIII, and her jewels and part of her money were restored to her, Maubreuil went unpunished. It is almost certain that this man had been hired for this purpose and that he was involved in a plot to kill Napoleon during his journey to the coast. On two occasions Joseph was able to warn Napoleon of the plans of would-be assassins, with the result that all suspicious characters in Elba were arrested before an attempt could be made. It is probable that the men behind these plots were members of the Tugendbund, the German liberation movement, and that none of the major powers were involved.

Alone among Buonapartes who had held on to power Murat and his wife were discovering that the role of renegade has certain handicaps. Nobody trusted them, certainly not their Austrian friends, and their treachery had earned them the hatred of all Buonapartists. It had also cost Caroline the good opinion of her mother, for Madame Mère found it difficult to forgive an act of such disloyalty to the family. Arriving in Rome soon after the abdication the old lady received a gift of eight beautiful horses from the royal stable of Naples. She returned them with the message, 'I have a horror of traitors and treasons.' But Caroline was exceptionally thick-skinned and made renewed overtures of friendship, declaring that what had occurred was not her fault, that she had had nothing to do with Murat's defection and that 'she had been unable to command her husband'. Madame Mère rarely laughed but she must have smiled at this excuse and if Napoleon's correspondence on the subject is to be trusted she replied, 'It was only over your dead body that your husband should have been able to pierce your brother, your benefactor and your master.'

In the political sphere all was far from well with the King and Queen of Naples. Their treaty with Austria had not been ratified and their position remained desperately uncertain, while the Pope continued to press for the return of the Neapolitan Bourbons. The lurid proclamation Murat had issued when he abandoned the Emperor had disgusted even those who were willing to see the Empire dissolved in order to save France from civil war. In this broadsheet Murat had declared that 'he had been forced to choose between crime and virtue'. Napoleon, who had identified the real traitor, subsequently excused Murat's part in the affair when commenting upon it at St Helena some years later. 'I always knew that Murat was wrong-headed' he said, 'but I thought he was attached to me. It was Caroline who was at the bottom of that betrayal.'

Jérôme, consoled by the prospect of a regular income under the terms of the abdication, followed Joseph to Switzerland when the Bourbons returned to Paris. It would not have excited much comment if Catherine had used this opportunity to desert him, for his reputation as a libertine was a byword in the courts of Europe but Catherine was the type of wife, by no means uncommon, who makes light of casual infidelities on the part of a good-natured husband. When her father ordered her to abandon Jérôme and return to Württemberg she refused, stating her reasons in a letter that goes some way to explain why Madame Mère regarded Catherine as her favourite daughter-in-law. 'Married to the king without knowing him, influenced at that epoch by great political interests, I attached myself to him,' she wrote to her father. 'I bear today his child in my bosom. During seven years he has rendered me happy by the most amiable and kindest conduct but even had he been the worst of husbands and made me unhappy, I would not abandon him in his misfortune. I shall never separate my interests from his. My resolution is firm upon the point; it is inspired by both affection and honour.' The letter does Catherine great credit and helps to explain why Jérôme, notwithstanding his reckless manner of living, his crazy extravagance and his sensuality, survived all the ups and down of life without making enemies.

Catherine's family, particularly her brother who had always

been welcomed in Westphalia, did their utmost to make her change her mind but she would not and when the pressure on her became intolerable she appealed to the Czar for passports to Switzerland. Alexander, always courteous towards ladies in distress, granted them and it was during Catherine's journey south that she was stopped and robbed by Maubreuil. She had to sit in the courtyard of an inn and watch her luggage ransacked and when the thieves had ridden off with her money and jewels she wrote a dignified letter of complaint to the Czar. Alexander, enraged that a woman bearing his passports should be so treated, arrested Maubreuil and his associates and recovered the jewels and part of the money. Luckily for the bandits they were released from custody before the Buonaparte faction regained control of the country.

In the meantime Catherine continued her journey to Switzerland and on the way she met the Emperor travelling into exile. They embraced affectionately and Catherine was greatly moved by the encounter. After a brief stay in Switzerland Jérôme and Catherine moved on to Trieste and were living there when news of the Emperor's escape was broadcast in the streets.

Louis did not take his brother's advice and retire to Switzerland but made his way to Rome and subsequently to Florence where he made his home. He occupied his time revising poems and novels he had written during his exile in Austria but presently a more congenial task occupied his attention, an acrimonious lawsuit waged against his estranged wife Hortense for the custody of their two sons, still living with their mother in France. Hortense had little inclination to separate herself from her children and less to be reconciled with the husband she detested, so the suit dragged on and on until the law decided in favour of the father. The decision, however, was not implemented, for with Napoleon's return all thought of sending the boys out of France was forgotten and Louis remained alone in Florence to brood on his wrongs.

The summer of 1814 was a gloomy season for Hortense. Not long after Napoleon had gone into exile Josephine died very suddenly at Malmaison. The discarded woman had enjoyed a brief Indian summer of popularity after the abdication and in her role as a wronged wife she was patronised by all the sovereigns and high-ranking officers who arrived in Paris as conquerors. The Czar himself called upon her and so did the King of Prussia, and as summer advanced her château became a rendezvous for everyone of note in the capital. Then, on May 25th, she was taken ill with diphtheria and four days later she was dead. The Czar behaved extremely well towards her sorrowing son and daughter, so well indeed that Napoleon, on his return, regarded Hortense's stay in France as an act of personal disloyalty to him.

With Josephine's death the long feud between the Beauharnais and the Buonapartes would have ended had it not been for the tug-of-war Hortense and Louis were waging over possession of their children. As it was the quarrel continued in a minor key and Hortense, in her memoirs, struck some telling blows at the men and women who had tried so hard and for so long to ruin her mother. Final honours in this sordid squabble go to Josephine, for on the day she was taken ill she was to have entertained the Czar who – more than any one person – had reduced the Buonapartes from ruling sovereigns to pensioners of State.

Nobody welcomed the end of the war so cordially as did Lucien. For more than three years he had been the social lion of rural Worcestershire and Shropshire, writing and presenting his plays, polishing the cantos of his epic poems, drawing up educational schedules for his family and making the most of his comfortable detention in England. However, he was really bored with the life and was beginning to tire of the eager provincials who visited him, and he yearned for the sophisticated society of Rome and for Italian sunshine. The day after the news of the abdication had reached him he wrote to Pius asking for a papal title and His Holiness obliged, creating him Prince of Canino and saying he was welcome to return to Italy if he wished. Lucien was overjoyed. He packed, marshalled his family and set off at once for Rome and here, for the first time in years, he was able to embrace various members of his family, including his mother, Louis and Caroline, all of whom were happy to welcome him back to the family circle. He possessed more wealth than any of them except Joseph and shortly after his arrival devoted some of his tremendous energy to the smelting of iron. It was the latter interest which proved the means of healing the breach between the two brothers, for Elba was rich in iron deposits and Lucien wrote to Elba's new sovereign for a supply of ore to use in his furnaces. The exchange of business letters laid the foundation for a reconciliation and the old quarrel, buried under the magnitude of the disasters that had overwhelmed the family, was patched up. From then on it was Louis, Lucien's understudy, who remained at a distance.

Elisa was nursing a new grudge against her sister Caroline. When Murat had declared for the Allies his troops had invaded his sister-in-law's domains and Elisa had been obliged to take refuge in Bologna where she was captured by the Austrians. The presence of Madame Mère, backed by that eternal hanger-on, Uncle Fesch, effected a reconciliation during the uneasy period that followed the abdication and private quarrels were forgotten in the general eclipse of family fortunes. Notwithstanding the general amnesty, however, Elisa must have found Caroline's survival as a queen very hard to accept in view of her own losses in rank and income.

In October, when Europe had begun to settle down and the powers were engaged in unravelling the tangle into which European affairs had drifted since the first triumphs in Italy nearly twenty years before, Pauline made good her promise to share Napoleon's exile and joined her brother and Madame Mère on Elba. She had, perhaps, less to thank him for than any of her brothers and sisters but she had the warmest heart in the family and was genuinely sorry for him. Her arrival in Elba was a sensation and soon the little island was a whirl of balls and carnivals that bewildered the simple islanders, already dazed by Napoleonic reforms. Napoleon delighted in his sister's company and it is on the strength of an intercepted letter from Elba that denigrators of Napoleon claim proof of an incestuous relationship between brother and sister. Pauline is supposed to have expressed boredom with life on the island and complained of a shortage of lovers, remarking

'Since I've been here I've only this rotten old man.' The Bourbon faction made the most of this remark but those who took it at face value were probably unfamiliar with Pauline's curious sense of humour and in any case it has come down to us via Mounier, a former secretary, who got it from Bougnot, a police agent. Because of its doubtful source the slander has been rejected by most historians.

Pauline had managed to salvage her fortune in the general ruin that surrounded the family and her money was extremely welcome to Napoleon, for so far not one five-france piece of the promised pension had reached him in Elba and he was forced to borrow large sums from his mother and sister. In handing over her hoarded pension Madame Mère might have reminded her son that she had warned him a time would come when he would have reason to be grateful for her thrift.

The stupidity of the Bourbons prior to the Revolution was equalled and even surpassed by their tactlessness and arrogance on their return to France. During the twenty odd years that they had been absent the country had produced a race of heroes and not all of them were dead. Three hundred thousand prisoners of war, many of them veterans who had contributed to triumphs at Austerlitz, Jena and Wagram, returned to France under the terms of the armistice and men who had been fêted and pampered by the Empire now found themselves penniless outcasts, fortunate if they could steer clear of the police and earn enough money to keep alive. Marshals of the Empire, whose names had become legends in their lifetime, were snubbed by the émigrés and saw their wives reduced to tears by contemptuous nobles who had been abroad since the days of the Terror. Frustrated and angry, the rank and file of the army were soon disenchanted with legitimacy and gathered in cafés to reminisce about the great days, their memories of the Russian campaign and disasters in Spain and Germany, climaxed by the unpleasant present. And all the time the man on Elba, and his hundreds of agents scattered through France and Italy, watched and listened, weighing the chance of converting popular discontent into a rising against a royal family restored to the throne by foreign bayonets. Word came from Lucien in Italy that Italians in the north were not taking kindly to the restored Habsburgs and Murat, afraid that his treaty with Austria would not be ratified, began to consider what he and Caroline should do if one day France invited Napoleon back to Paris. Joseph, living quietly in Switzerland, compiled his reports and Jérôme, in Trieste, continued to employ three aides-de-camp in spite of near-penury. Louis kept to himself, muttering threats about the woman who had deprived him of his children. Caroline and Murat did their utmost to recapture the confidence of the Buonapartes, explaining over and over again why they had been compelled to side with the enemies of France. Pauline, who had never wasted a thought on politics, beguiled the island with her wit and social graces. In Vienna the powers wrangled and argued, seemingly unaware that they were rebuilding the old order on the peak of an active volcano. Then, to the terror of the congressmen, the delight of the veterans and the amusement of the unconcerned, it happened. On the night of February 26th eleven hundred men, the entire army of Elba, were secretly embarked on seven small vessels and by March 1st, less than ten months after he had been cast out, Napoleon landed near Cannes and began his march on Paris. Pauline had been coaxed into politics after all. On the night Napoleon and his Guard slipped away she gave a spectacular ball, a diversion that deceived every enemy agent on the island.

There had never been a more audacious adventure. Not even the attack on Egypt or the passage over the Alps, compared with this, a gamble in which the stakes were all or nothing. Perhaps the best illustration of Napoleon's progress north can be found in a French newspaper that summarised the reaction of the royalist press. Here is the calendar of events, as published at the time:

February 25th: The *Exterminator* has signed a treaty offensive and defensive; it is not known with whom.

February 26th: The *Corsican* has left the island of Elba.

March 1st: *Buonaparte* has disembarked at Cannes
             with eleven hundred men.
March 7th: *General Buonaparte* has taken Grenoble.
March 10th: *Napoleon* has entered Lyons.
March 19th: *The Emperor* reached Fontainebleau today.
March 19th: *His Imperial Majesty* is expected at the
             Tuileries tomorrow.

People flocked to him everywhere but few more swiftly or un-
conditionally than his family, that assortment of ex-kings and imperial princesses who, in his brief absence, had already begun to
slip into obscurity.

Joseph, Lucien, Caroline and Murat were undoubtedly aware
of Napoleon's intention to make a bid for the Bourbon throne at
the earliest opportunity, but they had no precise foreknowledge
of the actual time and place and the first reliable news of the
event reached them as Napoleon entered Grenoble and the land-
slide in his favour had begun. Joseph, for once, acted promptly.
He wrote urging Murat to declare war on his new Austrian friends
and then set off to Paris, arriving only two days after Napoleon's
entry. Julie, his wife, was already in the capital, having gone there
shortly before Napoleon left Elba to try to regain possession of
Montefontaine, their château. She was therefore on the spot to
welcome the Emperor when he made his way through hysterical
crowds to the Tuileries on the night of March 20th, the fourth
anniversary of the birth of the King of Rome. Lucien arrived
shortly afterwards and very little seems to have been said about
the prolonged quarrel between the brothers. Joseph reoccupied
his seat in the House of Peers and Lucien would have joined him
there had not some pedant pointed out that Lucien had never been
an active Imperial Prince and was therefore unqualified to sit
among the elect. This quibble would have touched off a family
explosion in the old days, now it passed unnoticed. Lucien was
content to take up his duties in the Chamber of Deputies and here
he set about the familiar task of consolidating Buonaparte interests. During the next few weeks both he and Joseph stood like
rocks against conflicting tides of public opinion.

Jérôme's rush to Paris was chequered with adventures. Hearing the great news in his retreat at Trieste he said goodbye to the faithful Catherine (who had just presented him with an heir after seven years of marriage) and left in disguise, sailing to Naples, where he met his mother and sisters; then, for some unexplained reason, he went on to Florence where he narrowly escaped capture by the Austrians. Eluding them he withdrew to Naples and after a conference with his mother and Cardinal Fesch all three decided to risk a return to France by sea as the least dangerous alternative. They went via Corsica, dodged the British patrol vessels and landed at the exact point on the coast where Napoleon had put ashore on March 1st.

From here on Jérôme's journey north became a repetition of his brother's triumph. People pressed round him and at Lyons he ran into Barras, the man who had headed the Directory in the days before the *coup d'état* in 1799. The old schemer was annoyed by the royal airs Jérôme was giving himself as he walked about amid the cheering crowds exclaiming, 'Ah, we Buonapartes are on the mend again!' On reaching Paris, accompanied by his mother and uncle, the ex-King of Westphalia was received with great cordiality by his brother. All the old disagreements were forgotten in the dramatic circumstances of the family reunion and at the gathering in the Champ de Mai three brothers supported the Emperor, Joseph and Jérôme as kings on his right and Lucien, the old republican, on his left. The three girls remained in Italy, Caroline trying without success to rouse the martial spirit of the Neapolitans. One wonders what Madame Mère thought of this latest adventure and whether it warmed her heart to see her children working in harmony again. Before Napoleon had left Elba he had asked her advice and she had replied, enigmatically, 'Follow your destiny, my son.' Of all her children only Louis remained aloof in Florence, adamant in refusing to recommit himself, but even he wrote a long, pompous letter to Napoleon which the exile was to recall with sardonic amusement on St Helena. 'It was almost an ultimatum' Napoleon reflected, 'laying down the conditions on which he would return' and like an ultimatum it was rejected, for Louis had demanded that he should now be allowed to divorce Hortense and Napoleon would not hear of it. He preferred to resign himself to the loss of Louis' friendship and announced that his brother's conduct 'was caused by the chronic state of his health which had warped his outlook and paralysed him on one side'.

Louis could be dismissed as a misanthrope but good advice on how to cope with the present situation came readily from Joseph and Lucien, both of whom urged Napoleon to forestall reaction from the Great Powers by reabdicating in favour of his four-year-old son. At first he was inclined to agree with them, saying that he had returned to France not as a conqueror who wished to turn Europe upside down again but as guarantor of the gains of the Revolution. There were, however, considerable difficulties in the way of his adopting his brothers' advice. The King of Rome was now a closely-guarded prisoner in the hands of his Austrian grandfather and news came that Marie-Louise had no wish to return to her husband, having been professionally seduced by a man attached to her household for this very purpose. The seducer was a one-eyed Austrian cavalryman called Neipperg and the person who gave him his brief was Francis, his victim's father, an autocrat who had once described Napoleon Buonaparte as 'The Beast of the Apocalypse'. In these circumstances Napoleon had no choice but to submit to the popular clamour of his more enthusiastic supporters and reject the plan of standing down in favour of his son. He was obliged also to defend himself because the Allies, particularly Britain and Prussia, remained implacable and their armies were already on the march.

He set about organising the army with his customary energy and ex-prisoners of war who had rotted in English hulks and German fortresses flocked to his eagles in their thousands. At the head of one division of veterans he placed his brother Jérôme, giving him a third chance to win glory on the field of battle.

It was a very subordinate command, that of a mere general of division under Corps Commander Reille, but Jérôme did not complain. Like Lucien he was alive to the urgency of the moment and for once he could swallow his pride in the common cause.

Before leaving Paris for the trial of strength south of Brussels

Napoleon, who had forgiven Hortense for her flirtation with the Czar, took his stepdaughter aside and proposed that they should make a sentimental journey to Malmaison where Josephine had died ten months previously. Together they entered the château but at the door of the room in which his wife had died he told Hortense to wait and went in alone. When he emerged she noticed that his eyes were red with weeping.

He was away again, up the road to Charleroi to drive a great wedge between Wellington and Blücher. Behind them, the foremost of his enemies, were the vast armies of the Czar and of Austria and to the north was the Swedish infantry of the renegade Bernadotte, Joseph's brother-in-law. The crowds cheered him as he left Paris, but in the city were many secret doubters and not a few potential traitors. He was aware of this and had guarded against a reaction as best he could. Joseph and Lucien remained in Paris to hold together the tenuous threads of political support and at the Ministry of War was the one Imperial marshal whose record proved that he could be trusted, no matter how much pressure was applied. For here, holding Paris in a watchful grip, was the Iron Marshal Davout, the bald-headed martinet who had bullied Jérôme into handing over his entire income to pay for the French garrison of Westphalia and who had later resisted all the blandishments of the Bourbons to desert the man whom he had served with complete fidelity since the French had chased the Mamelukes up the Nile in 1798.

For the rest trusted friends were few among the leaders of the best-equipped army France had ever fielded. Soult, the stubborn defender of the Pyrenees, was serving as Chief of Staff and Ney, the hero of the Moscow retreat, commanded a wing. Suchet was in the south, Mortier was loyal but down with sciatica and all the other marshals were dead, neutral or opposed to him. Of his family only Jérôme rode beside him and Jérôme was moving towards a time and place where a single day's fighting would go a long way towards rehabilitating him as a man, a soldier and a brother.

On June 14th Napoleon's wing smashed the Prussians at Ligny whilst Ney's command attacked the British at Quatre Bras, a few miles away. General Reille's corps was actively engaged in this battle and at the head of division, exposed to the full blast of British musketry, was Jérôme, whose conduct that day was that of a front-line soldier. Time and again Jérôme's division attacked the British squares, inflicting and sustaining severe losses. Among the casualties in the ranks of the enemy was the Duke of Brunswick, whose inheritance had been taken from him to form part of the kingdom of Westphalia. In 1809 the Duke had led his 'Legion of Vengeance' on its epic march through Germany to the sea and had escaped to Britain to wait for better times. So Jérôme had his revenge after all, for it was the Duke of Brunswick's success on this occasion that had so enraged Napoleon and all but permanently destroyed their friendship. Yet Quatre Bras, notwithstanding the severe damage inflicted upon the British, was not a victory and Wellington's mixed army withdrew to the plateau of Mont St Jean. Jérôme, after having a wound dressed, retired from the field and took supper at the 'King of Spain Inn' close by.

It was here that a chance piece of information reached him via a waiter and if it had been put to good use it might have altered the course of history. On the previous day Wellington had eaten at the same inn and the waiter had overheard an English aide-de-camp mention that the British hoped to join up with the Prussians in the Forest of Soignés. The next morning, whilst Napoleon was at breakfast at Le Caillou, Jérôme came in with the report but Napoleon, convinced that he had thoroughly defeated and scattered the Prussian army at Ligny, dismissed the information as an impossibility. The two wings of the French army reunited and orders were given to advance on Brussels.

Jérôme's conduct on the field of Waterloo was that of an extremely courageous subaltern but an over-enthusiastic general of division. Reille's corps, to which he was attached, was given the task of demonstrating against Hougomont, a château outpost on the right of the British line, but the attack was never intended to be more than a demonstration to occupy the enemy's attention whilst the main French assault was launched against Wellington's centre.

The château was strongly garrisoned and when the 6th Division advanced, led by Jérôme in person, it was received by heavy fire. Bauduin, commander of the 1st Brigade, was killed at once but Jérôme continued to advance until his men had gained the Hougomont wood and orchard, which was cleared after an hour's fighting. At 1 am, two hours after the main battle had begun, the French infantry were within thirty paces of the château's walls and Jérôme had achieved his objective. All he needed to do was to consolidate and keep the British right wing engaged, but glory had eluded him for too many years and reckless enthusiasm took possession. Against the advice of his Chief of Staff he launched his men in another furious attack, bringing up the 2nd brigade and sending the survivors of the 1st off to the left to attack on the flank. The hand-to-hand fighting in and around Hougomont gate proved the fiercest of the day. Reckless of their losses the French advanced to the walls and actually battered down the gate but they were massacred as they entered the courtyard and when four companies of Coldstream Guards rushed up to reinforce the hard-pressed garrison the French had to retreat to the wood, leaving half their numbers under the walls.

Preoccupied with the main assault Napoleon did not call Jérôme to his side until almost the whole of Reille's corps had been committed, and from beginning as a feint the attack upon Hougomont had become a major battle. The fury of the attack continued to mount all the afternoon until the château and most of the farm buildings had been burned and the garrison driven to the chapel and gardener's cottage. The price paid by the attackers for this partial success was the sacrifice of vital French reserves and the consequent failure by Ney to breach Wellington's centre. Furiously assaulting the plateau later in the day the hero of the Russian retreat sent urgent requests for reserves, and Napoleon, looking over his shoulder at the blazing Hougomont, snapped, 'Reserves? Where does he think he can find them?' The failure of the attack, however, and its disastrous effects upon the outcome of the battle as a whole, was not solely due to Jérôme's impetuous conduct. Part of the blame was Reille's, for as an experienced corps commander he should have checked the wastage. Quite apart from this the individual recklessness of a rank and file with so many old scores to pay off is another factor to be taken into consideration. Be that as it may, Jérôme's conduct on this day did much to vindicate his character and the story of his gallantry at Waterloo passed into legend. In a long letter written to his wife soon after the battle Jérôme speaks of Napoleon's reaction to his conduct and says the Emperor exclaimed, 'It is impossible to fight better! Now that you are reduced to two battalions stay in order to go wherever there may be danger!' It is a theatrical comment from a man engaged in a life-and-death struggle but Napoleon was undoubtedly, delighted with Jérôme's last-minute appearance as a hero.

It needed more than one man's heroism, however, to save the day for Napoleon. By dusk the splendid cavalry of the Imperial Army had been squandered in useless charges against the British squares and what reserves remained were dribbled away in attempts to check the advance of Blücher on the French right. The final assault of the Old Guard was a complete failure and by ten o'clock the rout had begun, the victors of Austerlitz, Jena, Friedland and Wagram streaming down the road to Charleroi to the cry of 'Sauve qui peut'.

For a final, graphic description of that night of panic we turn again to Jérôme's letter to Catherine, written during the retreat. He says: 'The Emperor was carried along, there was no one to give orders. I reached Avesnes next day, having been at the rearguard with one battalion and one squadron. I found here neither Emperor nor the marshals who had gone on before. I made unheard-of efforts to rally the remains of the army and at length succeeded in rallying 18,000 infantry and 3,000 cavalry, with twelve guns with which I arrived at Laon on the 21st.' Here Soult took command and Jérôme made for Soissons and then Paris, where they were already crying news of Napoleon's second abdication in favour of his son. En route the battered and breathless ex-king of Westphalia received a letter praising his conduct in the field. The author was Marshal Davout who had once plagued him for the revenues of his fairy-tale realm.

CHAPTER THIRTEEN

*'I see one man between us and peace; let him speak and the country
will be saved!'*

Lacoste, addressing the Chamber
of Deputies, June 1815

HE CAME RUMBLING into Paris on the morning of June 21st, three
days after the battle, an exhausted, hesitant, semi-hysterical man
without an army, and, if one discounts some bedraggled officers
and a few old grenadiers, even a guard. He was already talking of
abdication and this for the third time in a matter of fifteen months.
On the morning after disaster, from Phillipville, he had written
to Joseph in his familiar strain of fantasy, declaring 'all is not
lost . . . when I reassemble my forces I shall have 150,000 men . . .
I will use carriage horses to drag the guns . . . raise 100,000 men by
conscription and arm them with muskets taken from royalists',
but now reaction had set in and he saw the future for what it was,
black with dissolution and defeat. What he craved at that moment
was not advice on how best to meet a new invasion but a bath, a
hot bath of the kind that had restored him so often in the past.
He went to the home of Caulaincourt, the man who had been his
sole companion on that fantastic sleigh-ride across Europe in
December 1812, and while he was bathing Caulaincourt assembled
the Imperial Council to discuss what should and could be done.

Joseph and Lucien came at once, the one solemnly loyal, the
other in a state of suppressed excitement that reminded those
about him of the Lucien who broke the tensions of Brumaire, in
1799. Joseph said very little but Lucien harangued his brother on
the wisdom of audacity, urging him to disperse both chambers
and make himself supreme dictator with direct access to the nation.

It was strange that Lucien, the diehard republican, should give such advice but stranger still that Carnot, a survivor of the plotters against Robespierre, should second the proposal. Napoleon listened, rejecting an appeal to make a personal appearance before the Chamber of Deputies and still half-resolved to make a second end of it all by standing down in favour of his four-year-old son, the prisoner in Vienna. The Chambers, they told him, were in a state of chaos with deputies stopping every fugitive from Waterloo and trying to assess the magnitude of the disaster. Opinions varied sharply. Some said all was lost and that no French troops stood between Paris and the Anglo-Prussian army, others that Marshal Grouchy was still in command of sixty thousand men and that Soult and Jérôme were assembling more every hour. But whatever was true of the military situation there seemed to be at least four distinct currents of opinion within the Chamber of Deputies. Some were for trading with the Allies on the basis of Napoleon's abdication in favour of the King of Rome, for this at least would keep the Bourbons out of France. Others favoured the Orléanist branch of of the royal house, while a third section sided with Lucien and urged a backs-to-the-wall defence of Paris. There was a fourth faction, recruited from men who had helped to make the Revolution when Napoleon was a lieutenant of artillery, and these advised the establishment of a federalised republic. Lucien was sent to try and subdue the uproar and soon proved that years of retirement from the politcal scene had not impaired his skill as a rhetorician. The plan, or apology for a plan that had emerged from the deliberations of the Imperial Councillors, was to submit the final decision to a committee of ten deputies, five to be chosen from each chamber, but when Deputy Lacoste openly attacked Napoleon, insisting on his immediate withdrawal from the country, Lucien ceased juggling with motions and amendments and rushed to his brother's defence. In reply to a charge that France was now at the mercy of the Allies he shouted, 'What? Shall we still have the weakness to believe the words of our enemies? When victory was for the first time faithless did they not swear, in the presence of God and man, that they would respect our independence and our laws? Let us not fall a second time into the snare set for our trust and credulity! Their aim, in endeavouring to separate the nation from the Emperor, is to disunite in order to vanquish us and replunge France more easily into that degradation and slavery from which his return delivered us!' It was heady stuff and in 1799 it might have carried the day. Not now however; it needed far more than Lucien's oratory to convince deputies that Napoleon was not necessarily synonymous with fresh conscriptions, fresh wars of conquests, more demands upon the blood and purse of the nation. Far too many young men had marched off to die in foreign lands and many listening to Lucien's impassioned speech could remember when the crowned heads of Europe had quarrelled instead of forming an alliance against the common enemy, General Buonaparte. One such man, the famous Lafayette who had fought beside the American colonists a generation ago, reminded his colleagues of the tremendous sacrifices France had made to sustain the ambition of the man awaiting the outcome of this debate. 'You accuse us of failing in our duties towards Napoleon,' he said, quietly. 'Have you forgotten all we have done for him? Have you forgotten that we followed him to the sands of Africa and in the deserts of Russia, while the bones of our sons and brethren everywhere attest our fidelity?'

At this deputies everywhere sprang to their feet and in the ensuing uproar it was impossible for any one man to sway the assembly either for or against Napoleon. The motion to appoint the Committee of Ten was carried but it was soon evident that a majority in the chamber would demand his deposition if he did not voluntarily abdicate. Napoleon's resolution to remain Emperor and defy the advancing Allies was shaken when the chamber adjourned for an hour in order to give him time to consider and then, as though he was suddenly persuaded that he was flogging a dead horse, Lucien admitted that further resistance to the clamour was useless. Backed by Joseph he advised qualified submission and Napoleon, his nerves at breaking point, accepted their advice. 'Write to these gentlemen to make themselves easy,' he said, 'they shall soon be satisfied.'

So Lucien wrote. In the years that had passed since he had gone into exile in Rome rather than sacrifice his wife to Napoleon's ambition he had gained great experience in literary self expression. Now, without help or advice from any of them, he composed the deed of renunciation, beginning 'Declaration to the French people'; and no document composed under such severe emotional stress could be more lucid or explicit. It was brief but it said everything that needed to be said. The King of Rome was appointed Napoleon's successor, a Council of Regency was proposed to govern during the child's minority, and the document concluded with an appeal to all to work for the safety and continuance of an independent nation. Napoleon read it through and signed without comment. It was the 22nd day of June. Only four days had passed since the opening of the cannonade at Waterloo.

In the event the formal renunciation was not taken seriously. The deputies continued to wrangle, and no one knew what would happen when Wellington and Blücher appeared at the gates. Only a few resolute men showed the steadiness of professional gamblers and one of these was Fouché, once Napoleon's Chief of Police and himself a former terrorist. Fouché had long since abandoned the terrorist creed and was now a strong supporter of the brother of the man he had helped to send to the guillotine. Enormously experienced in the art of survival, he saw clearly that nothing could be solved so long as Napoleon remained in Paris. He was seconded by Talleyrand, another who had mastered the art of remaining afloat whilst others drowned. Between them Fouché and Talleyrand persuaded the Buonaparte family to leave for Malmaison.

Napoleon raised no objection. He offered his services to the provisional government as a commander of its military forces (promising to retire as soon as they were victorious) but when this offer was rejected he and his forlorn few drove off to the house where Josephine had received the conquerors of 1814. The immediate problem was where the Emperor should go now. Blücher had sworn to kill him and the most optimistic among them realised that the King of Rome would never rule as Napoleon II. Yet there was still evidence of loyalty and unselfishness among the fugitives who gathered round him at Malmaison. Joseph and Lucien were there and Madame Mère, and Hortense, who offered to sew a diamond necklace into his belt, and Hortense's lover, de Flahaut, now a general. Plans were put forward, considered and rejected. A Mr Willing, one of those curious Americans who flit across the stage of every European tragedy, offered him a valet's passport and a specially built hogshead in which he could hide until an American vessel had passed the danger zone, but he could make no provision for Napoleon's friends and on these grounds the offer was refused. It would have been refused in any case. One cannot ask a man who has been flattered by kings and emperors to disguise himself as a valet and hide in a hogshead half-full of water. Charles II cheerfully performed such antics after Worcester, but Charles had a great sense of humour.

With the Allies on the point of entering Paris there was no profit to be gained by debating various possibilities beside Josephine's flower-beds at Malmaison. Deputies were already arriving at the château with instructions to keep Napoleon under surveillance and Hortense, who could be relied upon to improve upon any dramatic situation exclaimed: 'O my God! That Napoleon should be a prisoner at Malmaison!' On June 29th, four days after the arrival of the Imperial nucleus, he took to the road again, this time for Rochefort via Tours, Limoges, Cognac and Saintes. The journey was not without its dangers although there was no repetition of mob violence on the scale of the journey south the previous year, and the provincials treated him with respect. Lucien did not accompany him, for he and Madame Mère had decided to return to Rome. Before Napoleon entered the carriage that was to carry him across France for the last time mother and son took dignified leave of one another. They never met again and at Saintes, near the end of his journey, Napoleon said a final goodbye to the last of his family, Joseph, who had followed him and had been arrested and released en route.

If Waterloo had been Jérôme's hour this was Joseph's. The eldest Buonaparte had already come to share Madame Mère's doubts about the future and had made his own arrangements to sail to America. Now, with Napoleon still undecided what to do and where to go, Joseph came forward with an offer that stamps him, notwithstanding his many egregious failures, as a man of character. Pointing out the similarity of features between himself and Napoleon he proposed that they should change places, that Napoleon should board the American brig reserved for Joseph and that he – disguised as the fugitive Emperor – should try and run the British blockade in the Atlantic. Napoleon was touched but he refused the offer pointblank and Joseph left him, not for a port of embarkation but to hang about in the immediate area awaiting definite news of his brother's fate. Only when he was told that Napoleon had surrendered to Captain Maitland of the *Bellerophon* did he leave for Bordeaux and board his brig for Charleston, South Carolina. He crossed the Atlantic alone. Julie could never be persuaded to brave the voyage and join her husband in exile.

Two French cruisers awaited him off La Rochelle and if he had been able to obtain a safe-conduct he would have sailed at once, but this was refused and the coast was swarming with British warships, each on the lookout for the biggest prize of all. Various schemes were discussed and some might have had a chance of success, but each proposal entailed a sacrifice of dignity and dignity was all that was left to him now. A Danish captain offered him a passage and a group of naval cadets fitted out a small craft with a concealed cavity in which he might hide while his crew of boys ran the gauntlet. In the end he made up his mind to surrender to Britain and sent an aide-de-camp to the Prince Regent with a letter pledging himself to retire to a country estate in the manner of Lucien after his capture in 1811.

The aide-de-camp was not even allowed to land and Captain Maitland, although courteous, could make no promise beyond that of conveying the Emperor as prisoner to England. It was now almost a month after Waterloo and the Bourbons and their fol-lowers were swarming in Paris. The family was dispersed again, Joseph on his way to Charleston with a cargo of brandy, Lucien and Madame Mère asking for papal protection, Jérôme a fugitive travelling through France in disguise, the girls and Louis in Italy, Hortense reviewing the wreck of her fortunes and being snubbed by her former patron, the Czar of Russia. On July 15th he went aboard with his little suite and the next day the *Bellerophon* set sail for the Lizard. At Plymouth men who had been at war with him for almost twenty years and boys and girls who had been taught to regard him as the devil put out in small boats to row round and round the anchored vessel to get a glimpse of Boney, the Corsican Ogre whose name had been used to frighten them in their nurseries. He stood on the poop deck waving his hat at them and they waved back, shouting excitedly.

By now Joseph had got away, reaching not Charleston but New York where, after being mistaken for Carnot, he was received with courtesy and given the best suite in the City Hotel. Lucien, Madame Mère, Elisa and Pauline had been granted protection by that amiable man, Pius VII, who refused to bear the family a grudge and extended a warm welcome to all. Louis was still in Florence and in no need of protection for he had played no part in the last adventure. Jérôme, who had fought at Waterloo and was therefore in a different category, was appealing, so far in vain, for access to his wife and child in Württemberg. In the immediate period following Waterloo it was Caroline, Queen of Naples, whose future was more uncertain than that of any of them, excluding the prisoner in the *Bellerophon*, for Murat was also a fugitive and his Queen was alone in a city about to welcome its hereditary sovereign.

Murat's impulsive attack upon his new friends, the Austrians, had been a disaster. Even had Waterloo proved a victory for the French it is doubtful whether the Gascon King of Naples would have avoided the penalty for this his second act of treachery. As soon as he heard of Napoleon's flight from Elba Joseph had urged him to throw in his lot with his countrymen but Napoleon, showing more realism than his brother, had written offering to guarantee Murat's realm in return for renewed allegiance, but counselling extreme caution in the handling of his relations with Austria. Murat, as one might expect, took the more dramatic course and on March 16th, barely a fortnight after Napoleon had landed in France and started his advance on Paris, the pantomime king had attacked the Austrians and driven them back on the Po.

Musing on his impetuous action during his exile on St Helena Napoleon commented, 'He first ruined us by abandoning us and then by espousing our cause too warmly!' It was a just conclusion. Murat's attack ruined whatever chance had existed of the powers accepting Napoleon's return without renewing the war and although a brilliant tactician Murat's strategic talents were those of an excitable drummer-boy. Having recovered from the initial surprise the Austrians counter-attacked and soon Murat's Neapolitan army faded away. As their leader galloped for France he may have recalled the opinion Napoleon had once expressed of his Italian troops, 'You can dress them in green, red or blue but they'll run away just the same!' He reached France and waited in Toulon for a summons to Paris, but what came was not a promise of reconciliation but news of Waterloo. Almost alone he took refuge in Corsica and in the meantime Caroline did what she could to stem the tide of reaction in Naples, riding a horse on parade and dressing herself in the uniform of the National Guard. Waterloo extinguished all hope of success however, and when the garrison deserted she followed her brother's example and surrendered to the British, boarding the *Tremendous* and sailing as prisoner to Trieste. On the way there she passed a vessel which was given a royal salute. It carried King Ferdinand, the half-witted king whose throne Caroline and Murat had occupied ever since they succeeded Joseph in 1808. She did not remain in Trieste but was transferred to Vienna and here she assumed the title of the Countess of Lipona, Lipona being an anagram of Napoli. It was here, in late October, that she read in a newspaper the story of Murat's final act of stupidity. It told her that she was now a widow.

Ever since he had rushed across Paris to fetch the guns Napoleon needed to disperse the Paris mob in 1795 the Gascon innkeeper's son had regarded himself as his patron's understudy. He had always, by reason of his marriage to Caroline, taken precedence over the other marshals and once a king nothing could persuade him that he was not Napoleon's equal in statecraft and personal magnetism. The fallacy was to cost him his life. Skulking in

Corsica he let his imagination dwell upon the Emperor's sudden return to France, and his mind toyed with the dramatic possibilities of imitating the Emperor's challenge to troops sent to bar his advance. It seemed to him that this would be an ideal way of regaining his throne, and he began to recruit a band of local Buonapartists to land on the Italian mainland. Just before he was ready to leave he was given a letter from the Austrian Chancellor, Metternich. It was a very patronising document, setting out a list of conditions under which the gracious Austrian Emperor would be prepared to receive him, not as a king but as a private citizen pledged to remain on Austrian soil and taking no part in politics. As a sop Francis added that if he complied with these terms Murat might style himself 'Count of Lipona'.

Distracted, almost penniless and with less than three hundred men under his command, Murat was still the man who had led the cavalry of the Grand Army into action and had ridden, as a conqueror, into half the capitals in Europe. 'A prison then is to be my asylum?' he told the emissary. 'Then it seems there remains nothing but to die like a soldier!' He embarked with his forlorn expedition and landed with twenty-eight companions on the desolate coast of Calabria, but he was not received like a local Napoleon. Instead the Civic Guard rushed on the tiny band, shot some, drove the rest back to their boats and conducted the former commander of the cavalry of the Grand Army to the local lock-up. The Corsicans who had escaped the first volley fled, leaving Murat to his fate. He was stripped of his jewels, wounded in the face, insulted and hustled off to the castle at Pizzo close by. Within four days of his capture a panel of military judges tried him on a charge of treason and their verdict was a foregone conclusion. Within hours of the sentence the prisoner was backed against a wall and shot.

Composure had escaped Joachim Murat all his days but in the face of death he found dignity. A captain was chosen to defend him but the ex-king refused to assist his prosecutors in their attempt to make his trial appear legal. Rejecting the services of the defending officer he said, 'This is not a trial but a condemnation. My accusers are my executioners. I prohibit you to speak in my defence,' and to the 'judge' who asked his name, 'I am Joachim

Murat, King of the Two Sicilies and yours!' In a final letter to his four children, Achille, Letitia, Lucien and Louisa, he said, 'Remember what you *are*, not what you have been.' It was the best advice he ever gave them. He was a Gascon up to the very last moment. As the muskets were levelled he said, 'Aim at the heart, spare the face!' Round his neck was a cameo containing his wife's portrait and he held miniatures of his four children in his hand. He was buried in a chapel that he had ordered to be built when he was king. So the Neapolitan Bourbons disposed of a brave, impulsive, amiable fool, a man who was without either judgment or malice. Two months later, in the garden of the Luxembourg Palace, they shot another celebrated hothead, Marshal Michel Ney, and when an account of Ney's conduct during the Russian campaign was published a year or so later the daughter of Louis XVI exclaimed: 'Oh, if only we had known!' They should have known. They should have made it their business to know.

On October 15th, almost the same hour as a volley closed the life of King Joachim of Naples, the man in whose name these two soldiers fell stepped ashore on a rock in the South Atlantic to begin an exile that was to last five years eight months and end in his death at the age of fifty-one. Of the kin he left behind only Jérôme had difficulty in riding out the last Napoleonic storm.

After Waterloo the Bourbons showed no mercy to the men who had rallied to Napoleon during the Hundred Days. Jérôme's wife Catherine had been practically kidnapped by secret police agents after her husband left Trieste to join his brother, and when he tried to contact his wife Jérôme's position was perilous and there was talk of having him shot like Murat and Ney. He left Paris openly, returned secretly and then went into hiding in the home of a Corsican shoemaker. Eventually, through the good offices of Fouché, he reached the safety of Switzerland and here, after some delays, he obtained permission to re-enter Württemberg. The King had conveniently forgotten the favours he had accepted from Napoleon in the days when France was invincible, and treated his son-in-law severely, laying down harsh conditions which Jérôme must observe if he wished to live with his wife and child. Jérôme accepted the strictures and after a separation that had lasted five months he rejoined his wife at Elgangen. He took the title of Count of Montfort and as such remained in polite detention until his father-in-law's restrictions became so irksome that he preferred to withdraw from Württemberg and to live in Austria. In spite of the reversal of Buonaparte fortunes he had more money than when he was King of Westphalia, for he was able to buy a château near Vienna and a house in Trieste, generally living in Trieste. His income in the post-Waterloo period stemmed from two sources. After fear and hatred of the Buonapartes had subsided somewhat, Catherine managed to persuade her father to grant her an allowance and then she was lucky enough, or persistant enough, to extract a supplementary pension from her cousin, the Czar. On these two incomes Jérôme maintained a comfortable style of living and Catherine kept the debtors at bay. Never, at any time, would she hear a word of criticism against her husband. As long as he remained with her she was happy. At Trieste they sometimes had company. Elisa, the former Grand Duchess of Tuscany, now the Countess of Campignano, had finally left her husband Felice and salvaged a private fortune from the wreck of her fortunes. Always a practical soul and possessing her mother's prudent habits, she now lived in wealth and luxury and it is probable that Jérôme (who continued to live well above his means) borrowed from her when he was unable to borrow from his mother. Old age had not loosened the old lady's purse-strings. Taxed with yet another appeal for funds from her reckless son she replied, 'No! Do as I do! Retrench!' It was advice Jérôme had often been given but had never once taken. Loans notwithstanding, the relationship between the eldest and youngest of the Buonaparte family remained affectionate to the end and when Elisa lay dying it was Jérôme who sat by her bedside and held her hand.

Joseph, now known as the Count of Surveilliers, was well received in America. Soon after his arrival he bought a large country estate on the banks of the Delaware near Bordentown in New Jersey, and began to interest himself in farming. He too possessed a large fortune, the proceeds of prudent investment whilst reigning in Naples and Madrid, and by some means he was able to transfer a large part of his capital to the States where he invested it in public securities and real estate. He lost money on real estate but on the whole he prospered and was able to buy ten farms to add to his property, which became a treasure-house of busts, statues, pictures and antiques of every description. Always a man of taste he indulged it to the full and was soon accepted as one of America's most prosperous and distinguished citizens.

Lucien suffered no penalty for his quixotic championship of Napoleon during the Hundred Days. His close friendship with the Pope stood him and all the other Buonapartes in good stead and he lived mainly in Rome, occupying himself, as of old, with literature and archaeology. By now he had a very large family, two daughters by his first wife and five sons and four daughters by the second. Both marriages had proved ideally happy so that in one sense he was the most successful of the family in spite of or because of the long estrangement that had kept him clear of tumbling thrones. As a writer he never produced anything of note but as an archaeologist he contributed some valuable finds in the field of Tuscan research.

Louis also lived on in Rome where he spent all his time writing novels and historical works, the latter mainly concerned with the Dutch. He also wrote an opera, a tragedy, a romance and a book of poems, but he took no part in political or social life and remained estranged from Hortense. He had at last obtained possession of his elder son, Napoleon Louis, who was a complete stranger to him, and he devoted much time and thought to the boy's education, ultimately marrying him to his first cousin Charlotte, Joseph's second daughter. Pauline remained in Italy after the Hundred Days and Caroline made the best of her enforced residence in Austria, so that by 1820 it looked as though the Buonaparte family would spend the remainder of their lives in cushioned retirement. And so indeed it proved as far as six of them were concerned. Only the seventh, Jérôme, lived on to take his place among the greying veterans and dignitaries whom Napoleon III used to buttress an Empire built on heroic memories.

*

Far away in St Helena the gunner-cadet who had led the children of the Revolution from Lisbon to the Kremlin and back again, was fighting his final and most brilliant campaign. His heir was a prisoner, his family a group of pensioners, his wife the mistress of a one-eyed cavalryman, and he himself was followed wherever he went by redcoat sentries and the malice of his British gaoler, but he did not despair. He fought on with words, hints and complaints, with the ostentatious sale of plate to raise money that he did not need, with broadsides against an excellent climate that was supposed to be digging his grave. Some thought it a dirty and undignified campaign for so distinguished a general but it was his only means of keeping his name alive and his party active and as such it proved remarkably effective. Lucien wrote to him, giving him the kind of news he was allowed to hear and in this way, or through some other channel, he learned of the death of his sister Elisa, the first of the family to die.

Elisa was taken seriously ill at Trieste and died on August 9th, 1820, aged only forty-three years. Jérôme, so the story goes, watched by her bedside for fourteen days and nights. She was the least remarkable of the family and the closest in character to her disciplined, tight-fisted mother. When he learned of the event Napoleon said, 'I thought death had forgotten the family, but since Elisa has been taken I shall soon follow.' He had always been inclined to make fatalistic pronouncements but this one was prophetic. He followed her to the grave within nine months.

He had been growing much stouter but his corpulence was not caused by the sudden cessation of the extremely active life he had led in the past. He was suffering from the disease that had killed his father and was to kill other members of the family, a cancer of the stomach, and from time to time he was in considerable pain. By the early spring of 1821 he was aware of approaching death and fully reconciled to it. He had made his will, a massive document disposing of a great deal of money that he did not possess, and towards the end of April his brain began to cloud so that periods of clarity were interspersed with fantasies and he called on dead friends to attack phantom armies. They watched beside him, the doctors, the quacks and the nonentities who made up his little court, but although news of his failing health had reached the mainland no member of his family was present at the end. It was not for want of trying. Pauline, who loved him, plagued the British authorities for permission to go to St Helena and comfort him as she had done in 1814, and although her own health was poor she wrote to the British Prime Minister begging for a passport to join him without delay. Catherine, Jérôme's wife, also tried but with as little success. Only at the last moment did Lord Liverpool relent and Pauline was given permission to sail, but by then it was too late. Before arrangements could be made word came that he was dead.

The news stunned them all, the family, the marshals, his former subjects and his captors. For more than a generation the word 'Napoleon' had conjured up visions of the Apocalypse, of columns of men pouring across the frontiers, of maps being drawn and redrawn, of splendour and misery, triumph and death, and the bulletin from St Helena brought to those born before the year 1789 a sense of stillness, like the sudden cutting-off of the roar of a torrent. Of all who had flinched from the impact of his gigantic personality perhaps his brothers and sisters were the first to benefit from the change. The tension that had surrounded them eased almost at once and the restrictions that had been laid upon them by nervous governments were relaxed so that they could move about more freely, entertain more openly and put on paper some of their recollections of the last thirty years. And with this new freedom came the glow of reflected glory so that the least of them acquired a new kind of distinction, a direct legacy of their relationship with the Titan.

Joseph, in New Jersey, had already gathered round him a miniature court made up of former courtiers and servants and here he might have remained, had not his usual bad luck followed him across the Atlantic. On January 4th, 1820, the mansion on which Joseph had lavished so much money and taste was destroyed by fire. The owner's American neighbours managed to save most of the contents, an effort that earned them a letter of thanks addressed to the local magistrate, William Snowden. Joseph was very surprised by the prompt return to him of all the goods salvaged from the fire. As King of Spain he had been closely associated with such expert looters as Marshals Soult, Augereau and Masséna. Neither one of them would not have missed a splendid opportunity like this.

Some time after the death of his famous brother Joseph received a deputation offering him the crown of Mexico. His reply delighted the Americans. He said, emphatically, 'I have worn two crowns and would not take a step to wear a third! Every day I pass in this hospitable land proves more clearly to me the excellence of the republican institutions of America. Keep them as a precious gift of Heaven!' So he had again travelled full circle, back to the days when he had infuriated Napoleon by walking the streets of Paris 'in a round hat and brown surtout extolling the virtues of republicanism'. Yet he was a little disappointed when, after the Paris revolution of 1830, the French chambers replaced Charles X by a member of the Orléanist branch of the family instead of reverting to the House of Buonaparte. The family was still barred from returning to France and after the death from consumption of Napoleon's son, in 1832, Joseph visited England where he was joined by Lucien, Jérôme and his nephew, Louis Napoleon. He was now real as well as the titular head of the family and the three brothers discussed the future and the issues of the day, Joseph opposing an attempt to oust the Orléanists. By now the family had been reduced from eight to five. In 1825, at the home of her husband, Camillo Borghese, Pauline died after a death-bed reconciliation with the man who had shared her follies in the days when they had lived like Renaissance princes in Turin and spent a king's ransom on fêtes, masques and entertainments of one sort or another.

When her frantic attempts to get permission to join Napoleon on St Helena ended with his death Pauline, then forty but still one of the most beautiful women of her time, returned to the round of pleasures that had been her life since she had escaped from the horrors of the St Domingo campaign. She and Camillo had finally separated, he retiring to his splendid palace in Florence, she to an equally splendid home in Rome, and here she entertained on a lavish scale. Her villa was the resort of every spendthrift in the city. She had two homes in Rome, a Borghese palace and a smaller villa called the Villa Paolina, and both were famous for their elegance and expensive furnishings. Every week without fail Pauline was hostess at a spectacular ball, a concert, a soirée or a play and her extravagance must have appalled Madame Mère, who lived close by and was still imploring her surviving children to retrench. One of Pauline's most regular guests at this time was old Cardinal Fesch, Letizia's half-brother, who could always be found tagging along behind his nieces and nephews and seconding their capacity for display. The Cardinal had a talent for survival equal to that of Talleyrand and rode each successive crisis with equanimity. Very few could withstand Cardinal Fesch who was bland, genial and extremely tolerant with the weaker of his flock, but in his old age he showed an obstinacy that baffled the enemies of the Buonapartes. He categorically refused, for instance, to surrender the archbishopric of Lyons after Napoleon's fall and the Bourbons were obliged to appoint the Abbé de Rohan, an émigré, over his head. The Pope then prohibited Fesch from exercising spiritual jurisdiction in his former diocese but the old man had never concerned himself much about spiritual failings, his own or anyone else's. He continued to regard himself the real Archbishop of Lyons and went on adding to his magnificent collection of pictures until his gallery filled three floors of his palace in Rome. His taste was impeccable, embracing the work of Italian, Dutch and Flemish masters. Fat, liberal and entirely without rancour, he was popular wherever he went and his company was much sought after at Pauline's parties.

Early in 1825, Pauline, now forty-five, fell seriously ill and was taken to Pisa for the baths. The waters did not restore her health and as it deteriorated she developed a conscience about her treatment of Camillo and begged to be taken to him. Borghese must have been disconcerted by her deathbed piety but he readily granted her request and she was carried to his palace in Florence, dying (or so it is said) in the arms of the man whose character was so similar to her own.

Two of the sisters had gone but Caroline lived on, an exile in Austria who was strictly forbidden to set foot on French or Italian soil. Napoleon had found it in his heart to forgive Murat his treachery but Madame Mère found it very difficult to show the same spirit of forgiveness towards her youngest daughter. When the family reassembled in Rome after the second restoration she had refused to receive the ex-queen of Naples and as time passed she did not relent. During the last years of Napoleon's exile on St Helena Caroline wrote from Vienna asking her mother for a loan. It was refused with the comment, 'All the money I have is for Napoleon! It was from him I received it!' There was a partial reconciliation some years later, when it was thought that Madame Mère was dying. Caroline obtained permission to pay her a visit lasting one month. When the month was over she returned to Austria where she continued to live in straitened circumstances. The Bourbons had confiscated all her French property and Ferdinand of Naples appropriated everything left behind in Italy as the spoils of war, so that Caroline was without a regular income. It was not like her, however, to submit tamely to a life of penury. When Louis-Philippe became King of France and showed a more lenient attitude towards the exiles by permitting the re-erection of Napoleon's statue in the Place Vendôme, Caroline took advantage of the mood and hurried to Paris where she claimed a State pension as sister of the former Emperor. To everyone else's surprise she obtained it, the Chamber of Deputies voting her the equivalent of £4,000 a year. She returned in triumph to Italy, if not as a queen then at least as someone who could afford to dress well and be seen in polite society again, but she did not enjoy her good luck for long. On May 18th, 1839, Caroline died in Florence at the age of fifty-seven, the least mourned of all the Buonapartes. Perhaps, in the end, her mother forgave her for her treachery in 1814 but Buonapartists who remembered the great influence she had wielded in the councils of her husband continued to look upon her as a traitress whose guilt was far greater than that of the man who had died at Pizzo with her portrait round his neck.

When the last of her daughters died Letizia had already been dead more than three years. Ever since her retirement to Rome after Waterloo the old lady had shared a home with Cardinal Fesch, in the Palazzo Falconnieri. She took no part in social activities and received no one but her family and a few old friends. She could have returned to France at any time but she refused to accept clemency so long as one of her children was forbidden to set foot in Paris. Everybody respected her and although still disposed to hoard she was a good friend to the local poor. She had outlived her husband Carlo by more than fifty years and her famous son by fifteen. Antommarchi, the surgeon who had attended at Napoleon's deathbed, paid her a visit on his return to Europe and she made him describe every detail of her son's last hours. Towards the end of her life her eyesight began to fail but she remained upright, vigorous and the mistress of a dignity that none of her sons or daughters inherited. Traces of her remarkable beauty remained to her in her eighties and her stern features never lost the composure they had worn throughout her life. On February 2nd, 1836, she died as she had lived, quietly and without fuss. She was in her eighty-sixth year.

The year after his mother's death Joseph, now almost a septuagenarian, returned to America but as he grew older he became homesick and after a brief stay in his rebuilt home at Bordentown he returned to Europe for good, visiting England and Germany in search of health and exploring with his nephew, Hortense's youngest child, the possibilities of reviving Buonaparte interests. The next year, 1840, he suffered a paralytic stroke and after trying several spa cures he drifted south into Italy to resume his interrupted retirement with Julie and his brothers. He obtained permission to settle in Florence where he hoped his health would mend, but it did not and he began to sink. Occasionally his mind would be agitated by the injustice of the Bourbons in maintaining the ban of exile on the Buonaparte brothers and he would probably have considered it a boon to be allowed to return to France to die. Louis and Jérôme saw a good deal of him but Lucien had already preceded him to the grave, dying at Viterbo, in 1840.

Lucien's last years had been pleasant and uneventful. The fires of the Revolution had long since burned out in him and in his closing years devoted almost all his time to excavating the site of the Etruscan city of Vetulonia, which happened to be within his estates. He kept well clear of politics and his brief sally in 1815 proved his final exercise in oratory. In 1831 there was an insurrection within the Papal States but Lucien took great pains to keep clear of it and encouraged his family to do the same. He had had more than enough of revolutions and riots and having survived so many upheavals was not disposed to challenge fate in his old age. He died on July 29th, 1840, respected, envied and, to a limited extent, admired by former colleagues. Napoleon excepted, he had more talent than any of his brothers or sisters but what endeared him to his intimates was not his ability to make impassioned speeches, or his undoubted ability in literary or administrative fields, but the fact that he had once sacrificed material advancement in order to remain loyal to his second wife. It may be that his brother Jérôme thought of this when he attended Lucien's funeral.

Joseph, aged seventy-six, died in Florence on July 28th, 1844, four years after he had returned to his family. He too was mourned by many friends, most of whom had forgotten his performance as King of All the Spains. There is not the slightest doubt that without Napoleon as a brother Joseph would have led a quiet, ordered and unremarkable life and the nineteenth century would never have heard of him at all. For twenty-nine years he had been banished from France and had never ceased to complain that Bourbon malice allowed so many patriots to die in exile. Alone among her family Madame Mère had at last been given permission to return. 'I will gladly do so when the same indulgence is granted my children!' she had said not once but many times after Napoleon's death in 1821.

Both Joseph's daughters married their first cousins, one the eldest son of Lucien, the other the eldest son of Louis, who would have been Napoleon III had he not died in 1830. It is pleasant to record that Julie, Joseph's loyal if unremarkable wife, was his companion during his declining years. Five decades had passed since Julie Clary's dowry had rescued the Buonapartes from penury and now the money that had once helped to provide Elisa and Pauline with enough to eat returned to her, for Joseph left everything he possessed to Julie and her daughters.

*

Only two of the original family were left and soon there was but one. On June 25th, less than a year after Joseph's death, Louis, the implacable invalid, died at Leghorn, in his sixty-sixth year. Louis' declining years had not been free from the domestic strife that had plagued him since his youth, but although regarded as the least robust of the family he had survived all except Jérôme. Louis' troubles towards the end of his life stemmed from the erratic behaviour of his youngest son, Louis Napoleon, who became head of the family on his father's death and was ultimately successful in restoring Buonaparte fortunes and founding the Second Empire. Louis' favourite, the second son he had left behind when he abdicated the throne of Holland in 1810, had died at Forli in the 'thirties and the young man's death was a source of great grief to his father, who had regarded him as the prince most likely to restore the name of Buonaparte to its former glory. The third son, fruit of Napoleon's last reconciliation between Louis and Hortense, had already made two abortive attempts to regain the imperial crown and the second ended in his arrest and imprisonment at Ham. Louis, with his usual pessimism, regarded both these attempts as ridiculous episodes but he was very upset by the refusal of the British and French Governments to allow his son to visit him before he died, and therefore had a grudge to nourish him during his final moments. His instructions were that his body was to be taken to France and buried on his estate at St Leu and this was allowed, a large assembly of Buonapartists obtaining permission to attend the funeral. So many years had passed since Napoleon had terrified the crowned heads of Europe that restrictions on the family were now sufficiently relaxed to enable a large number of the second generation to see Louis interred. Another sign of the times at the funeral was the presence of veterans of the Old Guard, a very few of them perhaps men who had been Louis' companions-in-arms when he had rushed across the bridge at Arcola to rescue the young man who was conquering Italy.

Of the Buonaparte family Louis was the one whose early promise achieved the least. As the lonely little boy who had shared his brother's lodgings in garrison, and as the adolescent who had fought beside him in Italy and Egypt, Louis could have been his brother's favourite if he had not been suspicious by nature with a curious streak of cussedness. It was because of this that Napoleon took the part of Hortense in the dismal record of marital strife that continued, one way or another, all their lives. Louis' apologists excuse his awkwardness and pessimistic nature on grounds of ill-health and there may be justification for this, for there is not much doubt that Louis contracted syphilis in his youth and suffered from the effects of the disease all his life. Louis' sourness towards friend and foe sets him apart from his brothers and sisters. Even Caroline, the most like him, quarrelled with people for material reasons, but Louis seemed to go out of his way to make enemies.

Hortense had died more than eight years before, at her villa at Arenemburg, on the shores of Lake Constance. She had been closely involved in her sons' participation in the revolt of the Papal States in 1831 (a revolution that Louis had studiously ignored) and when the elder of the two boys died the survivor was banished to America. Hortense had written her memoirs by then and the sentiments expressed in them were unlikely to recommend her to the Bourbons. She had always been a fanatical Buonapartist and remained so, extolling the glories of the Empire in every page that she did not devote to denouncing Louis as a husband or justifying herself as an injured wife. By this time she had presented her lover de Flahaut with a son, although the boy's true paternity was never openly acknowledged. The child, born soon after Louis' abdication, grew up to become the Duc de Morny and played a prominent part in the establishment of the Second Empire. He was a talented young man and this is not surprising for his father, de Flahaut, was almost certainly the illegitimate son of Talleyrand, while he himself was a Beauharnais so that he possessed a very remarkable pedigree indeed. During her retirement Hortense occupied herself with painting and music and when she was dying her surviving son was given permission to return to Europe for a visit. He arrived just before she died and arranged that Hortense should be buried beside the mother she had adored, in the chapel near Malmaison.

So Jérôme was now alone, the last survivor of the fugitives who had come ashore at Toulon in the summer of '93, a paunched man of sixty-two, whose sardonic features showed the marks of a dissipated life. For a single moment, in a picture gallery in Florence, a chance encounter had lifted a curtain that had fallen on the early part of Jérôme's life in 1803. Taking advantage of the comparative freedom of movement gained by the death of Napoleon in 1821, Jérôme and his wife Catherine returned to Italy. They were admiring pictures in the Pitti Palace when a fashionably dressed woman wandered by, engaged in the same pursuit. Jérôme stared hard at her but the stranger moved on without a glance or a word. It was Elizabeth Patterson, the Baltimore girl whom young Lieutenant Buonaparte had married after a whirlwind courtship when they were both twenty years of age. Some men would have been desperately embarrassed by the coincidence but Jérôme had survived worse shocks. With a smile he pointed to the retreating figure and said, 'You see that woman, my dear? It is Elizabeth, my American wife!' Nobody has recorded what the faithful Catherine said in reply.

With the passing of time, and a general easing of political tension in Europe, Jérôme and Catherine were permitted to travel more freely and to spend more of their time in Italy. Jérôme had never quite abandoned hope of winning custody or control of his son by Elizabeth Patterson. Efforts to obtain guardianship of the boy had failed when he was King of Westphalia and his embittered mother continued to keep a jealous hold on him, as if he was all she had to prove how close she had come to being an Imperial Princess. From time to time Elizabeth visited Europe and on her third visit she brought young Jérôme Napoleon with her, sending him to school in Geneva. She stayed on in Italy and during a break in his studies he came to visit her. He was now sixteen and most of the Buonaparte family were still living in Rome so that when the proposal was put to her Elizabeth raised no objection to him paying them a visit. He called upon Madame Mère, his grandmother, on his uncles Lucien and Louis, and even visited his notorious aunt, Pauline. They received him warmly, complimenting him on his bearing, his good looks and pleasant manners. Madame Mère recognised him as Jérôme's eldest son and there was even talk of a marriage between him and Charlotte, Joseph's eldest daughter, who ultimately married another cousin. Aware of his father's improvidence Letizia was strongly in favour of finding the boy a bride with a large dowry and when the project was discussed Camillo Borghese (who was still making Pauline a handsome allowance) promised to contribute 300,000 francs from his will. Nothing came of the plan, however, and eventually 'Bo' as the boy was known, left Europe to study for a period of three years at Harvard. It was not until 1826, when Jérôme was over forty years of age, that he met his American son and the meeting, longed for on Jérôme's part, took place in Rome, Elizabeth remaining in Florence. 'Bo' wrote home to his grouchy grandfather in Baltimore, 'My father received me with great cordiality and treated me with all possible kindness and affection . . .', but despite his welcome the boy was homesick for the States and said he did not wish to remain in Europe for good. He must have been an observant young man for in his letter home he added a footnote that caused his grandfather considerable satisfaction. 'Everyone of the Buonapartes' he remarked shrewdly, 'is living above their means, the only exception being grandmother!' Three years later he married in America, but the Buonapartes had not yet seen the last of him. In 1854, when Napoleon III was seated on the Imperial throne, he turned up again, this time with a grown son of his own, also called Jérôme. Bo's half-brother, Jérôme senior's eldest son, was so jealous of the favourable impression the Americans made upon the Emperor that he did his best to get them sent out of France and Bo's legitimacy was never established in the French courts.

In the years immediately preceding the Second Empire, when he was to come into his own again, Jérôme was able to persuade Italian society that he was still a king, albeit one lacking a kingdom. Westphalia had crumbled but Jérôme posed as the victim of a temporary reverse and in the main his bluff succeeded, despite the comment of one contemptuous witness that he was no more than a superannuated lady-killer.

Jérôme's eldest son by Catherine, born during the dark days of 1814, was being educated at Siena and his father encouraged him to wear the insignia of the crown of Westphalia in his buttonhole. He spent money as freely as ever, pledging his wife's two pensions and borrowing gaily from anyone who was unable to withstand his blarney. He built an expensive villa on the shores of the Adriatic and continued to entertain a succession of mistresses, although without causing the tolerant Catherine a moment's disquiet. In 1835 his luck ran out again. The gentle Catherine died, proclaiming her adoration for him to the last. 'What I loved most in this world was you, Jérôme,' she is said to have told him just before she died. Jérôme had never loved her in the same way but was distressed by her death, for in addition to losing a loyal companion, who had remained by his side through all his troubles, he also lost his pensions and was soon in very straitened circumstances. He had sold his Adriatic villa at a loss when his enemies forced him to move north during the Papal revolt and now his Florentine establishment was put on the market to pay some of his debts. When Madame Mère died she left him a large share of her savings but although the legacy included a share in a gold dinner service it was not enough to keep Jérôme more than one jump ahead of his creditors. The following year, however, following the pattern that is often found in the lives of inveterate spendthrifts, the graph of his fortunes shot up again, boosted by the marriage of his daughter Mathilde to a wealthy Russian noble and then his own third marriage to an equally wealthy Florentine widow, the Marchesa Bartolini-Badelli.

The Marchesa was forty, good-looking and very tolerant. Although Jérôme had nothing to offer but a mountain of debts and a rather faded charm she consented to a morganatic marriage. Once again he was able to conduct himself like a Prince and in 1847 came news that he had been awaiting since Waterloo. The ban of exile was lifted and Louis-Philippe, in the final year of his reign, allowed Jérôme, last of the Buonapartes, to return to his native soil.

He arrived just in time for the revolution of '48 and was ready with a proclamation that would have done credit to Lucien during the latter's republican days: 'Gentlemen,' it announced, 'the nation has torn up the treaties of 1815! The old soldier of Waterloo, the last brother of Napoleon, returns at this moment to the bosom of his great family! The time for dynasties has passed for France. The law of proscription which struck me down has gone with the last of the Bourbons. Pray receive, Members of the Provisional Government, my expressions of respect and devotion!' He then sat down and wrote a letter to the King of Württemberg and signed it 'Citizen Buonaparte'.

From then on everything was plain sailing for Jérôme. As an old soldier of Waterloo the republicans could hardly do less than appoint him Governor of the Hotel Des Invalides. The compliment delighted him and so did the salary. It was 45,000 francs a year. His nephew, Louis Napoleon, the only surviving son of Louis and Hortense, was made president of the new republic and Jérôme pocketed an additional 12,000 francs a year as a reinstated general. Having, as it were, made sure of his social, political, military and financial status, Jérôme now embarked upon an Indian summer of romance and although sixty-five soon showed his Italian critics that he was far from being 'a superannuated lady-killer'. His gallantries, strenuous though they were, did not occupy all his time. Sometimes, with a male companion, he would patronise freak theatrical shows and on one occasion he sat in a box at the theatre and watched a performance of a play called *Napoleon at Schönbrunn* in which there was a scene depicting the former Emperor lecturing his improvident younger brother. The promoters, informed of Jérôme's presence, were frightened out of their wits but they were soon reassured. Jérôme was helpless with laughter.

Honours were heaped upon him as a Prince of the Empire and legends gathered about him as a survivor of the days when the French lancers of the Guard had stormed the Sierra Somo through a tempest of grapeshot or crossed the Danube to drub the Austrians at Wagram. His single day's glory, outside the château of Hougomont, was magnified into a lifelong career of soldiering and when stories of his prowess on the field were challenged by cynics there were always plenty of anecdotes about his adventures at sea. There was now hardly a trace of the smooth-featured boy who had wooed Elizabeth Patterson and looked so handsome in the uniform of a naval lieutenant. His hair was grey, his features coarse and flesh bulged from behind his satin waistcoat, but his heart remained young and there was still a gleam of mischief in his eye. The boy who would never grow up was now the old rake whom nobody wanted changed. The new Emperor, himself a great success with the ladies, looked upon his uncle with amused affection and all who had marched with the great Napoleon over the Alps and across the bogs of Poland treated the old reprobate with respect.

At last, at the age of seventy-five he began to fail, and when he died at his château at Villegenis, on June 24th, 1860, Paris mourned him as the final link with a glorious past. He was given a State funeral and every important veteran and dignitary of the Empire came forward to pay their last respects. Debauched, untrustworthy, a prodigal spender of other people's money, a faithless husband to two wives and the betrayer of a third, Jérôme was surely the biggest failure of them all yet something of his irresistible charm and impudence has survived in portraits and memoirs to this day and one is left with a conviction that, if forced to choose a boon companion from the eight Buonapartes, Jérôme would be preferable to any of his brothers and sisters, including the man whose explosive genius kept Europe in a turmoil for nineteen years.

EPILOGUE

One hundred and sixty-three years have gone by since this bizarre family captured, for a moment of time, the attention of everyone who knew them or heard about them. Across a century and a half of wars, revolutions and so-called progress which has led humanity to the edge of an abyss of self-destruction, we are able to look upon their antics with detachment – Joseph's plodding, well-intentioned posturing, Lucien's hoarse appeals to mass hysteria, Louis' rumbling complaints, Jérôme's madcap follies, the greed and selfishness of Caroline, the steady pursuit of power by Elisa, the wildly extravagant displays of Pauline – and they are seen for what they were, the squeals of deprived children hoping to attract a little attention and a little deference. In an age of machines, when temporal power rests with men who, at the touch of a button, are able to destroy millions they seem as harmless as a gathering of clowns. One should not forget, however, that in exchange for money and power each was ready and willing to bring colour and sparkle to those around them. This is more than can be said of presidents and prime ministers who solicit our votes at stipulated intervals and give, in exchange, the maximum number of clichés for the minimum amount of security.

BIBLIOGRAPHY

I have never been much impressed by bibliographies. I recall the late A. G. Macdonell, one of the more amusing of writers on the Napoleonic Saga, pointing out that nothing was easier than to pay a visit to the British Museum and compile a list of acknowledged authorities on one subject or another and therefore, like Macdonell, content myself by saying that every word appearing here – apart from comment and some deductions – has appeared in a work of history, memoir or biography over the last one hundred and fifty years.

I would not, however, seek to deprive a reader who finds himself more than lightly interested in the subject, of an opportunity to explore sources. They are all there, in any good library, the millions of words written by men and women who took pride in recalling that they once associated with members of this fantastic family. Memoir-writing was even more popular in the second and third decades of the nineteenth century than it was among generals and ex-prisoners of war after the Second World War. Almost everyone of note wrote and published their impressions of the Buonapartes, and since then there has been an ever-increasing spate of books about the brief period when the French rode into almost every capital in Europe. As to the vast correspondence of Napoleon, the quotes from his estimated total of 54,000 letters (written in fifteen years!) were taken from the excellent translations of J. M. Thompson, published by Dent and issued in the Everyman Series. For the rest I went to the inimitable Madame Junot, to the family themselves, to soldiers, soldiers' wives, diplomats, secretaries and even police spies for information on one or other of the four brothers and three sisters of this human dynamo. A few of these books are dull and all of them are highly controversial but in the main they are fascinating reading to anyone like myself who gazed at Napoleon's coach in Madame Tussaud's at the age of six and went home with a curiosity about him that has lasted a lifetime.

R.F.D. Sidmouth, Nov., 1963

INDEX